Professional Practice in Governance and Public Organizations

"Professional Practice in Governance and Public Organizations" offers cutting-edge insights and practical guidance for professionals in the areas of economics, politics, public policy and public administration, and those working at international organizations. The series features concise and accessible books on the latest developments in governance, organizational and political strategies, institutional policies, policy instruments, public management, and finance. Leadership and digitalization issues are a core topic throughout the series. All volumes are written by practitioners, experts and leading authorities from think tanks, non-governmental organizations, and public and international organizations. While the books are explicitly intended for professionals in the above-mentioned fields, students of economics, political science, public policy and public administration will also benefit from these practical guides for their future careers.

Detlef Eckert

40 Years of European Digital Policies

Forgotten Lessons

Springer

Detlef Eckert
Bertem, Belgium

ISSN 2731-9776 ISSN 2731-9784 (electronic)
Professional Practice in Governance and Public Organizations
ISBN 978-3-031-61640-2 ISBN 978-3-031-61641-9 (eBook)
https://doi.org/10.1007/978-3-031-61641-9

This Springer imprint is published by the registered company Springer Nature Switzerland AG
The registered company address is: Gewerbestrasse 11, 6330 Cham, Switzerland

In memory of my parents
Anny and Kurt Eckert

Foreword

Why is Europe more market-driven than the USA in some areas? How did Europe provide more equal and less expensive access to certain services such as telecoms? Thomas Philippon analysed the deregulation of airlines and telecoms in his book *The Great Reversal* [1]. He explores how Europe managed to stick with liberalisation, while former monopolies fought back in the USA, and prices rose. A question raised by the industry recently is whether the market may in fact be too competitive to allow for sufficient investment.

Meeting in Lisbon in 2000, European leaders decided to turn the EU into "the most competitive and dynamic knowledge-based economy in the world". The results of this highly ambitious Lisbon Agenda appeared satisfactory. However, Wim Kok, a former prime minister of the Netherlands, chaired the assessment group, and its findings were clear. The implementation was a disappointment.

One exception stood out: significant progress was made in the spread of ICT and the use of the Internet at schools, universities, administration, and commerce. For instance, households were rapidly connected to the Internet. At that time, 12 out of the 15 EU member states achieved their objectives.

Why did ICT do so well? European policy made a substantial difference. Liberalisation of telecom industries, including local loop unbundling, was critical. There were also member states eager to lead, but once encoded in European regulation, the changes had to be applied everywhere. Incumbent operators resisted, but ultimately lost the regulatory battle over control of the "last mile" when the competence for competition policy was entrusted to the European Commission, making it harder to water down decisions.

Detlef Eckert has written an impressive book recounting the 40-year history of European digital policies. From GSM to digital sovereignty and artificial intelligence, the story takes in regulatory reforms, research and promotional programmes to provide an exceptional insight into this crucial EU policy area. It also demystifies the Union's complex decision-making process for outsiders.

Inevitably, Commission staff did not get everything right during those years, even if their thinking was often ahead of its time and forward-looking. Some shifts were missed, such as the move from technology to applications in the early 2000s.

How will information and communications technology affect our prosperity and well-being? This is a fundamental question. In the long term, this will hinge on its impact on productivity growth. As Nobel Prize-winning economist Robert Solow observed in 1987, the computer age is visible everywhere except productivity statistics.

The early 2000s saw the widespread adoption of the Internet and the dotcom boom. Many anticipated a significant boost to productivity growth. What has transpired in the two decades since? A recent research paper, "Why is Productivity Slowing Down?" [2], suggests that while part of this decline may be due to the end of convergence and a return to "normal" rates of growth at the frontier, "it remains puzzling in view of its scale, and considering the context of continued deployment of new digital and other technologies".

Robert Gordon had already made a cautious assessment in the early 2000s. He now says that the era of great innovations is behind us, and improvements from now on will be incremental, leading only to slow productivity growth. AI looks set to be the next contender to challenge this view.

Richard Baldwin has written on supply chains and how they have shifted away from "the old globalisation" and the first phase of unbundling, in which manufacturing links were primarily confined to Europe and the USA [3]. However, the second phase of unbundling from the 1990s saw the dispersal of the production process, as components and prefabricated parts could be purchased from specialised suppliers. These, in turn, were able to spread their own production in a similar fashion. Supply chains became global, and they grew longer. Information and communication technologies made this development possible, and the wage gap made it profitable. ICT and globalisation have become intertwined.

One significant shift has been the increased economic dominance of major technology corporations. The "winner-takes-all" principle means they can conquer a large share of global markets and earn extremely high incomes. At the beginning of 2024, the market capitalisation of Alphabet, Meta, Apple, Amazon, NVidia, and Microsoft jointly represent about 50% of US GDP.

The European Commission has played an active role in this area with its competition policy. The first major litigation was launched in 2001 against Microsoft, following an investigation of a 1998 complaint by Sun Microsystems and concluding in 2004. Many other cases have ensued over the two decades since.

A new period started in March 2024, when the Commission opened non-compliance investigations under the new Digital Markets Act (DMA). The investigations concern Alphabet's role in steering Google Play self-preferencing on Google Search, Apple's rules governing its App Store and the default choice of browser, and Meta's pay or consent model.

Did the EU assess all factors correctly when the ICT revolution began or when China became part of the world trade system? No. The EU's assessment did not foresee all the outcomes, revealing the unpredictable nature of technological and global economic shifts.

Globalisation and technological development represented a major step forward. But nothing comes for free. Many countries either failed to react to the exclusion of a growing number of individuals from the labour market and a widening income gap or reacted too late.

Clearly, not everything unfolded as hoped. Now, Europe's challenge is to find ways to gain competence and leadership in technology while keeping its societies inclusive.[1]

Helsinki, Finland | Erkki Liikanen
30 March 2024 | European Commissioner 1995–2004

References

1. *The Great Reversal. How America Gave Up on Free Markets*, Harvard University Press, 2019.
2. Ian Goldin, et al., "Why is productivity slowing down?", *The Oxford Martin Working Paper Series on Technological and Economic Change,* Working Paper No. 2022-8.
3. *The Great Convergence. Information Technology and the New Globalisation*, Harvard University Press, 2016.

[1] Daron Acemoglu and Simon Johnson have explored this theme in its historical context: *Power and Progress*, 2023, Basic Books, UK.

Preface

If you want the present to be different from the past, study the past.
Benedict de Spinoza (seventeenth century)

I.

Forty years of European digital policymaking make quite a story. This book starts its tale in the 1980s when big mainframes ruled the business world with office workers in front of dedicated terminals, and personal computers were only beginning to appear in private homes. Today, digital devices are all around us, wherever we are. We take the Internet for granted. An entire generation has only experienced a world with smartphones, and their lives have been shaped by digital technologies. For four decades, technological breakthroughs largely dictated the agenda, but meanwhile, the process of European political integration offered policymakers an increasingly significant role in determining outcomes. Looking back over this interplay of technology and policy is critical to envisaging the future.

The book offers a comprehensive perspective on the noteworthy array of policies with which the EU has so far sought to be a catalyst for Europe's digital transformation. Few would be well-served by a detailed account of all policy initiatives undertaken or measures adopted. If libraries were solely physical, they would overflow with books and articles on the subject: just the development of telecommunications generated hundreds of legal measures. Therefore, several programmes and some legislation, such as the Media programme, the Computer Programs Directive, the global e-business dialogue, the IPv6 initiative, or, more recently, the data strategy, are not covered in this story. It was a tough choice necessary to keep the narrative flowing and avoid overloading it with everything that occurred in this broad field.

In narrating this story, I aim to identify the key moments and decisions that have shaped digital policy. I delve into the rationale behind policy actions, defining these critical junctures and the factors that determined success or failure.

When learning from the past, it may not be possible to replicate precisely what worked well. Conversely, what might have been a failure could prove effective today. Historians may forgive me, but no straight line connects the past with the present and even less with the future. Nonetheless, by identifying patterns and trends, we can navigate the unpredictable nature of disruptive events, which occur more frequently than policymakers and their advisers often anticipate. Although we cannot necessarily extrapolate from these events, we can factor in the probability of their exerting a critical influence on what is to come. The narrative of the book confronts this inconvenient reality of life.

II.

The book unfolds along a chronological timeline spanning four decades since the 1980s, with interwoven narratives.

Chapter 1 reflects on the early years, encompassing the 1980s and early 1990s. It starts with the inception of GSM, a pivotal success in Europe's digital policy. The chapter then delves into the initiation of ICT-related research programmes, the liberalisation of telecommunications, and shifts in broadcasting policy.

In Chap. 2, the focus turns to the emergence of the Information Society, a policy framework aimed at harnessing the potential of ICT. Stemming from the Delors Whitepaper on employment and growth, this framework, although thought-provoking, overlooked the rise of the Internet. The chapter ends with the story of the people who brought the Internet to Europe.

Chapter 3 revisits the inaugural information society action plan, which led to the complete liberalisation of the telecommunications sector and the adoption of the initial privacy directives. It details how the Internet evolved into the dominant infrastructure of the digital age, significantly shaping both narrative and legislative agendas.

Chapter 4 details the ambitious macroeconomic agenda outlined in Lisbon in 2000, which laid the foundation for the comprehensive eEurope 2002 Action Plan. This period saw the implementation of a revised telecommunication framework, establishing principles and methods that persist today. The introduction of the .eu domain name, the establishment of the cybersecurity agency ENISA, and the promotion of ADSL broadband through local loop unbundling were notable outcomes of this phase.

Chapter 5 scrutinises the impact of the fledgling Lisbon Agenda, the euro crisis, and a noticeable loss of competitiveness in the digital economy, revealing Europe's increasing lag. The i2010 strategy introduced the concept of a common information space, laying the groundwork for the subsequent digital single market approach. Concurrently, broadcasting and media regulation adapted to the era of convergence, and the 7th Framework Programme implemented significant measures to enhance the effectiveness of research policy.

Chapter 6 relates the digital agenda, a pivotal component of the 10-year Europe 2020 strategy to reinvigorate Europe's growth trajectory. While the comprehensive digital agenda marked a breakthrough in setting targets, its true value lay in paving the way for the digital single market strategy.

Chapter 7 delves into the intricacies of the digital single market, a substantial effort to surmount fragmentation in the online economy. Legislative initiatives spanned privacy, telecommunications, delivery services, online contracts, network security, copyright, and media. While the EU was busy implementing legislation, the world progressed, ushering in the age of AI.

Chapter 8 explores the European reaction to the significant advancements in AI that have captivated public interest, particularly highlighted by the release of ChatGPT. It analyses the EU's AI Act, which addresses the risks associated with AI technologies by establishing product safety regulations. The chapter discusses Europe's competitive situation, deals with global efforts to regulate AI, and analyses AI's potential effects on employment and productivity. It calls for a strategy that includes leveraging Europe's industrial strengths and mobilising public procurement to support its fledgling ecosystem.

Chapter 9 propels the narrative into the early 2020s. Amidst global tensions, the COVID-19 pandemic, climate change, and the Ukraine war, the concept of digital sovereignty emerged. The digital decade strategy, maintaining the tradition of framing policies within a 10-year perspective, saw the enactment of various legislations, including the Digital Services Act, the Digital Market Act, and the Chips Act.

Chapter 10 discusses the prospects for a gigabit society. In early 2024, a White Paper, a Commission Recommendation to national regulators on how to regulate access to high-speed networks, and a revision of the Broadband Cost Reduction Directive opened what would be a deep discussion about the evolution of telecom regulation. The chapter ends where the book began—with mobile communications, spanning a remarkable journey from GSM to 5G over four decades.

The book concludes with an Epilogue (Chap. 11) juxtaposing policymakers' aspirations with the harsh realities. While not framing success versus failure, it reflects on the lessons from the past that could inform future digital policies. The narrative emphasises the importance of productivity growth, which should become the overarching objective for future digital strategies. The text highlights the importance of understanding the Solow paradox for realistic digital policies. The analysis aims to identify previous non-typical patterns that can guide us in navigating what lies ahead.

III.

If you need to become more familiar with the distinctive vocabulary of the European Union, the following terms and explanations are provided to assist you in navigating the intricacies of European institutions and their policymaking.

The EU functions as a supranational construct, wherein member states relinquish national powers to common institutions, namely the Commission, Parliament, and Council. This transfer of sovereignty distinguishes it from intergovernmental arrangements like ASEAN or the African Union.

The competencies of the EU are defined in Treaties ratified by the Parliaments of all member states. When acting, the EU must specify the legal basis within the respective Treaty Articles. Exceptions are possible but require the approval of all member states.

The Treaty on the Functioning of the European Union (TFEU) lays down the rules for decision-making, answering questions of who decides what, when, and how. Two points merit consideration.

First, the Commission holds the exclusive right to make legal proposals, known as the "right of initiative", while the Parliament and Council decide. In most cases, decision-making in the Council involves a qualified majority, which requires approval by at least 55% of member states representing at least 65% of the total EU population.

Second, EU legislative acts vary in their legal consequences. Apart from Decisions and Recommendations, the two most significant are:

Regulations, such as the GDPR, constitute a directly applicable law. Regulations often allow member states some leeway to adjust certain rules.

Directives, such as the European Electronic Communication Code, instruct member states to alter their laws or administrative practices in specific ways to achieve well-defined objectives.

The TFEU has established mechanisms to ensure that its legislation remains adaptable to changing circumstances without necessitating amendments to the legislation itself. These mechanisms, known as Implementing Acts and Delegated Acts, grant the European Commission the authority to modify certain aspects of implementation. This authority must be explicitly defined in the legislative act, including the conditions under which the delegation is granted and can be revoked.

The European Union was established by the Maastricht Treaty in 1992. Until then, the EU was the European Communities, referring to Treaties from the 1950s establishing three Communities—Economic, Nuclear, and Coal and Steel. I generally used today's terminology, including euro, instead of ECU. However, at some places, at the beginning of the book, it was more appropriate to use the historical term of a European Community.

The book centres around the policymaking activities of the European Commission. Politically, the Commission comprises 27 Commissioners acting as a college. Their interactions with the services, mainly organised as Directorates-General

(DGs), are crucial for the work of the Commission as an institution. The DGs prepare the political decisions and manage their implementation.

DGs can be compared to national ministries but are run by civil servants, the Director-Generals who report to one or more Commissioners. Besides their titles, DGs used to be known by a Roman number, which was changed into alphabetic abbreviations during the Prodi Commission. For example, DG IV became DG COMP for competition. DG XIII became DG INFSO for information society and later DG CNECT for communication networks, content, and technology. DG CNECT is commonly known as DG Connect, as it sounds better.

Over the four decades, DG Connect was managed by only five Director-Generals, guaranteeing consistency during political transitions: Michel Carpentier, Robert Verrue, Fabio Colasanti, Robert Madelin, and Roberto Viola. I had the privilege to work with all of them.

Digital policies were overseen by ten Commissioners and two Vice-Presidents: Étienne Davignon, Karl-Heinz Narjes, Rudolfo Pandolfi, Martin Bangemann, Erkki Liikanen, Viviane Reding, Neelie Kroes, Günther Oettinger, Andrus Ansip (VP), Mariya Gabriel, Thierry Breton, and Margrethe Vestager (VP).

IV.

This book incorporates biographical elements but is not a personal memoir. Throughout much of the narrative, I played a role as one of the participants, allowing me to provide insights from an insider's perspective. In writing the book, I drew upon my experiences in both the public and private sectors, my exposure to technology, and my academic background as an economist.

I commenced my tenure as a civil servant at the European Commission on 1 September 1988 and concluded my service on 1 September 2017. For 17 years, I engaged in digital policymaking within what is now DG Connect. Between 2002 and 2006, I took personal leave to work with Microsoft on trustworthy computing. In the final five years of my Commission career, I served as the Director overseeing employment policies, skills development, and vocational training. Additionally, I played a role within the European Semester team, contributing to policies addressing structural reforms following the financial crisis in 2008. Following retirement, I spent two years in China working with Huawei's global government relations team.

The inspiration for this book emerged post-retirement. To my knowledge, beyond the scope of domain-specific literature, no comprehensive narrative exists spanning the entire lifespan of Europe's digital policies. Recognising the significance of these policies, I believed it worthwhile to compile them in one place as both a historical account and a resource for policymakers and academics seeking a broad perspective.

Bertem, Belgium Detlef Eckert

Acknowledgements

This book marks the culmination of years of experience and reflections on the intricate world of digital policies, whose results represent the collective wisdom, work, and creativity of many remarkable individuals in European institutions, member state ministries and agencies, industry, academia, and civil society groups. I had the privilege of working with many of them, which enriched my worldview. Through them, I learnt to keep learning and be ready to shift perspective as circumstances change.

The book itself owes its existence and depth to the encouragement, expertise, and insights of several individuals whose contributions were invaluable.

I am grateful to Robert Madelin for his encouragement and advice throughout the writing process, which provided the initial impetus and ongoing support for this project.

Hugh Barton-Smith's revisions and drafting suggestions were instrumental in refining the narrative, ensuring clarity and coherence in the presentation of complex topics.

Michael Niebel shared memorable insights on crucial events, adding a valuable dimension to the historical context of our discussions.

Karl Falkenberg spent time with me explaining the intricacies of the Uruguay Round in relation to audio-visual services.

I am particularly thankful to Erkki Liikanen and Ilkka Räsänen for their insightful comments on the 2002 telecom reform, especially regarding the local loop unbundling regulation.

The discussions on cybersecurity were significantly enriched by the input from David Aucsmith, Ronny Bjones, Taher Elgamal, Bart Preneel, and Andrea Servida. Their expert commentary and perspectives added considerable depth to the narrative.

I also thank Georges Metakides for his background discussions about the early days of the ICT research programmes.

My appreciation also extends to Georg Serentschy for his insights into telecommunication regulation.

I also learned from conversations with Wolfgang Boch on the FET flagship concept and Kurt König on ISDN.

I want to give special thanks to Christopher Kuner for sharing his expertise in privacy regulation, which has greatly enhanced my understanding of this critical aspect of the digital age.

Each contribution has been a building block in the creation of this work, and I extend my sincere thanks to all involved for their support and expertise.

Contents

Chapter 1
The Beginning

The GSM Story

In Paris, 8 October 1980, a group of telecommunications experts met to discuss a standard.[1] None of the participants imagined their work would lead to one of the biggest successes of Europe's digital industry and go on to shape societies around the world over the coming decades.

Europe's digital policy started as a pan-European and inter-governmental exercise. In 1982, the Conference of Postal and Telecommunications Administrations (CEPT) set up a working group called Groupe Special Mobile (GSM). This group was tasked with specifying the technical characteristics of a new and digital mobile communication standard to operate in the 900 MHz band.

The telecom sector in those days looked significantly different. Younger generations have never experienced a world with only one operator, one type of phone, incredibly expensive long-distance calls, and, of course, the absence of ubiquitous mobile phones. At the beginning of the 1980s, mobile services were analogue (with many different standards), of modest quality, geographically limited, and extremely expensive.

The CEPT's technical work progressed slowly. Developing telecom services depended on political decisions. In 1984, Germany and France signed an agreement to work on a common mobile communication standard. In practice, that meant spending money on joint research projects. A year later, Italy joined. In 1986, the United Kingdom was affiliated, making it a quadripartite agreement.

[1] 'It was the first time that officials from across Europe had sat down around a table and set out in any great detail what was going on in each country with their national public mobile services and the trend of thinking.' http://www.gsmhistory.com/the-beginnings/. This website presents a fascinating insight into the development of GSM. Do not miss the Rare Documents section.

D. Eckert, *40 Years of European Digital Policies*, Professional Practice in Governance and Public Organizations,
https://doi.org/10.1007/978-3-031-61641-9_1

Under the leadership of Prime Minister Margaret Thatcher, the United Kingdom had already deregulated telecommunications and privatised British Telecom. The United Kingdom's gambit of introducing competition in a future mobile communication market was met with broad-based scepticism (to be polite), a view that would eventually change.

What appeared, in retrospect, as a smooth process of alliance building was actually full of twists and power games. Netflix could make a good series out of it. After senior officials sorted out some divergent views, which almost led to a breakdown of the initiative, on 19 May 1987, in Bonn (Germany), ministers from Germany, France, the United Kingdom, and Italy met and eventually accepted a CEPT proposal with slight modifications. They instructed national operators to enter into an agreement (remembered as the Bonn compromise).[2] The combined weight of these four countries was crucial in convincing the industry to pour resources into developing an up-to-then immature technology.

On 7 September 1987, public telecom operators from 13 countries signed the GSM Memorandum of Understanding in Copenhagen.[3] This MoU turned out to be one of the most influential documents in the history of telecommunications. It rallied all key actors around a common goal with clear direction. A mobile communications ecosystem was in the making. Eventually, over 200 operators from more than 100 countries would sign the memorandum. Managing the MoU finally led to the foundation of the GSM Association, today's advocate for the global mobile industry.[4]

What was the role of the European Union in this inter-governmental initiative? The European Commission's support was critical. It quickly endorsed these activities and undertook two crucial actions. First, it established a Directive ensuring harmonised spectrum availability in the 900 MHz bands.[5] Early on, the United Kingdom pushed to add the 1800 MHz bands, broadening market space and allowing GSM technology to enter the US market. Second, it supported standardisation through the European Telecommunication Standardisation Institute (ETSI), founded in 1987. This was the beginning of a strategy to use European standardisation to underpin industrial policy objectives.

Finland, then outside the EU, became the hotspot of GSM development. The Finnish operator, Radiolinja, a competitor to the incumbent, Telecom Finland, launched the first GSM network in 1991. Nokia brought the first GSM handheld to market in 1992, the Nokia 1011.[6]

---

[2] http://www.gsmhistory.com/wp-content/uploads/2013/01/4.-Bonn-Ministers-Declaration.pdf

[3] http://www.gsmhistory.com/wp-content/uploads/2013/01/5.-GSM-MoU.pdf

[4] https://www.gsma.com/aboutus/who-we-are/our-history/

[5] Council Directive 87/372/EEC of 25 June 1987 on the frequency bands to be reserved for the coordinated introduction of public pan-European cellular digital land-based mobile communications in the Community. In those days, a Directive could make do with just five articles.

[6] https://www.theregister.com/2012/11/09/20_years_of_gsm_digital_phones/?page=1

The developer Neil Papworth of Vodafone sent 'Merry Christmas' as a short message to his colleague in December 1992—the first use of SMS. GSM not only brought affordable mobility in voice communication but also introduced a new form of communication—messaging on the go. Soon, millions of users would be torturing their thumbs. Vodafone sold the code of this SMS as a non-fungible token on 21 December 2021 for 107,000 euros and donated the money to charity.

By 1998, the world had racked up 100 million GSM subscriptions, half of which were in Europe. By 2001, there were a billion mobile phone users. A powerful driver was China, which adopted the GSM standard in 1994. At times, the country added one million subscribers to its GSM networks monthly. The mobile revolution was well underway, and Europe had traced the path.

Not surprisingly, the GSM story has provided a blueprint for European digital initiatives for decades. They all tried the same mix of research, standardisation, and public–private partnership. Yet, its success has never been repeated to the same extent. Four factors made the GSM story special.

First, GSM operators benefitted from spectrum availability assigned to operators by national authorities essentially free of charge. Getting underway and building coverage were the objectives—not public revenues.

Second, with fewer operators, standardisation was more straightforward compared to today. Member states were fully committed to the project, sharing a real vision well beyond the run-of-the-mill instructions to the Commission found in many Conclusions of the European Council.

Third, governments agreed to allow at least one new entrant to the market. This differed from their intentions at the beginning of the standardisation process, but the Commission clarified that otherwise, it would be forced to act under competition rules.

Fourth, a group of competent and passionate senior officials in the four ministries of Germany, the United Kingdom, France, and Italy had the ears of their political masters. They overcame difficulties, struck compromises, and steered the process to a successful outcome.[7]

The idea that mobile communication could work seamlessly across borders and be affordable—thanks to one standard and roaming—was revolutionary. This vision was not pushed by telecom suppliers fearing the loss of their privileged national markets but rather imagined by policymakers and powerful public network operators. This has since changed: now, vendors are the driving force behind mobile technologies.

[7]These were Armin Silberhorn (Germany), Stephen Temple (UK), Philippe Dupuis (France) and Renzo Failli (Italy). http://www.gsmhistory.com/who_created-gsm/

ESPRIT: The First European Response to the IT Revolution

The European Strategic Programme on Information Technology (ESPRIT), launched in 1984, played a prominent role in establishing what we recognise as digital policy today.[8] Because of its size and its approach based on industry-university cooperation, ESPRIT paved the way for a series of research framework programmes (FPs) up to the current FP9 (Horizon Europe).

Its key elements have remained in place over the years: cross-border cooperative and pre-competitive research projects focusing on exploitation and innovation. Whenever the European Commission developed an initiative aimed at a specific technology or industry, a substantial part consisted of deploying such programmes. The basic idea was to bring companies, investments, and resources together around a common aim of building critical mass. This started with ESPRIT.

Back then, the EU was still the European Communities with ten member states. When Spain and Portugal joined in 1986, it became a bloc of 12 countries. Also, in 1986, the member states agreed to an ambitious goal: to complete the Common Market—envisaged by the Rome Treaty—by the end of 1992. The Single European Act—once all member states had ratified it—came into force on 1 July 1987. It established qualified majority voting in the Council for several policy areas, particularly those relevant to the Internal Market—the famous Article 100a.

It also introduced research and development (R&D) as a European Community objective, institutionalising technology initiatives. Thus, the political climate was ready for ambitious initiatives, and the charismatic Belgian Commissioner, Étienne Davignon, seized the opportunity. Exciting times would follow.

Davignon had already spearheaded a political discussion at the European level about the importance of information technology (IT) in the late 1970s. His arguments still make sense today: Europe is falling behind its competitors, i.e. the United States and Japan. In those days, Japan was the rising star and much feared as a competitor, a role now attributed to China. At their meeting on 21 and 22 June 1979, in Strasbourg, the Heads of State and Government 'declared that the dynamic complex of information industries, based on the new electronic technologies, offered a major source of economic growth and social development' (quoted from the ESPRIT Decision). It would, however, still take a preposterous 5 years until member states agreed to a research funding programme—ESPRIT. Speed has rarely been a salient characteristic of EU decisions.

In 1982, the Commission set up an internal Task Force. The natural place for this team would have been the Directorate-General for Industry. However, Davignon felt that an innovative policy required a set-up independent of the hierarchical strings of a traditional Directorate-General—modern management at work. The Task Force prepared several policy papers, which the Commission submitted to the Council to push for a European response to improve Europe's weak position in IT, putting the

[8] Council Decision 84/130/EEC of 28 February 1984 concerning a European programme for research and development in information technologies (ESPRIT).

emphasis on microelectronics. Member states were, in principle, positive but still hesitant. Even the industry had doubts: could these bureaucrats run an industry-driven research programme? The first victory for the Commission's persistence was the Decision of the Council on 21 December 1982 to start a demonstration phase with a budget of 23 million euros (ECU at that time). The response from industry across the Community exceeded all expectations and cleared the way for a full-fledged research programme.[9]

Meanwhile in Japan

One trigger for ESPRIT occurred in Japan. In October 1981, the Japanese government announced its Fifth Generation Computer Systems (FGCS) initiative. This programme is well-known amongst artificial intelligence (AI) experts as it injected life into AI research and helped end the first AI winter. The AI hype—yes, there was hype before ChatGPT—from the late 1950s to the early 1970s about what computers could do to reach human intellectual performance was not matched by any fundamental advances. Funding for AI research dried up between 1973 and 1980, primarily prompted by an influential and devastating report written for the British Science Research Council by James Lighthill about the limited prospects for this technology.[10] You might be tempted to watch an impressive public debate about this report and compare predictions with historical knowledge.[11]

Japanese researchers conceived the future of computing in knowledge-processing machines. The FGCS programme was Japan's vision of how computers would alter the economy and society in the 1990s, opening the gate to a prosperous post-industrial society. No doubt you have the impression of having read something similar recently.

The programme aimed to build a computer that could infer decisions from a knowledge repository and have an intelligent user interface, such as talking and understanding voice commands. The Japanese chose PROLOG, a logic programming language, as the underlying software. PROLOG was a European development that competed with LISP, the more popular US variant of such logic programming. LISP was developed by John McCarthy, a pioneer of AI who introduced this term to the scientific community in the 1950s.

The government established a dedicated institute (ICOT) to conduct most of the research. Kazuhiro Fuchi, an unconventional scientist, became the director of ICOT, staffed with about 40 researchers, mainly delegated from the eight supporting companies: Fujitsu, Hitachi, Mitsubishi, NEC, Oki, Toshiba, Matsushita, and

---

[9] Commission Communication COM (83) 258 final of 2 June 1983 concerning Esprit: First European Strategic Programme for Research and Development in Information Technologies.

[10] https://www.aiai.ed.ac.uk/events/lighthill1973/lighthill.pdf

[11] https://media.aiai.ed.ac.uk/Video/Lighthill1973/1973-BBC-Lighthill-Controversy.mp4

Sharp, and a 10-year budget equivalent to $450 million. Fuchi became an enigmatic figure, a kind of computer science pop star.[12]

With hindsight, we know the objectives were never attainable, neither with computing as it was back then nor with the resources available. This had already become clear halfway through the programme, but Japan pursued it until its planned ending in 1992. The Japanese built several prototypes but never a commercial fifth-generation computer. Two so-called 'parallel inference machines' are displayed in the National Science Museum in Tokyo.[13]

The American Reaction

The announcement of the FGCS programme triggered anxious reactions in the United States. They perceived the programme as a significant challenge, even as a threat. Japan had successfully conquered global markets, such as automobiles and consumer electronics. The fear was that US computer companies would become another target in the aggressive strategy of MITI, the notorious Japanese industry ministry.

The American counterpart of Kazuhiro Fuchi was Edward Feigenbaum, a professor at Stanford University, an AI pioneer, and a vigorous proponent of expert systems. 'Knowledge is power, and the computer is an amplifier of that power', he would say.[14] He co-authored an influential book, *The Fifth Generation. Artificial Intelligence and the Japanese Challenge to the World*, published in 1983. Feigenbaum convinced the US government, even addressing the US public through TV appearances, about the need for a reaction.[15]

The US defence agency, DARPA, launched a 10-year Strategic Computing Initiative (SCI) with a budget of $1 billion. Yet, it quickly abandoned AI research and focused on technologies relevant to military purposes. The US computer industry also organised itself. In late 1982, 13 companies (amongst them Control Data, Motorola, DEC, and Sperry-Univac) founded the Microelectronics and Computer Technology Corporation (MCC) to pool research activities to counter the FGCS programme and located operations in Austin, Texas. Over time, participation and objectives shifted, and the companies involved ended the cooperation in 2000. What remained, however, was one of the most important IT hubs in the United States, i.e. Austin, Texas.

---

[12] https://www.airc.aist.go.jp/aitec-icot/ICOT/Museum/InvitedResearcher/InitialStage/1982-1.pdf

[13] http://museum.ipsj.or.jp/en/computer/other/0002.html#:~:text=The%20system%20had%20a%20large-scale%20parallel%20hardware%20system,and%20it%20came%20to%20an%20end%20in%201992

[14] https://computerhistory.org/profile/edward-feigenbaum/

[15] The Computer Chronicles – Fifth Generation Computers (1984). https://youtu.be/Mu8zyHh4vTg

By 1987, funding for AI was no longer the principal aim of both initiatives. In addition, over the following years, most, if not all, companies that had built commercial expert systems, such as LISP Machines, Symbolics, and Thinking Machines, went out of business. PCs offered more performance for less money than special LISP-based hardware. The second AI winter would set in, much to the disappointment of AI enthusiasts, and this would last until 1993 when increasing computer power and better algorithms would stir a more extended period of progress. How did Europe react?

The United Kingdom and the Alvey Programme

Inspired by the Japanese computer initiative, the United Kingdom launched the Alvey Programme for Advanced Information Technology, which lasted 5 years, from 1983 to 1988.[16] The United Kingdom invested £200 million plus £150 million from industry (about a billion euros today). It was a pre-competitive programme like ESPRIT. As Margaret Thatcher, the conservative prime minister, was instinctively against subsidies to companies, many commentators were surprised she agreed to this programme. The threat of the Japanese initiative was significant enough to overcome ideology.

A programme evaluation concluded that technical objectives had been met with a positive impact on IT research. The report of programme director Brian Oakley was blunter: projects were too focused on academic research, and the strategic objectives to consolidate the industrial structure and breed commercial successes were not achieved. The United Kingdom did not launch a follow-up programme and focused on participation in the ESPRIT programme.[17,18]

In 2018, the House of Lords commissioned a review of the Alvey Programme to find out what could be learned to inform the AI strategy of the United Kingdom, a highly recommended read—and already forgotten. According to this evaluation, the Alvey Programme was not sufficient, and complementary investments and measures would have been necessary for a breakthrough.[19] This is a crucial insight. Technology policy can address specific problems but generally does not achieve major goals by itself. Generations of European research managers would relive this experience repeatedly, beginning with the ESPRIT programme.

[16] It was named after the chairman of the committee that led to its formation, without John Alvey taking any role in the programme.

[17] https://publications.parliament.uk/pa/ld201719/ldselect/ldai/100/10018.htm

[18] https://blog.policy.manchester.ac.uk/posts/2018/05/to-every-thing-there-is-a-season-lessons-from-the-alvey-programme-for-creating-an-innovation-ecosystem-for-artificial-intelligence/

[19] House of Lords, Select Committee on Artificial Intelligence, "AI in the UK: ready, willing and able?", 16 April 2018.

La filière électronique

The political situation in France was the opposite of the one in the United Kingdom. The socialist government under President François Mitterrand had launched a nationalisation programme for strategic industries and big companies. Most IT companies were under government control. Thus, when the government launched a comprehensive strategy called *la filière électronique*, it was a public-sector initiative. Its *raison d'être* was the international position of French industry, in other words, market share globally and nationally.[20]

French (over-)confidence was partly based on the considerable success of Minitel terminals, which offered videotext via telephone connections. Launched by the national operator in 1980 and only retired in 2012, the service gave users access to the telephone directory, train timetables and reservations, news, online chat services (notably the infamous *messageries roses*), and even text-based games, not unlike the very early web but in black and white—and at highly profitable metered usage rates.

Industrial policies are not detached from macroeconomics. The French economy was not immune to a general deterioration across Europe in the early 1990s. When the country's conservative party won the 1993 legislative election, the socialist President (in France, this is known as *cohabitation*) adjusted course and loosened state control of companies. The French supported ESPRIT, in principle, but were afraid of losing technological advantage to their neighbours. Ultimately, they joined and brought their philosophy into the European programme. Recent French and European digital initiatives are descendants of this early approach to bolster a strategic industrial sector.[21]

The German Non-reaction

Germany (to be precise, West Germany) did not launch programmes comparable to the size and ambition of the FGCS or Alvey. It did not carry out an industrial policy *à la française* either. Previous governments had run relatively modest 'data processing programmes' during the late 1960s and 1970s. Germany's computer companies, Siemens, Nixdorf, and Telefunken, struggled relative to their US and Japanese competitors. The Siemens mainframe computer, for instance, was *de facto* a Fujitsu computer.

In 1982, German political leadership changed from a more interventionist government to a conservative-liberal coalition. The focus shifted to horizontal support of

---

[20] Marc Humbert, "L'électronique française sur le fil du rasoir", *Revue d'économie industrielle*, 1985 (32): 1–27. https://www.vie-publique.fr/discours/153840-cm-28-juillet-1982-la-filiere-electronique

[21] https://www.conseil-national-industrie.gouv.fr/comites-strategiques-de-filiere/la-filiere-industries-de-l-electronique

R&D activities, for instance, through tax benefits, irrespective of the underlying technology.

Germany's industrial core has remained traditional sectors such as chemicals, automobiles, and machine tools. Many middle-sized and family owned companies, the *Mittelstand*, characterise the economy. Thus, the business culture leans towards incremental innovation and not risky investments. Even SAP, founded in 1972 and Germany's most successful IT company, took over 20 years to become a world leader.

ESPRIT 1

> Eight out of ten personal computers sold in Europe are imported from the USA: nine out of ten videotape recorders sold in Europe come from Japan. European-based integrated circuit manufacturers supply 30% of their own home market and represent 13% of world production, half of which is manufactured in the USA by subsidiaries of European companies.
>
> Council Decision launching ESPRIT in 1984.

Davignon and the task force, under the leadership of senior French official Michel Carpentier, intensified the involvement of the 12 leading ICT companies. They joined forces and convinced member states of the urgency of an active European IT policy.

Let us recall the major names in European IT at the time: Siemens, AEG Telefunken, Nixdorf Computer (Germany), Honeywell-Bull, Compagnie Générale d'Electricité, Thomson (France), General Electric, ICL, Plessey (UK), Olivetti, Società Torinese per l'Esercizio Telefonico (STET) (Italy), and Philips (Netherlands). The Commission could base its proposal for the complete ESPRIT programme on the authority of these companies in their role as national champions.

Despite the growing sympathy for a full-scale European programme, member states were still dragging their feet on the size of the budget. This has remained a problem until today: member states agree to EU action, but not too much, as it might overshadow national programmes or hurt their pride. To overcome this last bastion of resistance, Davignon threatened to withdraw the entire proposal, a tactic that worked. With the full backing of the industry, the Commission stuck to its proposal and won. On 28 February 1984, the Council adopted the first ESPRIT programme with a total of 1500 million euros (750 million euros from the Community budget).[22]

It was structured in six domains covering microelectronics, software, office systems, computer-integrated manufacturing, and information processing. These areas still form the architecture of the latest research programmes, albeit with different names, such as nano-electronics, super-computing, robotics, and AI.

[22]Council Decision 84/130/EEC of 28 February 1984 concerning a European programme for research and development in information technologies (ESPRIT).

AI was implicitly part of the 'information processing' section, which encompassed knowledge and expert systems and the PROLOG software. Thus, ESPRIT was also a direct response to Japanese AI ambitions.

Unnoticed by the designers of the various programmes in the United States, Japan, and Europe, in 1986, Geoffrey Hinton and colleagues published a paper outlining the backpropagation algorithm for training neural networks [1]. This shows how difficult it is to identify promising ideas. Geoffrey Hinton received the 2018 Turing Award for his AI contributions and gained wide publicity in 2023 when he warned about the potential existential risks of AI. More about that later.

ESPRIT II and Creating DG XIII, the Forerunner of DG Connect

In February 1986, the Task Force was merged with an existing Directorate-General based in Luxembourg, forming DG XIII (Telecommunications, Information Technologies, and Innovation) with Michel Carpentier as Director-General. By then, Jacques Delors had become President of the European Commission, considered by many as the most influential leader of European integration. The Commissioner in charge of DG XIII was Karl-Heinz Narjes, a German politician.

After a favourable evaluation, the ESPRIT programme was due for a second phase. On 11 April 1988, the Council adopted ESPRIT II with a Community budget of 1.6 billion euros—a total of 3.2 billion euros over 5 years was envisaged for the programme. ESPRIT II contained basic research with an explicit AI and cognitive science component.[23]

Unlike ESPRIT I, each research area had an *ex ante* budget allocation, indicating the programme was more 'managed'. On the one hand, it made it easier to satisfy a growing number of stakeholders. On the other, the programme lost flexibility, and the budget looked thinly spread. This lack of focus would become a common criticism of all follow-up programmes to ESPRIT and beyond. The ESPRIT management argued that it is difficult to pick winners, and pre-competitive research had a search function for winning ideas. Sadly, no such winners showed up. On the contrary.

In 1990, Fujitsu acquired 80% of ICL. This event caused the 'Breydel' building in Brussels, the headquarters of DG XIII, to shake. The reaction was outright negative. The Commission excluded ICL from the Club of Twelve. To make matters worse, Siemens allied with IBM on chip technology. And Philips abandoned its computer business. The vision of an independent European world-class IT industry was slowly disappearing in the dust of commercial realignments.

[23] Council Decision 88/279/EEC of 11 April 1988 concerning the European strategic programme for research and development in information technologies (Esprit).

A debate started on whether ESPRIT and similar programmes would be sufficient to achieve industrial policy objectives. Everyone agreed that ESPRIT had achieved a deeper integration of European research and lifted it to higher levels, but critics could not see any major successes. Defenders pointed to the number of patents, publications, and contributions to standards. In any case, ESPRIT, representing only a small portion of the research efforts of the entire industry, would have needed more capacity to make a difference.

DG XIII concluded that pre-competitive research programmes were too far from the market and that the next phase of ESPRIT needed to focus more on innovation. A second conclusion was that Europe's competitors benefitted from structural advantages, mainly through fewer obstacles to trade and a lower cost of capital. This was the moment I joined DG XIII's policy analysis unit.

Our analysis showed that improving these factors was crucial for industry policy to be successful. However, attempts to establish a pro-active market access policy ended nowhere, and the focus shifted to the ongoing international trade negotiations, the Uruguay Round, aimed at removing trade barriers.

Another conclusion was that market intelligence and understanding customers were more important than technology policy advocates tended to assume. For example, one of our studies revealed that, despite Canon's lead in the technology, Hewlett-Packard had become the market leader for laser printers. This is not unlike what happened two decades later to technology leader Nokia following the innovation of the iPhone, with its far more Internet- and user-friendly software.

EUREKA

Geopolitically, the 1980s were characterised by the Cold War. In 1983, US President Ronald Reagan announced the Strategic Defence Initiative (SDI), an ambitious and futuristic (Star Wars) research programme to develop a defence shield against a nuclear attack by ballistic missiles using satellites equipped with laser weapons.

This initiative generated intensive political debate in Europe. Besides the security and military aspects, European governments feared this project would lead to massive subsidies for the US industry. It could also attract top researchers away from Europe to the United States.

This fear was not entirely unfounded. For instance, in the 1990s, Motorola used its SDI participation to launch Iridium, providing satellite mobile phone services, although the project failed. Parallel to this, while not related to SDI, Teledesic, a project sponsored by Bill Gates, unsuccessfully aimed to provide broadband Internet access via satellites. Some ideas are ahead of their time, as 30 years later, Elon Musk seems to have found a business case with his Starlink project.

Putting the lengthy and animated political debate aside, in 1985, French President François Mitterrand proposed a substantial European civil research programme as a common response: EUREKA. Jean-Paul Karsenty, then a technology policy adviser to the government, recalled the emergence of EUREKA in a fascinating interview in

2006.[24] The programme was established on 17 July 1985 with the Paris Declaration, sponsored by Mitterrand and German Chancellor Helmut Kohl.

Mitterrand wanted a direct national response, free from bureaucratic rules in Brussels and closer to the market. The Commission was puzzled as EUREKA could undermine the credibility of Community research. I remember Michel Carpentier being very nervous and appointing a colleague to follow every project meticulously. It took a while until a working relationship was established and Community research programmes could participate in EUREKA.

In 1989, the biggest EUREKA project was born: the Joint European Submicron Silicon Initiative (JESSI), which would run until 1996 with about 3.8 billion euros of funding. The amount is strikingly higher than the EU budget to be invested in chip technology following the 2023 Chips Act. Neither JESSI nor its follow-up programmes, MEDEA, MEDEA+, and CATRENE, significantly changed Europe's global market position in semiconductors. However, Europe still is the home of a few exceptional companies.

In the shadow of ESPRIT and JESSI, the Dutch giant Philips (the company pulled out of JESSI quickly) helped—hold your breath—to set up a small company focusing on lithography. This technique is used to transfer intricate circuits onto silicon wafers in chip production. ASML, founded in 1984, is the world leader in this field today. They have a near monopoly in 'extreme-UV stepper' lithography, allowing edging of an incredible 7 nm and less in mass production. ASML participated in several European projects, both ESPRIT and EUREKA, but while this involvement was never decisive for their success, it did help nurture the European ecosystem.

EUREKA gradually lost its strategic importance but is still running, with 41 associated countries from all over Europe and the world.[25] Its vision of a *Renaissance technologique de l'Europe* is still present in today's digital policies.

SDI was shelved by President Clinton in 1993.

ESPRIT Reloaded

The third phase of ESPRIT had already begun in 1991, overlapping with ESPRIT II. This made it possible to synchronise ESPRIT with the third Framework Programme for Research (FP3). Hitherto, ESPRIT had had a life of its own. An Italian Commissioner, Rudolfo Pandolfi, responsible for both DG XII (Research) and DG XIII, was keen to have one policy framework and management structure for all programmes.

[24] https://www.mitterrand.org/du-cesta-a-la-creation-d-eureka.html#easy-footnote-4-338

[25] https://www.eurekanetwork.org/

ESPRIT III, by and large, was a continuation of the previous programme (with a budget of about 1.5 billion euros over 4 years).[26] It also contributed to EUREKA, particularly the JESSI project and COSINE, a project supporting Open System Interconnection (OSI) standards.[27] You will read more about OSI in Chap. 2.

In November 1994, as part of FP4,[28] the fourth phase of ESPRIT began, with a duration of 4 years and a budget of about 1.9 billion euros.[29] The designers of ESPRIT IV responded to criticism that funding was being spread too thin. They introduced the concept of 'focused clusters' around selected themes. One was the Open Microprocessor Initiative, and another was the High-Performance Computing (HPC) and Networking cluster. Thirty years later, the concept of clusters reappeared in Horizon Europe. HPC and microchips have remained a priority.

Language Technologies: Back to the Future

Everyone is stunned by the performance of Large Language Models and their applications, such as ChatGPT. It may surprise you that all ESPRIT programmes funded projects dealing with language technologies, multi-linguistic applications, and human–machine interfaces. For instance, one project supported by ESPRIT II attempted 'to develop improved algorithms for speech recognition in the presence of noise and to build a hardware real-time demonstrator' (Adverse-Environment Recognition of Speech, ARS).[30]

Yet, a breakthrough in language processing originated in academic research. The German Sepp Hochreiter developed Long Short-Term Memory (LSTM) at the University of Munich in 1997, an improved Recursive Neural Networks architecture that has underpinned many applications up to the present day [2]. The US Internet giants used it extensively. Hochreiter once quipped that Amazon people invited him for a mojito to thank him for his technology input, which was easily worth a few billion dollars. In 2024, Hochreiter released a significantly improved version of

[26] Council Decision 91/394/EEC of 8 July 1991 adopting a specific research and technological development programme in the field of information technologies (1990 to 1994).

[27] The OSI model is a conceptual framework developed by the International Organisation for Standardisation (ISO) to standardise and guide the design and implementation of network protocols. ISO was established in 1947 as a non-governmental organisation to facilitate international collaboration and standardisation to support trade and innovation.

[28] Decision No 1110/94/EC of the European Parliament and of the Council of 26 April 1994 concerning the fourth framework programme of the European Community activities in the field of research and technological development and demonstration. Official Journal L 126, 18/05/1994 pp. 0001–0033.

[29] Council Decision 94/802/EC of 23 November 1994 adopting a specific programme for research and technological development, including demonstration, in the field of information technologies (1994 to 1998).

[30] https://cordis.europa.eu/project/id/2101

LSTM, aiming to compete with the Transformer models behind the recent large language models. To be introduced as a reference: Maximilian Beck et al (including Sepp Hochreiter). "xLSTM: Extended Long Short-Term Memory", arXiv 7 May 2024. https://doi.org/10.48550/arXiv.2405.04517.

A similar story occurred in computer vision, an area also supported by ESPRIT. Yann LeCun, a French researcher, co-authored a paper in 1998 advancing Convolutional Neural Networks, which are ideal for image recognition [3]. In fact, many of the foundations for modern AI were laid in the 1990s, with significant contributions by Europeans.

We can find more examples of projects that pursued interesting ideas ahead of time, with commercial success eventually going to the Americans. For instance, one project in ESPRIT IV, Mining the Internet for Marketing Intelligence, aimed 'to give online shopping malls the ability to market their products and services effectively by providing information tailored to individual customers'—as in the 'recommendation systems' used by digital platforms today.[31]

ESPRIT can be praised as a programme that pushed European research cooperation to a new level. It created European-wide ecosystems between private and public actors. By 1998, the EU had invested almost 6 billion euros in IT projects. As impressive as this figure sounds, it was too little and spread across too many domains to prevent the European IT industry from going into decline. Entire sectors went to Asia (consumer electronics, hard disks, LCD screens, memory chips) or the United States (computers, software, microprocessors). Europe remained a bystander as the PC industry, one of the success metrics for ESPRIT, took off elsewhere. It could not keep pace in semiconductors and had to watch how Japan and the United States fought that battle.

Semiconductor Dispute Between the United States and Japan.

Worries about computer chips are not new. In the late 1980s, the United States was baffled by the success of the Japanese semiconductor industry. Under pressure from the American industry, which claimed unfair practices, the United States entered negotiations and achieved better conditions for its companies to compete. The 'semiconductor agreement', a *de facto* cartel sponsored by the two governments, lasted from 1986 to 1992, during which Japan vowed to increase the US market share in Japan from 10 to 20%.

In parallel, with financial support from the US government, 14 chipmakers such as AMD, Intel, and Texas Instruments set up the Semiconductor Manufacturing Technology (SEMATECH) organisation located in Austin, Texas, which began

[31] European Commission. ESPRIT Information Technologies RTD Programme. Domain 6: High-Performance Computing and Networking. Summaries of projects. Fourth Framework Programme 1998, p. 151.

operations in 1988. Critics argued that there was a substantial risk of replacing company funds with government money. They also feared that young companies with no access to government funds would be at a disadvantage [4]. In 1996, SEMATECH renounced government subsidies and gradually included more companies from other parts of the world.[32] The organisation eventually dwindled and was absorbed by SUNY Polytechnic in 2015, but its example was an inspiration for the approach of the 2022 US Chips Act.

During the 1990s, Japan's global market share declined, with the Americans taking the lead as their chipmakers benefitted from the fast-growing domestic PC industry. Intel shifted entirely away from low-margin memory chips to more profitable microprocessors [5]. Europe was left behind.

Liberalisation of Telecommunications

> Information, exchanges of knowledge, and communications are vital in economic activity and the balance of power in the world today.
>
> Green Paper 'On the Development of the Common Market for Telecommunications Services and Equipment', 30 June 1987.

On 11 December 2018, EU legislators offered the European Commission an early Christmas present by adopting its proposal for a Regulation to overhaul and bring together the entirety of telecommunications legislation under one roof—the European Electronic Communications Code. The Code forms the peak of a four-decade mountain of regulations. While telecommunications and its regulation will undoubtedly continue to evolve, as we will see in Chaps. 9 and 10, the Code marks the primary endpoint of the era launched by the 1987 Green Paper.

The Green Paper

Up until the 1980s, state-controlled monopolies provided telecommunications services within closed borders under national rules in most countries. Public telecom operators (PTOs) dominated the entire value chain, from networks and services to terminals. They tended to work exclusively with national manufacturers—where available—to supply network and terminal equipment: for instance, Siemens and Alcatel in Germany and France, respectively. Then, perceptions shifted.

Computers arrived in networks, changing the dynamics with which services could be offered. Introducing IT in telecom exchange centres was one thing—Siemens, for instance, offered a world-class product, the EWSD digitalised telephony switch—but imagining what is involved in the merger of public telecom networks and private

[32] https://web.archive.org/web/20130702191328/http://www.sematech.org/corporate/history.htm

computer systems required a different mindset. This mindset was slow to develop, a lag that would haunt Europe from when the Internet started its meteoric rise and persists until today. More on this below.

Because of digitalisation, telecom services beyond making phone calls grew in importance. Data services became essential for businesses. It slowly dawned on policymakers that the necessary service quality, price levels, and innovation required a competitive market structure, and across the Atlantic, the course was soon set.

In 1984, the United States sent a shockwave through the telecom sector by breaking up AT&T, then a private monopoly, into seven regional monopolies (which were then barred from entering other businesses than local exchanges) and introducing competition for long-distance calls. Within a short time, several hundred resellers (buying phone capacity with a discount and reselling individual calls to end users) entered the market. Prices for long-distance calls fell dramatically. The signal was clear: the era of national monopolies in the telecom sector was about to disappear.

In Europe, the United Kingdom took the first steps almost in parallel. In 1984, as part of a general privatisation initiative to turn more citizens into investors, the Thatcher government privatised British Telecom. It introduced competition in long-distance calls by granting a licence to the company Mercury.

Against this background, the Commission published its Green Paper—a massive work of over 250 pages and full of details. Only nerds interested in the history of telecom regulation would like to read the entire oeuvre today. But it is a historical document.

The Commission had long been eager to include the telecom sector in an Internal Market regime, particularly with the magic date of 1992 in sight. It felt that purely nationally regulated telecom markets developing at different speeds and directions would distort the functioning of the Internal Market. It considered the gradual introduction of competition as the only way to provide the economy with innovative services at internationally competitive prices.

Member states, albeit to different degrees, shared this view in principle. They were, however, afraid of the consequences of too rapid structural change. They feared the implications for the revenue streams of their PTOs, concerns expressed officially as the need to preserve financial stability. Trade unions also pressured their governments to protect monopoly positions. Naturally, why agree to tough competition when living within a monopoly is pleasant? Lastly, member states argued that universal service needed to be guaranteed. This was also linked to the conviction that local calls were more important for most citizens and, therefore, could be justifiably subsidised through high tariffs for long-distance calls considerably above their actual costs. Thus, the member states only wanted to move as before, step by step, maintaining consensus, preferably based on non-binding Recommendations, and preserving national prerogatives. The Commission felt a greater sense of urgency and decided to make use of its power.

The Power of the Commission

This power lies in Article 106, and subsequently Article 90, of the Treaty. Public monopolies are exceptions, and exclusive rights must be justified to the Commission. Until then, the Commission had never used this role as an arbitrator to curtail exclusive rights granted to certain entities. The first target was the market for terminal equipment. Only PTO-certified terminal equipment like phones, modems, and fax machines could be hooked into the network. Many capable users already connected modems to their telephone lines to access data services and email. This practice was often illegal, a telling example of how telecom monopolies hindered the development of new services.

The situation was incompatible with the Internal Market and not justified by any public service obligation. Herbert Ungerer, one of the key architects of telecom policy in the 1980s and 1990s, recalled that the use of Article 90 needed the agreement of three Commissioners: Peter Sutherland for Competition, Karl-Heinz Narjes for Telecom, and Lord Cockfield for the Internal Market [6]. Based on Article 90, the Commission issued Directive 88/301/EEC instructing member states to open their terminal and equipment markets by 1993. To be clear, this Directive did not need the approval of either the Council or the Parliament.

While member states agreed to open their terminal equipment markets to competition, some of them—with France leading the charge—opposed the legal instrument and brought the affair before the European Court of Justice. In 1990, the Court decided broadly in favour of the Commission's interpretation and confirmed the power of the Commission. The Court also stipulated that Article 90 and Internal Market Directives are compatible and could apply simultaneously. Europe would not be Europe if no compromise had been found before the legal outcome. The Commission agreed to seek political agreement before further use of Article 90 [7].

Based on such an agreement in the Telecom Council, the Commission adopted a second Article 90 Directive liberalising certain telecom services, which would serve as the legal basis for the future.[33] DGXIII's telecom team cleverly drafted the Directive (in conjunction with DG Competition, formally the lead DG) by liberalising all telecom services except public voice telephony. The exclusion of voice telephony was justified by using the argument that the revenues were needed to ensure 'financial stability' and 'universal services'.

Framing this as a derogation would make it much easier to liberalise later—just remove the exception. The Directive ensured that entities other than PTOs could offer data and value-added services. Voice services could be provided between regionally dispersed entities of companies. Objectively, it was a small step, as derogations were also offered to some member states, but the legal basis was laid and waiting to be used.

[33] Commission Directive 90/388/EEC of 28 June 1990 on competition in the markets for telecommunications services.

Article 90 Directives also instructed member states to separate operations from regulators. The administration of PTOs was part of government ministries, and their employees were typically civil servants. This functional disconnection contributed to changing the status of PTOs from civil servant organisations to public corporations, although these steps would take time. France Telecom became a *Société Anonyme* in 1990, but Deutsche Telekom AG was only founded in 1995. The measures also laid the foundation for National Regulatory Authorities to act as implementers and guardians of regulations and rules.

Striking the Balance Between Liberalisation and Harmonisation

Liberalisation was undoubtedly the most spectacular development in telecom policy, but only half of the equation. Harmonisation measures based on Internal Market rules were a necessary complement. These legal acts were also politically essential to achieve institutional equilibrium. The Court cases showed how unhappy member states were with Article 90 Directives, although the Commission was simply taking its role as guardian of the Treaty seriously. The Commission adopted its Services Directive the same day the Council adopted the Open Network Provision Directive.[34] Symbols are important in politics.

Open network provision (ONP) was the most critical harmonisation measure. To allow new entrants to offer services, they had to connect to the network and the PTOs' services. The Directive established rules for non-discriminatory access based on transparent and objective criteria.

For the Commission, these three Directives were only the beginning. It carried out a review of the telecom sector in 1992, and with its publication, the first phase of European telecom policy ended.[35] The review paved the way for further liberalisation and harmonisation. In it, the Commission presented options for proceeding along this path. Two influential studies drafted by Arthur D. Little and Analysys Mason accompanied the review. They predicted a positive economic impact of a continuous and orderly liberalisation process. Arthur D. Little predicted a quadruple increase in telecom revenues by 2010, which, with hindsight, was a pretty accurate prediction. The message to the PTOs was clear: do not worry about losing market share, as the market will grow much faster.

---

[34] Council Directive 90/387/EEC of 28 June 1990 on the establishment of the internal market for telecommunications services through the implementation of Open Network Provision (ONP).

[35] Commission Communication. SEC (92) 1048 of 21 October 1992 on 1992 Review of the situation in the telecommunications services sector.

A Brief History of ISDN

What GSM was for mobile networks, ISDN was supposed to become for fixed networks. Digitalisation had already reached the telephone exchanges in the central offices of operators, but the transmission of phone calls was still analogue. The technical committee of the United Nations (today the International Telecommunication Union (ITU) in Geneva) proposed a standard in 1984 for an Integrated Services Digital Network (ISDN). The idea was to use ISDN to establish end-to-end digital communication.

ISDN used ordinary, twisted copper wires to transmit digital traffic on two channels, each offering 64 Kbps. The control and signalling information were carried by a separate D channel at 16 Kbps. This basic connection could be aggregated to combine (in Europe) 30 channels for a total bandwidth of 2048 Kbps. These 2 Mbps would become the first quantified marker for broadband—and still used in the 2010 Communication 'A Digital Agenda for Europe'. Standards regarding terminal devices and network equipment had yet to be developed and agreed upon.

The European Commission jumped on the bandwagon, not least because operators and vendors saw a good business case. Already in 1986, the Council, acting on a proposal by the Commission, recommended the coordinated introduction of ISDN across the Community.[36] Led by the Commission, the EU deployed its entire arsenal of policy instruments over the next 10 years: mandates for standardisation, financial support for research and pilot projects, annual progress reports, and coordination efforts. As with GSM, a memorandum of understanding was used to coalesce key actors around a joint implementation strategy.[37]

The immediate advantage for the user was better-quality phone calls from using two channels simultaneously. The vision was to integrate all services into one network, but no additional service was standardised or successfully implemented beyond the existing possibilities of phone calls, fax dispatching, and data transmission modems. Ideas of Euro File Transfer or Videotelephony services never materialised. Time passed, and technical developments buried ISDN as a future network. It remained in service for some time but is switched off in most countries.

In parallel with the promotion of ISDN, the European Commission and the telecom industry began to focus on another technology. No, not the Internet, which would have changed history, but Asynchronous Transfer Mode.

[36] Council Recommendation 86/659/EEC of 22 December 1986 on the coordinated introduction of the integrated services digital network (ISDN) in the European Community.

[37] https://www.iris.berlin/IMG/pdf/memorandung_of_understanding.pdf

RACE: The Vision of Integrated Broadband Communication

> Telecommunications is a critical area for industrial and economic development: a telecommunication network is the nerve system of modern society. New telecommunications services will profoundly affect industrial activities, their geographical location, the efficiency and nature of services and the level of employment.

The above is from a 1988 report about the RACE programme. It could easily figure in one of the latest digital policy papers—add Internet and 5G, and you have it.

Then (as today), digitalisation and new transmission technologies, such as coaxial cable, satellites, and fibre optics, opened the potential for more powerful communications networks. A political consensus emerged that the development of advanced communication systems for the future is vital for modern societies. As the ESPRIT programme mainly addressed IT and computer companies, it became clear that a complementary programme was needed.

After a definition phase of 18 months, on 14 December 1987, the Council agreed to a full-fledged RACE programme (Research and Development in Advanced Communications Technologies in Europe) with a duration of 5 years and a Community budget of 550 million euros.[38]

The vision of RACE was Integrated Broadband Communication (IBC). A distinct feature of the programme was its 10-year horizon, with milestones and coordinated research tasks. The ambition was nothing short of supplying Europe with world-class telecom infrastructure. Deployment was scheduled to start in 1995. RACE was to develop the network architecture, protocols, and key technologies, such as optoelectronics, super-fast switches, and other electronic components, coupled with standards to enable interoperability and economies of scale. The programme was tightly managed under its visionary director, Roland Hüber.[39] Tasks were related to each other, aiming for a common goal. RACE people thought they had a superior approach to the other pioneer research programme, ESPRIT, generating a healthy (or unhealthy) spirit of competition between the teams.

A digital switching technology played a key role: Asynchronous Transfer Mode (ATM), for which the ITU first published the specification in 1980.[40] The RACE programme brought European players into a leading position to use ATM as an underpinning technology for IBC. Initially developed as a backbone protocol, RACE elevated ATM to become the technology underpinning end-to-end communication. Unlike today's Internet business model, it allowed user and service-specific

---

[38] Council Decision 88/28/EED of 14 December 1987 on a Community programme in the field of telecommunications technologies—research and development (R&D) in advanced communications technologies in Europe (RACE programme).

[39] https://www.linkedin.com/pulse/personal-tribute-roland-h%C3%BCber-director-research-dg-cnect-santucci/

[40] Though ATM is a packet-switching standard, it can establish a virtual end-to-end connection. It is called asynchronous because it has no fixed transmission speed, which makes it flexible, as the protocol negotiates capacity depending on network and service features. Its transfer mode consists of a fixed cell length, which makes network behaviour predictable.

billing, potentially making it a lucrative source of revenue for PTOs. Moreover, it ensured a high degree of service quality, adapted to the needs of service categories, for instance, video conferencing as opposed to file transfers. DG XIII officials dreamed of intelligent networks, but eventually, the 'best-effort' Internet became the future.

RACE: An Unaccomplished Mission

The second phase of RACE started in 1991 as part of FP3 with a budget of 554 million euros.[41] It ran until 1994, when IBC was expected to be rolled out on a large scale. PTOs were supposed to invest billions in ATM-driven fibre networks. This did not happen. Surprisingly, there was no serious discussion about why it was not economical. Research programmes are not big politics and are left to specialists. The 'insiders' were already shifting their attention to the follow-up programme.

The Advanced Communications Technologies and Services (ACTS) programme, with 630 million euros of funding up to 1998, targeted various technologies and resembled ESPRIT.[42] It still pursued the objective of high-speed and smart networks (continuing to build on ATM) but no longer focused on deployment goals. Photonics took a prominent place. It supported mobile communication, although with only a loose reference to the successor to GSM, which became known as UMTS. The section with the most budget was Interactive Digital Multimedia Services, the technologies that underpin online services, digital TV, and satellite services.

The idea of an integrated programme with a 10-year mission was striking and taught some lessons. Betting on one technology is risky, as it may not reach maturity or be overtaken by emerging alternatives. Moreover, the era of top-down and politically driven investments was declining as competition and business cases took precedence in determining where the money flowed. The liberalisation of telecommunications was, finally, incompatible with the philosophy of the RACE initiative.

Broadcasting

Culture versus Commerce

On 1 January 1984, commercial TV (private television) started in Germany.
TF1 in France was privatised on 16 April 1987.
US-owned Sky Television began operation from the UK in 1989.

---

[41] Council Decision 91/352/EEC of 7 June 1991 adopting a specific research and technological development programme in the field of communication technologies (1990 to 1994).

[42] Council Decision 94/572/EC of 27 July 1994 adopting a specific programme for research and technological development, including demonstration, in the field of advanced communication technologies and services (1994–1998).

After World War II, television emerged as the predominant media influence in every household. The norm was terrestrial analogue broadcasting, offering only a limited number of channels. Iconic TV towers, like the *Fernsehturm* in Berlin, Shanghai's Oriental Pearl Tower, and the CN Tower in Toronto, became not only landmarks but also symbols of prestige. In many European countries, public television organisations held a *de facto* monopoly in producing and broadcasting content. Public TV was funded directly by the government or through mandatory fees, and in some countries, advertising also played a role.

The privileged position of public TV underwent a transformation with the advent of satellite and cable networks, introducing many channels and attracting private operators. The rapid proliferation of commercial channels ensued. With satellite beams covering vast territories, television evolved into a European issue. Accessing television programmes from other countries became a novelty for viewers. While governments could not prevent signals from reaching their territories, they could impede commercial activities related to satellite receivers, marketing, or advertisements, making them challenging or illegal.

Since the early 1970s, the European Court of Justice had made it clear that broadcasting would fall under the provisions of the Treaty, i.e. freedom to deliver services. Thus, a European regulation became necessary. The Commission launched a discussion with a voluminous Green Paper in 1984,[43] and on 3 October 1989, the Council adopted a Directive of international relevance: the Television without Frontiers Directive 89/552.

On the one hand, it established the freedom to provide services across the EU and associated countries. On the other hand, it set rules regarding the protection of minors, transparency, and time restrictions for commercials, prohibition of tobacco advertising, limitations on alcohol commercials, rules about sponsorship, and a right of reply. It also established a 50% quota for European content. However, this content was limited to the showing of feature films, i.e. conventional movies. It did not cover documentaries, music videos, news, or advertising.

This quota provision became a trade issue as the United States had substantial interests (meaning Hollywood) in the European media market. Initially, the quota was unconditional and was supposed to reach 60% gradually. This did not find a majority in the Council, and a clause, 'where applicable', was introduced. France was the only country that meticulously implemented this provision, while, for example, the United Kingdom and Germany broadly ignored it. The quota lost relevance for private broadcasters because local content was inevitably produced as people wanted to watch it.

However, the audio-visual sector became a contentious issue during the GATT negotiations, which were part of the renowned Uruguay Round that established the World Trade Organisation (WTO). The European film community, including producers, directors, actors, and technical support staff, vehemently argued for the

[43] Commission Green Paper "Television without Frontiers" COM (84) 300 of 14 June 1984 on the establishment of the common market for broadcasting, especially by satellite and cable.

exclusion of the audio-visual sector from trade negotiations, advocating for a 'cultural exception'.

Nonetheless, the Commission viewed this stance as a mistake, as it would not prevent potential future trade disputes in this sector, which would fall outside the scope of multilateral trade rules. Consequently, the Commission persuaded member states to accept an offer aligned with the Television without Frontiers Directive, particularly regarding granting market access for up to 49% of the European market.

In December 1993, tensions peaked during the final night of negotiations in Geneva. The US delegation rejected the EU's offer, threatening unilateral measures to compel the European market to open. However, their own industry, represented by the Motion Picture Association of America (MPAA), later pressured them to backtrack in the morning, unwilling to jeopardise their largest export market. The US delegation resubmitted their offer for an open market.[44]

In parallel, during the night, the EU delegation swiftly formulated a defence strategy, which was approved by all member states by morning. The EU retracted its offer but retained the audio-visual sector within GATT, reserving the right to impose trade restrictions in the media sector in response to any unilateral measures imposed by trading partners. The initial offer could no longer be reintroduced once news of the US reversal began to circulate.

This outcome was celebrated by member states committed to safeguarding their media sector. Karl Falkenberg, one of the key Commission negotiating officials who later served as Director-General for Environment, recalls how the French delegates received accolades from their government while the Commission really did the job.

HDTV: The Japanese Did It Again

By the 1980s, the Japanese consumer electronics industry had risen to dominate world markets. Europe still had two major players (Thomson and Philips) and a couple of innovative medium-sized companies. One of them, Telefunken, invented and successfully implemented the PAL colour TV back in the 1960s. Japan became the first country to broadcast its home-grown HDTV MUSE system on 4 June 1989.

The apparent superiority of Japan in HDTV worried Europe's two big manufacturers and French and Dutch politicians. A substantial EUREKA HDTV project had already specified a European standard, HD-MAC, with an interim standard, D2-MAC, allowing it to broadcast in 4:3 and 16:9 screen formats (the latter deemed essential for HDTV). The Commission proposed making the standards mandatory

[44] As the most competitive country, the United States foresaw no difficulties in eliminating all trade barriers. Nevertheless, their offer included the caveat that any film production in the United States must involve local staff—well, nobody is perfect.

for satellite transmissions through a Directive, which was adopted in 1986.[45] However, broadcasters circumvented it to continue broadcasting in PAL using different satellites from those covered by the Directive. How shocking . . .

The progress of the Japanese industry led to nervous discussions within DG XIII. Only Roland Hüber, whom you know from the RACE programme, quipped that we should calm down as the future was digital TV anyway. Yet, colleagues remained enthusiastic about HD-MAC, established a showroom on DG XIII's premises, and placed a satellite dish on the roof to receive live broadcasting from the Barcelona 1992 Olympics.

Determined to make its policy successful, the Commission proposed a revised Directive fixing the loopholes. It was adopted in 1992 by the Council; however, it was amended with a compromise text that existing services could remain in PAL while new ones must move to D2-MAC/HD-MAC.[46] The Directive did not cover digital television. In addition, DG XIII began preparatory work for a massive 600 million euros support programme. So, it looked like everything was going according to plan. But, in 1993, things would change fast and dramatically.

Philips suddenly decided that analogue HDTV was not the way to go and focused on digital TV, as predicted by Roland Hüber. Indeed, analogue HDTV was inefficient because it consumed a considerable bandwidth of the scarce terrestrial broadcasting spectrum—it was only viable via satellite. Digitalisation provided the solution as the signal could be compressed. The industry started the Digital Video Broadcasting (DVB) Group that would define digital systems for satellite, terrestrial, and cable, all based on MPEG (Moving Picture Expert Group) compression standards.[47]

Also, in 1993, the German Commissioner, Martin Bangemann, took responsibility for DG XIII and quickly decided on a more market-oriented approach. He proposed repealing the Directive and replacing it with a less interventionist one, which was adopted in 1995.[48] He agreed to a support programme of 228 million euros to promote TV content for the 16:9 screen format, with the rationale of overcoming a chicken-and-egg problem: nobody would buy 16:9 TVs without content and vice versa.[49] Readers might still remember the black horizontal stripes on their 4:3 screens and the proud announcement before the broadcast 'Supported by the European Union 16:9 Action Plan'. This programme ended in 1997. As mentioned above, the Commission focused on supporting digital television through the ACTS part of FP4.

---

[45] Council Directive 86/529/EEC of 3 November 1986 on the adoption of common technical specifications of the MAC/packet family of standards for direct satellite television broadcasting.

[46] Council Directive 92/38/EEC of 11 May 1992 on the adoption of standards for satellite broadcasting of television signals.

[47] https://dvb.org/wp-content/uploads/2019/12/History-of-the-DVB-Project.pdf

[48] Directive 95/47/EC of 24 October 1995 on the use of standards for the transmission of television signals.

[49] Council Decision 93/424/EEC of 22 July 1993 on an action plan for the introduction of advanced television services in Europe.

The MUSE project failed. Digital technologies conquered television. French pay TV channel 'Canal+' began broadcasting based on the DVB-S standard in 1995. Technology neutrality would become the new mantra of the Commission.

The End of the Beginning

Here we are in the 1990s. The Commission had successfully established ICT research, telecommunications, and broadcasting as European policies. Over the next three decades, they would evolve into what we know as 'digital policy'. However, these sector policies would remain largely separate. Despite the various action plans and strategies launched over the next three decades, they maintained their own logic, stakeholders, and legal frameworks.

ESPRIT, launched with great ambition to establish a world-class computer and chip industry, struggled to meet expectations. It was doing fine as a programme but still needed to achieve its industrial aspirations. Within the Commission, there were different views on how to approach the challenge of competitiveness in ICT: the trade department (DG I) was worried about protectionism, which would distort the negotiation of the Uruguay Round of GATT (that would become the WTO). The competition department (DG IV) was against sponsoring national champions and was sceptical about mergers. The industry department (DG III) was still busy with the first phase towards completion of the Internal Market and worried more about the automotive than the computer industry. The ICT and telecom department (DG XIII) favoured an active industrial policy, looking eastwards with envy at the powerhouse called MITI.

Telecom liberalisation and harmonisation entered the 1990s with a relatively straightforward agenda. RACE was mid-term and still full of hopes. GSM was on its way to becoming a stunning success; only a few people predicted that it would become that successful. Many, if asked, would have considered ISDN more crucial for Europe. GSM developed as an inter-governmental process with the Commission as a supporting force. This tells us something important. Industry policy breakthroughs that make a difference require member states to be aligned and fully committed. The multiple action plans the Commission would propose to member states over the next decades would suffer from a lack of such commitment.

The first decade highlights two overlooked factors.

First, you need committed and visionary people in functions where they can make things happen. The people factor is among the most underrated in policymaking, where party affiliations, seniority, and show-off attitudes too often dominate decision-making.

Second, research programmes play an important role; they create an ecosystem, motivate researchers, and seed innovation for the future, but they are all unpredictable. The mistake is to repeatedly burden them with a 'save our industry' mission. There is no linear path from research to innovation, from spending public money to successful companies.

Nobody in DG XIII and the Commission noticed the emergence of a network protocol that only provided best-effort packet switching that any 'decent' telecom engineer would sneer at: TCP/IP, the foundation of the Internet. Nobody acknowledged the significance of Tim Berners-Lee's World Wide Web protocols (HTTP, HTML, URI) developed in 1990 at CERN in Geneva and his release of the first browser in 1991. We were all part of the telecom world as we knew it, expecting telecom operators to invent the future. This part of the story is told in the next chapter.

References

1. David Rumelhart, Geoffrey Hinton, and Ronald Williams, "Learning representations by back-propagating errors", *Nature,* 323: 533–536, 1986. https://doi.org/https://doi.org/10.1038/323533a0
2. Sepp Hochreiter and Jürgen Schmidhuber, "Long Short-Term Memory", *Neural Computation*, 9 (8): 1735–1780, 1997. https://doi.org/https://doi.org/10.1162/neco.1997.9.8.1735
3. Yann LeCun, Léon Bottou, Yoshua Bengio, and Patrice Haffner, "Gradient-based learning applied to document recognition", *Proceedings of the IEEE*, 86 (11): 2278–2324, Nov. 1998. doi: https://doi.org/10.1109/5.726791.
4. Bryan Johnson, *The U.S.-Japan Semiconductor Agreement: Keeping Up the Managed Trade Agenda.* The Heritage Foundation. January 24, 1991.
5. Gordon Moore, "Intel: Memories and the Microprocessor", *Daedalus*, 125 (2), Spring 1996.
6. Herbert Ungerer, "Liberalisation of telecommunications in the Nineties – when European competition policy went to its limits". https://ec.europa.eu/competition/compat60/memories/pdf/006-ungerer.pdf
7. Herbert Ungerer, "EC Competition Law in the Telecommunications, Media, and Information Technology Sectors", *Fordham International Law Journal*, 19 (3) Article 10, 1995.

Chapter 2
The Information Society

By the end of 1992, the EU had met its symbolic deadline for establishing the Internal Market, at least formally. However, it turned out to be a permanent task, with progress constantly marred by divergent views on what needed to be harmonised. Persistent fragmentation would remain a constant challenge to developing a more robust digital Europe.

Germany was unified on 3 October 1990. The Maastricht Treaty renamed the European Communities the European Union with a vision of ever-increasing integration, establishing the road to a common currency by 2000 and criteria for financial stability. The Treaty also formalised the meetings of the Heads of State and Government as The European Council.

The Soviet Union collapsed in 1992, and Bill Clinton was elected president of the United States. Jacques Delors obtained a third mandate, shortened to 2 years, so the Commission's mandate was aligned with the election cycle of the European Parliament, to which the Maastricht Treaty accorded co-decision power over many legal acts.

In 1992, Neal Stephenson coined the term 'metaverse' in his dystopian science fiction novel *Snow Crash*.

The Delors White Paper on Growth, Competitiveness, and Employment

> We have to "accept that the world does not owe us a living. The Treaty objectives of 'raising the standard of living and quality of life' and of a 'high level of employment and social protection' have to be earned; they are aspirations, not entitlements."
>
> UK Contribution to the White Paper Exercise, London, 30 July 1993.

D. Eckert, *40 Years of European Digital Policies*, Professional Practice in Governance and Public Organizations,
https://doi.org/10.1007/978-3-031-61641-9_2

Increasing unemployment had plagued Europe since the second half of the 1970s. In 1992, the EU's jobless rate shot above 12%. Jacques Delors decided to make the fight against unemployment the priority of his last mandate and to complete his already impressive legacy as Commission President.

He gave a presentation illuminating the economic situation to the European Council in Copenhagen in June 1993. The Heads of State and Government invited the Commission to present a White Paper in time for their December meeting.[1] Member states contributed to it in writing, but with some exceptions, their contributions were too focused on their national affairs to influence the drafting.

Preparation

The White Paper mobilised broad swathes of Commission services. Every DG wanted to participate and sought to have its policies represented. The result was a lengthy document full of suggestions, not always new ones but of great potential. It contained three interesting ideas that are worth remembering and still resonate today.

First, the White Paper proposed financing trans-European networks through Union bonds. This mechanism would take 30 years to become a reality with the Next Generation EU pandemic recovery funds.

Second, the White Paper suggested increasing taxation of the use of natural resources (to protect the environment and to reduce carbon emissions (sic!)) and simultaneously decreasing the non-wage costs of labour, which should create more jobs. This reads like a page out of the Green Deal book of the Commission in the 2020s.

The third idea, from Commissioner Bangemann and his team, was the introduction of the information society paradigm. Michael Niebel, then a cabinet member, saw this approach as a counterweight to the dominant industry-driven US policies.

The notion of an information society was not new; it had existed in literature for some time. Scholars wrote about a post-industrial future and the growth of a knowledge industry (for example, Daniel Bell's 1973 *The Coming of Post-Industrial Society* and Fritz Machlup's *The Production and Distribution of Knowledge in the United States* in 1962). Japanese scholars such as Yoneji Masuda (1905–1995) also predicted the information society in 1972 with *The Plan for Information Society: A National Goal toward the Year 2000*, published in English only in 1980.[2] He foresaw that the information revolution caused by computers would mass produce cognitive, systematised information, technology, and knowledge.

The information society narrative was broader than the scope of the White Paper, which squeezed the notion of a societal revolution caused by ICT into a document

[1]White Paper: COM (93)700 of 5 December 1993 on growth, competitiveness, employment. The challenges and ways forward into the twenty-first century.

[2]"The Information Society and Post-Industrial Society", Washington, 1980.

trying to reduce unemployment quickly. Michael Niebel worked closely with the Cabinet of President Delors to ensure a prominent place for this concept in the paper. The message: Europe should grasp the opportunities and confront the challenges of rapidly evolving digital technologies—quite a modern idea, although the concept of an information society is out of fashion.

The White Paper proposed hefty investments in communication networks, i.e. ISDN and Integrated Broadband Communication (IBC), and developing trans-European services, such as email. The Commission estimated that investments of 64 billion euros up to 1999 and a total of 150 billion euros by 2005 would be necessary. These figures were educated guesses and were both meaningless and wrong. They were pointless because the White Paper acknowledged that investments would come mainly from the private sector, and nobody knew how the market would evolve. They were wrong, as investments would not flow into IBC and trans-European telecom services but into Internet companies and the build-up of mobile communications. Unfortunately, the practice of underpinning policies with prominent and seemingly precise yet pointless figures has persisted.

Although DG XIII was not at the origin of the information society narrative, we brought something beyond telecom liberalisation to the table, which packed this narrative with concrete policy measures: the telematic programmes.

Telematic Applications

When envisioning a broadband strategy, it became clear that RACE needed a complementary demand component to answer the question of what we need high-performing networks for.

Three programmes, set in motion during the late 1980s, tried to answer this question. Starting as small-scale demonstration programmes,[3] they became part of the 1990–1994 third Framework Programme (with a budget of 398 million euros).[4] The AIM programme dealt with health applications, DELTA with distance learning, and DRIVE with transport management and navigation systems. They aimed to demonstrate the usefulness of ICT for applications in the public interest and to

[3]Council Decision 88/417/EEC of 29 June 1988 on a Community action in the field of learning technologies—development of European learning through technological advance (Delta)—exploratory action.

Council Decision 88/416/EEC of 29 June 1988 on a Community programme in the field of road transport informatics and telecommunications (Drive)—exploratory action.

Council Decision 88/577/EEC of 4 November 1988 on a Community action in the field of information technology and telecommunications applied to health care—Advanced informatics in medicine (AIM)—exploratory action.

[4]Council Decision 91/353/EEC of 7 June 1991 adopting a specific programme of research and technological development in the field of telematic systems in areas of general interest (1990 to 1994).

develop the necessary technologies and standards. Other programmes would follow over time, including solutions for disabled people, electronic interchange between administrations (predecessor of the ISA—Interoperability solutions for public administrations, businesses and citizens—programmes, now becoming the Interoperable Europe programme), and ICT for environmental protection.

These programmes gave us, in DG XIII, a knowledge base from which to make recommendations. We discussed the implications of ICT in these policy fields with respective Council formations. Sadly, our outreach did not generate overwhelming interest. For most policymakers, our ideas and suggestions were too technical and partly considered as 'not invented here'. Admittedly, we occasionally acted as ICT evangelists who constantly talked about a revolution just around the corner. Yet, the time was not ripe; the technology was not mature enough for many applications: no Internet, smartphones, or broadband.

I remember a project proposal from a German entrepreneur proposing a health card that would store essential data on an optical component (chips were not powerful enough) and provide access to an online repository. This was another idea ahead of its time, which did not reach a proof-of-concept phase.

And still today, despite technology no longer being an obstacle, many of these digital visions remain an aspiration. Think of telework: numerous projects, applications, and trials have been launched over the last 30 years, and yet only with the pandemic did the 'home office' become a noticeable reality. Similarly, it forced schools and universities to revert to distance learning, not the DELTA programme.

The concepts of the telematics programmes still live on, although under different names and integrated into sector policies rather than as separate ICT programmes. This makes sense, as the prospects for take-up increase when stakeholders feel ownership.

Bangemann Report: Europe and the Global Information Society

> Given its history, we can be sure that Europe will take the opportunity. It will create the information society. The only question is whether this will be a strategic creation for the whole Union or a more fragmented and much less effective amalgam of individual initiatives by Member States.
>
> Europe and the Global Information Society, Recommendations to the European Council, Brussels, 26 May 1994.[5]

When it came to the final drafting of the White Paper, the DG XIII team was pleased with the uptake of the broader concept of the information society. Our key target was to ensure that the White Paper and, later, the Council conclusions would

[5] https://op.europa.eu/en/publication-detail/-/publication/44dad16a-937d-4cb3-be07-0022197d9459/language-en

establish a high-level group of industrialists to flesh out the vision with concrete proposals. This required some social engineering behind the scenes, but political support was strong enough for us to achieve this goal.

The idea to set up such a group was born during the drafting period at a brainstorming meeting organised by Commissioner Bangemann in Brussels. Olivetti CEO Carlo de Benedetti dominated the discussion. He gave a deep analysis, eloquently presented, in which he argued for close involvement of the private sector and suggested establishing a group of personalities with enough authority to impress the top policy ranks of the EU. De Benedetti could be pleased with the outcome of the Brussels European Council of December 1993:

> The European Council requests that a report be prepared for its next meeting by a group of prominent persons fully representative of all relevant industries in the Union and of users and consumers, ... On the basis of this report, the Council will consider an operational programme defining the precise procedures for action and the necessary means.

Who should become a member? The group's composition illustrates nicely how Brussels used to and still does balance interests. We finally settled on this solution: two representatives were chosen from each of the five larger member states—Spain, Italy, France, Germany, and the United Kingdom—with one member each from the other seven. One question was whether to include the United States and Japan. The solution was to invite Peter Bonfield, CEO of ICL from the United Kingdom but owned by Fujitsu, and Hans-Olaf Henkel, CEO of IBM Europe, to represent Japan and the United States indirectly. With Martin Bangemann as chairman, it became a group of 20. As was quite normal then but inconceivable today, no women were involved. Amongst the group members were former Commission President Gustav Thorn, future Commission President and Italian Prime Minister Romano Prodi, and the CEOs of Olivetti (Carlo de Benedetti), Philips (Jan Timmer), Siemens (Heinrich von Pierer), Bull (Jean-Marie Descarpentries), Canal+ (Pierre Lescure), and former Commissioner and hero of DG XIII, Étienne Davignon.

My colleague Jack Metthey and I (I had been the assistant to Director-General Michel Carpentier since 1993) *de facto* assumed the group's secretariat. We hired two British journalists to ensure that the report would be written clearly and convincingly despite the unavoidable technicalities. The group set up two working groups: De Benedetti would chair the group dealing with applications, and Davignon would chair the one handling regulation.

At the first meeting, the group agreed that the report should address the 'global information society'. Hans-Olaf Henkel invited the group to the IBM headquarters in New York, where Lou Gerstner, newly appointed Head of IBM, organised a meeting with CEOs of several US companies. This event was a revelation for many group members and convinced everyone they had to develop something substantial and visionary. I recall three messages.

First, in his speech, Lou Gerstner said that the computer industry was changing so rapidly that (even the mighty—my words) IBM had to diversify and would predominantly become a service company. Second, Carlo de Benedetti announced that his company would move into telecommunications, which indeed happened later. His company, Infostrada, became a competitor to Telecom Italia, and, in the end, Olivetti ceased to be a computer company and, through mergers and acquisitions, became Telecom Italia. Third, several US company CEOs said the Internet would be the future. Did the group believe that? Not really. It was not even mainstream in the United States yet. Later, the Bangemann group report would mention the Internet as a fast-growing 'network of networks' that seemed to have potential and needed to be followed closely. Well spotted.

In Europe, the final meeting to adopt the report was held on 2 April 1994 at the Commission's HQ. Ahead of the meeting, in the middle of the night, we sent the draft to the group members via fax since no email was available.

The report's main messages were: we are witnessing a revolution that will change how we work and live; policymakers need to put faith in the private sector; they should set the right framework conditions to unleash market dynamism; in this context, full liberalisation of telecommunications, i.e. infrastructure liberalisation, is critical; Europe has no time to lose.

The report suggested ten telematics projects as private–public partnerships. A new idea was the smart city concept, with one member being the Mayor of Barcelona. The group supported our IBC vision but relied on private finance. It recommended various regulatory initiatives to address privacy, security, copyright, and media ownership. Maybe it's a little too market-driven for today's zeitgeist, but otherwise, it's a good approximation of the digital decade.

What did the Council, for which the report was written, say? The leaders agreed with the report at the Corfu European Council (24/25 June 1994). They underlined the importance of the information technology revolution, which '...opens up vast possibilities for economic progress, employment and the quality of life, while simultaneously representing a major challenge'.

The Council set up a permanent coordination instrument at the ministerial level to ensure a consistent approach to the various aspects of the information society. Finally, the Corfu Council asked for a 'programme' detailing the necessary measures to be examined at the next European Council in Essen. This led to the first European digital policy action plan.

Europe's Way to the Information Society

Following the Council conclusions, the Commission integrated the recommendations of the White Paper and the Bangemann report into a comprehensive action plan titled 'Europe's way to the information society', published on 19 July 1994.[6] In case you hadn't noticed, Europe is all about processes.

This action plan brought together the various policy strands that had been developing separately since the beginning of the 1980s: ICT research, industrial

[6]COM (94) 347.

policy, telecom regulation, media policy, privacy, and other aspects, such as copyright, under one roof. Unlike future action plans, it had a short timeframe; most actions would be undertaken by the end of 1995. It combined policy areas across the Commission services and various ministries in the member states and Council formations.

The Essen Council (9/10 December 1994) recognised the action plan as the basis for implementing the information society agenda. However, the leaders wanted more attention given to audio-visual services and related cultural aspects and requested a review of the Television without Frontiers Directive. They asked the Ministers for Industry and Telecommunications to coordinate further measures. This buried the idea of a special coordination instrument. The implementation of the agenda was firmly back within the existing institutional structure. Was someone talking about a revolution?

DG XIII, which was soon renamed DG Information Society, remained the centre of this policy within the Commission and has assumed the function of a coordinator until today. The role of the Parliament became increasingly important, not only through their co-decision power but also as a contributor to the policy narrative.[7]

G7 Conference: A Forgotten Highlight

> Progress in information technologies and communication is changing the way we live: how we work and do business, how we educate our children, study and do research, train ourselves, and how we are entertained. The information society is not only affecting the way people interact, but it also requires the traditional organisational structures to be more flexible, more participatory and more decentralised.
>
> Chair's conclusions from the G-7 Ministerial Conference on the Information Society, February 1995.

In July 1994, the Naples G-7 Summit adopted US President Bill Clinton's proposal to organise a ministerial conference on the information society. It took place on 25 and 26 February 1995, organised by the Commission in the new premises of the European Parliament in Brussels.

The conference started with a round table of 42 business leaders and three scientists from the G7 countries. Their statements reflected their optimism and conviction of being at the forefront of a technological and societal revolution, and the ministers were listening.[8]

Individual contributions touched upon themes that would remain on the agenda until the present day: avoiding over-regulation but seeking global rules to protect intellectual property rights, promoting the sharing of information and stressing the

[7] Report of the European Parliament A4–0244/1996
https://www.europarl.europa.eu/doceo/document/A-4-1996-0244_EN.html

[8] https://op.europa.eu/en/publication-detail/-/publication/a3426f7a-17fa-4327-80e1-8e1068f1fe52/language-en

great potential for education. Most striking was the intervention of H. Hultzsch, a board member of Deutsche Telekom, who predicted e-commerce, online video, and, most interestingly, social media, which he called tele-togetherness. Fascinating. Why on earth has Deutsche Telekom not become one of the Internet giants? And yes, what about the Internet? It was hardly mentioned. MIT professor M. Dertouzos pointed to the World Wide Web, but not many participants paid attention.

The conference featured impressive demonstrations that could have been the top attractions of any industry show: a 3D virtual walk-through of the Vatican, a multimedia whiteboard for schools, a GPS navigation ride with a car, and more. These are all standard today but were amazing eye-openers back then.[9]

The Ministers agreed to eleven projects to demonstrate the value of ICT, following the approach of the Bangemann report. In retrospect, these projects never fulfilled their promises. Such projects needed a dedicated budget, central management, and a communication plan. None of this was put in place, and while the projects may have led to some positive spillover effects, they remained largely unknown and irrelevant.

Nevertheless, media attention to the event was significant because US Vice President Al Gore addressed the conference. He had become an ardent supporter of ICT and liked to say that people would gain access to global information at their fingertips. Indeed, Google was founded 3 years later.

He compared information technology with Gutenberg's invention of the printing press in the fifteenth century and the cultural change it triggered. He was also an evangelist for the American approach to ICT based on free markets and competition. Let's take a closer look.

The American Information Superhighway

> All Americans have a stake in the construction of an advanced National Information Infrastructure (NII), a seamless web of communications networks, computers, databases, and consumer electronics that will put vast amounts of information at users' fingertips. Development of the NII can help unleash an information revolution that will change forever the way people live, work, and interact with each other.
>
> The White House, The National Information Infrastructure. Agenda for Action. Washington DC, 15 September 1993.

The Clinton administration, very technologically savvy, launched a strategy to catapult the country into a new age, the age of information, multimedia, and fast networks: the National Information Infrastructure (NII). It was also called the 'information superhighway', a term that became popular in Europe as *l'autoroute de l'information* in French or *Datenautobahn* in German.

---

[9] https://youtu.be/q-QVvPHGqAA
https://youtu.be/noXR8vvXEYk

The NII concept stressed the critical role of the private sector. The task of the government was to create the proper framework, which meant overhauling the Communications Act of 1934. As in Europe, reforming the telecommunication sector was the central piece of the initiative.

Adopted in 1996, the Telecommunications Act removed the barriers between telecom market segments, such as local and long-distance phone services.[10] It allowed telecom companies to compete with cable TV actors and enter the entertainment business. The Act opened the gate for mergers and alliances, leading to spectacular acquisitions. The seven local carriers began to merge until one bought AT&T; Ma Bell was swallowed by its daughter. The telecom equipment section of AT&T had already been divested, including the legendary Bell Laboratories, and a new company, Lucent, had been created.

The United States, as today, was leading in computers and high-end semiconductors, but who would lead the telecom world and build the information superhighway were still open questions. The IBC vision of the RACE programme was 7 years ahead of the NII initiative. It had even inspired the 'Al Gore Bill' (he sponsored it as a senator) in 1991, which aimed to finance a national research broadband network.[11]

In a speech at the World Telecom Conference in Buenos Aires in 1994, Al Gore made the NII popular worldwide.[12] It resonated in many countries and influenced their policies much more than the European approach. Countries like Korea, Singapore, Malaysia, and Vietnam developed their respective strategies. Besides the United States, we in Europe devoted most of our attention to Japan. How would the country, which had stirred up the world before with its FGCS programme, react?

Japan's NII Approach

Japanese policymakers and industry leaders saw the NII as a potential threat to their electronic and computer industries. The Japanese government set up a coordination instrument—the Advanced Information and Telecommunication Society Promotion Headquarters—chaired by the Prime Minister with all cabinet ministers participating.

From a Japanese perspective, multimedia was the focus point of its NII: multimedia computers connected via fibre optics. The government specified targets for fibre penetration in households: 20% by 2000 and 100% by 2010. It was the first government to do so, but in the end, Japan missed its targets by a significant margin. Fibre penetration reached about 35% in 2010, with broadband, including DSL and cable, accounting for the remaining 65%. The question arose: is connecting

[10] https://www.fcc.gov/general/telecommunications-act-1996

[11] https://www.govinfo.gov/content/pkg/STATUTE-105/pdf/STATUTE-105-Pg1594.pdf

[12] https://search.itu.int/history/HistoryDigitalCollectionDocLibrary/4.144.57.en.104.pdf

60 million households a national or commercial task? This fundamental question is one to which policymakers are still struggling to find an answer today [1].

Japan's consumers wholeheartedly embraced mobile communications. In 1999, Nippon Telecommunication and Telegraph (NTT) introduced the 'i-mode', a pioneering mobile Internet service.[13] It offered content, email, Internet access, payment services, and even mobile apps that users could download. Although i-mode's popularity declined over the years with the emergence of smartphones, it remains a noteworthy chapter in the history of mobile technology, and the emoji it created are still around.[14]

In those days, Japan was battered by macroeconomic problems, a long deflation period known as the 'lost decade'. A tragic earthquake that damaged the town of Kobe contributed to the difficulties. Against this background, a consistent NII strategy did not emerge; instead, various Japanese ministries, MITI for industry, MPT for telecom, and MOF for finance, pursued different strategies. This arm-twisting policymaking culminated in the reform of telecommunications, which meant deciding the future of Japan's dominant telecom operator, NTT.[15]

For many years, Japan struggled with the issue of whether it should follow the British and American approaches in breaking up its dominant operator, beginning with the privatisation of NTT in 1985. Since then, competitors have been pushing for better access to the network. A European type of open network provision (ONP) regulation did not exist. Eventually, in December 1996, the power play ended with the structural separation of local and long-distance business (under one holding) and permission for NTT to enter the international phone business, a domain up to then reserved for the company KDD.

However, these measures did not create a vibrant telecom scene, so tariffs across all services remained high, which became an obstacle to Internet uptake. The real change in the attitude of policymakers, not only in Japan, occurred when it became clear that an NII is nothing other than the Internet, whose history goes back over 60 years.

ARPANET

In the late 1960s, the US Department of Defence for Government Research Agency (DARPA) responded to scientists' desire to connect computers to make collaboration more efficient. It sponsored a packet-switched data network, the ARPANET. The path from the early ARPANET to the Internet would take another 20 years,

---

[13] https://www.global.ntt/our-history.html

[14] https://thehistoryoftheweb.com/before-there-were-smartphones-there-was-i-mode/

[15] http://www.fundinguniverse.com/company-histories/nippon-telegraph-and-telephone-corporation-history/

depending on your chosen milestone. It was far from a linear process, and success was never guaranteed, as competing architectures existed.

The decisive moment was the design of TCP/IP by Robert Kahn and Vinton Cerf. The initial problem Robert Kahn tried to solve was satellite and radio package communication with military needs in mind. It emerged as a more general task of connecting networks irrespective of their architecture and underlying technology. In 1974, he and Vinton Cerf published the TCP/IP suite concept [2]. The Internet Protocol (IP) gives every computer an address and provides a simple, best-effort routing method. The Transfer Control Protocol (TCP) ensures reliable data transmission. TCP resides at the endpoints, the user devices, and not within the network. The network has a simple task: route packets as fast as possible.

In 1981, with version 4 of IP, DARPA switched to TCP/IP for the ARPANET backbone. In parallel, other US departments ran their computer networks with incompatible protocols, several of which were funded by the National Science Foundation (NSF). NSF had its own network, and like ARPANET, it was a network of networks (internetworking). Eventually, NSF mandated TCP/IP for all networks it financed. ARPANET was decommissioned, and NSFnet became the *de facto* Internet. NSF status 'connected' became a precious label and was initially only given to US institutions.[16]

The Internet

The future is already here, it's just not evenly distributed.

Fiction author William Gibson also coined the term cyberspace in his book *Neuromancer*.

With hindsight, it is remarkable that the US NII initiative largely ignored the emerging Internet, recognising it only as a network for researchers. In his Buenos Aires speech, Al Gore did not mention the Internet once. The NII was perceived as emerging from big investments by competing big companies. Telecom, entertainment, and cable TV companies were writing the script, and the idea of open and interoperable networks did not fit into their business plans.

Time Warner's Orlando Project in 1994 was a good example of this vision. They planned to connect 4000 household TVs to a service platform via a set-top box and existing coaxial cables. The consumer would select services through a graphical interface, allowing them to download movies, shop, or play games. The expectation was that 'video on demand' would be the killer application on broadband networks. However, the price tag for the set-top boxes was prohibitively high. Time Warner abandoned the project in 1997, claiming it had learned a lot and saying it would focus on, strangely enough, the World Wide Web.

[16] https://www.internetsociety.org/internet/history-internet/brief-history-internet/

Even scientists who were developing the Internet thought it would be only one of many networks in the NII. In a remarkable report, Realizing the Information Future. The Internet and Beyond, published by the National Research Council in May 1994, the researchers conceived a public open data network (ODN) architecture. On page 18, the authors wrote: 'Yet the Internet's success may well be dwarfed by the promised returns from the far larger, more complex, and more integrated NII.'

One of the authors, David D. Clark, a co-designer of the Internet and MIT scientist, characterised the Internet as a 'hostile overlay' when viewed from the perspective of a telephone network. The IP layer decouples the network from applications. Despite the infrastructure being costly, most profits occur through applications. Researchers predicted operators would establish their own service networks, often called 'walled gardens'. This prediction aligned with initiatives such as Time Warner's attempts with Orlando. Additionally, the researchers anticipated the emergence of vertical integration, a phenomenon that unfolded later, albeit unsuccessfully in some instances, as exemplified by the AOL-Time Warner merger in 2001.

The report's authors erred in their pessimistic view about the future of the Internet, which quickly became apparent during the latter half of the 1990s. They were right that telecom companies would remain reluctant to invest billions in low returns from super-fast access networks while big Internet companies made huge profits. This has been at the core of the 'investment dilemma' in telecom regulation. If you wonder why the gigabit society is so complex to bring about, the answer was already there in that 1994 report.

The Internet developed through multi-stakeholder cooperation and private investments. Its rise was barely fostered by any government initiatives at all. However, central resources, such as the allocation of IP addresses and the management of the domain name system, were organised without a formal structure by academics, industry, and the US government.

The Clinton administration conducted a significant international dialogue and debate aiming to privatise and internationalise the management of these core Internet functions. We were involved in these discussions, focusing on shaping Europe's participation in the envisaged Government Advisory Committee. I recall our constructive discussions with Ira Magaziner, a senior adviser to President Clinton, who led the efforts on the US approach to promoting global e-commerce.

Eventually, the US government constituted a private non-profit organisation, ICANN, the Internet Corporation for Assigned Names and Numbers, under Californian law on 30 September 1998. The story of ICANN is fascinating and well-documented, including by ICANN itself.[17]

Over the years, the Commission has advocated for a multi-stakeholder model, emphasising the global and open nature of the Internet, and has not supported attempts to transfer ICANN's responsibilities to the ITU.

---

[17] https://www.icann.org/history

The Internet Comes to Europe

The enthusiasm and determination of a small group of academics brought the Internet to Europe towards the end of the 1980s, thus well before the information society initiative. Their story deserves to be told.

These people understood computer networking and belonged to the European UNIX[18] systems network, EUnet for short, set up in 1982. It was the mirror network of the American USENET, the centre of UNIX expertise. These networks connected computers or sites with several computers, allowing users to communicate by email and receive news and information. EUnet grew fast from ten connected computers in three countries to more than 500 in 1985. The Centre for Mathematics and Computing (CWI) in Amsterdam (Netherlands) functioned as the central network node and provided the cross-Atlantic gateway to USENET.[19]

The connections between the sites ran over ordinary phone and leased lines, which were slow and expensive, and some devices (such as auto-diallers) were not even legal in some countries. The Commission-enforced liberalisation of end terminals and telecom services, leading to more choices and lower prices, would inadvertently help these communities enormously.

In 1987, Daniel Karrenberg, a German managing the EUnet central computer at CWI, promoted converting the network to TCP/IP, which was already happening on the other side of the Atlantic. CWI managed to obtain IP addresses. A US start-up with just 20 employees, CISCO, provided routers and closed the missing link. Arguably, EUnet was the first customer to buy CISCO routers in Europe. After a couple of months, the first TCP/IP network was up and running in Europe, in part, ironically, over so-called Open Standard Interface (OSI) X.25 lines, which were underutilised. On 17 November 1988, CWI established a link to NSFnet in the United States and received the confirmation mail: CONNECTED. The Internet had arrived in Europe.[20]

Hang on a moment. This was a crucial moment, and yet, it is hardly known or celebrated. It is characteristic of historical events that you only realise their importance, if at all, in retrospect.

DG XIII was very sceptical about TCP/IP and kept putting its faith in 'official' standards endorsed by ISO, the ITU, or ETSI. The telecom standards of the future were supposed to be built around ISO's OSI, for instance, or ITU's X.25 for data

---

[18] UNIX is a multitasking operating system developed in the late 1960s by AT&T Bell Labs. Ken Thompson and Dennis Ritchie are particularly notable for their contributions. Thompson initiated the creation of UNIX, and Ritchie developed the C programming language, which was crucial for UNIX's development and portability to various hardware platforms. UNIX inspired the creation of Linux, a popular open-source operating system. UNIX's influence is pervasive in the computing world, underpinning many of the servers powering the Internet. Even Microsoft's Windows NT included some of its concepts, such as a hierarchical file system and support for multiple users, but it was not based on UNIX code.

[19] https://eunet.com/?page=vz

[20] https://www.cwi.nl/en/about/history/cwi-first-european-internet-connection/

communication. On top of that, TCP/IP was American, and the Commission aspired to defend the fledgling European IT industry—digital sovereignty at work.

European academic groups were eager to connect via TCP/IP because it worked, while OSI networks were inflexible and inefficient. Digital policies did not bring the Internet to Europe; on the contrary, traditional telecom stakeholders fought against TCP/IP, known by insiders as the 'protocol war'.

For many users, the first online experience was with 'walled garden' services, such as CompuServe, an online news and information service you would reach via an ordinary phone or ISDN line. When connecting to their server via a modem, you were greeted with a sneering voice saying, 'Welcome to CompuServe'. It was via CompuServe that I received the news of the 1993 military putsch in Moscow with the photo of Boris Yeltsin sitting on a battle tank. Al Gore mentioned this item in his 1994 speech, so the Vice President of the United States and a lowly European civil servant received the same information at the same time via the same service.

RIPE

On 24 May 1989, Robert Blokzijl, a scientist at the Dutch National Institute for Subatomic Physics, and Daniel Karrenberg organised a meeting in Amsterdam, attended by 14 people from 11 organisations, such as INRIA (France) and CERN (Geneva), to discuss how to coordinate the technical and administrative issues emerging from the fast-growing number of TCP/IP networks. Everyone could run a TCP/IP network internally, but as soon as it was connected via a backbone with others, coordination was needed, mainly to ensure the use of unique IP addresses. This was timely, as in the United States, a discussion was taking place on how to handle the Internet globally. Looking at the gigantic size of the Internet today, the fact that this emerged out of voluntary coordination coupled with open protocols and open access is more than impressive.[21]

Later, in 1989, the Amsterdam group established an informal organisation, *Réseaux* IP *Européens* (RIPE). The French-English word combination was *en vogue* in those days. Still, it was also to mock the umbrella organisation of national research networks, the *Réseaux Associés pour la Recherche Européenne* (RARE), an adamant supporter of OSI standards. Nevertheless, in 1992, RARE provided the legal framework for RIPE or, more precisely, the RIPE NCC (Network Coordination Centre), which only became a legal entity in 1998 (registered as a not-for-profit membership association under Dutch law).

RIPE NCC became the first IP Registrar outside the United States. It attributes IP addresses to operators and assumes the role of a neutral coordinator for Internet activities in Europe, part of Central Asia, and the Middle East. Before, everyone had to ask InterNIC in California for IP addresses. RIPE NCC would later take

---

[21] https://www.ripe.net/participate/ripe/history

responsibility for one of the thirteen DNS root servers (the K-Server). This notable achievement brought one of the main Internet infrastructure elements to Europe. Today, RIPE has over 5000 members from more than 70 countries.

Europeans were more involved in the development of the Internet than often assumed. Amazingly, in 1972, INRIA in France started the Cyclades project and developed packet-switched network protocols. Most importantly, they showed that transport control could be put at the network's endpoints. Their results were happily taken up in the United States, while the project was abandoned for political reasons in France in 1976.[22] However, Europe had something else up its sleeve. TCP/IP came to Europe, but the World Wide Web (WWW) went from Europe to the United States. This brings us to CERN in Geneva.

The World Wide Web

Computer networking is a big thing in an organisation like CERN, as several thousand scientists from over 100 countries want to share data and retrieve documents. This was difficult to achieve in an environment with incompatible computer systems, a high turnover of temporary staff, and data encoded in different formats.

In March 1989 and May 1990, Tim Berners-Lee published two concept papers in which he wrote: 'This is why a "web" of nodes with links (like references) between them is far more useful than a fixed hierarchical system.'[23] In November 1990, Robert Cailliau, a Belgian colleague of Berners-Lee, joined his efforts, and they pushed the project forward.

Tim Berners-Lee developed HTTP, the hypertext transfer protocol, by which a user could request a server to retrieve information. He designed HTML, hypertext markup language, a standard for presenting information. Finally, he introduced the concept of a URL (unique resource locator) that would give a page or a document a unique address, enabling the hyperlinks. Based on these protocols/standards, Berners-Lee wrote the software for a server and a browser and set it up inside CERN by the end of 1990. It became a stunning success.[24]

In 1993, CERN put the programme code in the public domain, free for everyone. Soon after, Mark Andreessen from the National Centre for Supercomputing Applications at the University of Illinois (NCSA) developed the Mosaic browser and made it available to the public.[25]

---

[22] https://www.inria.fr/en/our-history

The Cyclades project, hosted by IRIA, was launched in 1972. IRIA's contributions by Louis Pouzin, Gérard Le Lann and Hubert Zimmermann were quickly incorporated into the work that led to the transition from the Arpanet to the Internet. In 1979, IRIA was renamed as INRIA (*l'Institut national de recherche en informatique et en automatique*).

[23] https://cds.cern.ch/record/369245/files/dd-89-001.pdf. Page 5.

[24] https://home.cern/science/computing/birth-web/short-history-web

[25] https://web.archive.org/web/20070702183017/http://www.livinginternet.com/w/wi_mosaic.htm
https://new.nsf.gov/news/mosaic-launches-internet-revolution

Meanwhile, Robert Cailliau organised the first web conference in May 1994 in Geneva, the month we published the Bangemann report, followed by a second one in Chicago in October 1994.[26] At the same time, then working at MIT, Tim Berners-Lee set up the World Wide Web Consortium (W3C) in collaboration with CERN and with financial support from the ESPRIT programme and DARPA. This was the background for the remarks made by Michael Dertouzos from MIT referring to the web at the 1995 G7 conference. Georges Metakides, then Director of ESPRIT, promoted the project inside the Commission, and, slowly, the penny dropped.

I first saw the Mosaic browser when we visited Sun Microsystems in early 1994. At this point, it should have been clear to us that the Internet was the future. Yet, we considered the Internet important for researchers but not for the wider public. The wake-up call came a year later. Netscape (founded earlier by Jim Clarke and Marc Andreessen) released the Navigator browser. This browser was the most user-friendly among the many alternatives and gained rapid market share. On 9 August 1995, Netscape went public and was a big hit. We were stunned; how could a start-up with *de facto* only one software product trigger such a reaction from capital markets? Note that the browser was not free, so it needed to be purchased.[27]

The emergence of the web browser signalled what was to come: the dotcom economy. Yet, the EU and member states were still busy implementing the information society agenda. The future was already there—it was just not everywhere.

References

1. Yoshio Arai, "History of the development of telecommunications infrastructure in Japan", *Netcom*, 33–3/4, 2019. https://doi.org/https://doi.org/10.4000/netcom.4511
2. Vinton G. Cerf and Robert E. Kahn, "A Protocol for Packet Network Intercommunication", *IEEE*, Vol Com-22, No. 5, May 1974.

[26] https://www.w3.org/Conferences/Overview-WWW.html%25

[27] By the end of the 1990s, Navigator had a market share of around 90%. Readers might remember how Internet Explorer pushed Navigator out of the market when Microsoft bundled the browser with Windows and discriminated against other browsers. Today, Google's Chrome has taken the pole position.

Chapter 3
Responding to the Internet Economy

By the mid-1990s, the action plan 'Europe's Way to the Information Society' was being implemented but remained incomplete. Digitalisation and the emerging Internet economy introduced a host of pressing issues, including information security, data protection, copyright, e-commerce, and audio-visual services. There was still work to be done to complete the liberalisation of telecommunications. Our research programmes needed a more holistic approach to respond to a changing technological landscape.

The Commission dealt with these challenges without recourse to a further action plan or strategy. Some initiatives had already been set in motion but required refinements, such as data protection. Others were designed from the ground up, such as formulating encryption policies and regulations for e-commerce.

In 1996, the accession of Austria, Sweden, and Finland expanded the Union to a bloc of 15 member states.

Former Luxembourg Prime Minister Jacques Santer followed Jacques Delors as President of the Commission, and Martin Bangemann continued to serve as the Commissioner overseeing information society policies.

1998: Full Liberalisation of Telecommunications

After the political decision to liberalise all telecom services by 1998, the remaining issue was the opening of telecom infrastructure to competition. This had two components.

The first element concerned infrastructure owned by energy and water utilities, cable TV networks, and telecom lines alongside railways and motorways. These facilities were not initially authorised for public telecom services, prompting a fundamental question: why should such valuable assets, which we referred to as 'alternative infrastructure', remain dormant underground? One argument for

D. Eckert, *40 Years of European Digital Policies*, Professional Practice in Governance and Public Organizations,
https://doi.org/10.1007/978-3-031-61641-9_3

addressing this challenge stemmed from the excessive tariffs associated with leased lines. These high costs posed a significant barrier to data services. In some cases, these tariffs were up to ten times higher than those in the United States. Once the momentum initiated by the Bangemann report gained traction, the process of liberalising alternative infrastructure became relatively straightforward and was officially implemented on 1 January 1996.[1]

The second aspect focused on the freedom to build new infrastructure directly competing with Public Telecommunication Operators (PTOs). While replicating networks may seem inefficient initially, it aimed to address the issue of leased lines. The goal of encouraging competition in building connections was to reduce tariffs and enhance existing networks, expanding coverage and improving quality through innovation.

Two Green Papers prepared the final liberalisation steps.[2] On 17 November 1994, on the 14th floor of the Charlemagne Building, then the seat of the Council, telecom ministers agreed to remove all obstacles to infrastructure competition in line with the 1 January 1998 deadline. Some member states still voiced concerns about the timetable; for instance, the Spanish telecom minister, Josep Borrell, who would later become the EU's High Representative for Foreign Affairs, asked for a more extended transition period. Commissioner Bangemann predicted that none of the countries would eventually use their derogations to their full extent—an accurate prediction. The meeting was a highlight in the history of digital policies and European policy in general. Instead of reading out prepared interventions, ministers debated.

Infrastructure competition would not replace the need for Open Network Provision (ONP) regulation. We still wanted competition on the legacy plain telephone networks. A Directive ensured that authorised operators could access the incumbent's networks and offer competing services. The Directive obliged member states to guarantee universal telephone services, potentially including ISDN, and any co-financing schemes had to be transparent and cost-oriented.[3]

Who would be authorised to enter the market? A Directive established general authorisation as the default scheme instead of individual licensing. This made the EU

---

[1] Commission Directive 95/51/EC of 18 October 1995 amending Directive 90/38 8 /EEC with regard to the abolition of the restrictions on the use of cable television networks for the provision of already liberalised telecommunications services.

[2] Commission Green Paper COM (94) 440 of 25 October 1994 on the liberalisation of telecommunications infrastructure and cable television networks, Part One, Principle and Timetable, Commission Green Paper COM (94) 682 of 25 January 1995 on the liberalisation of telecommunications infrastructure and cable television networks, Part Two, A Common Approach to the Provision of Infrastructure for Telecommunications in the European Union.

[3] Directive 97/33/EC of 30 June 1997 on interconnection in Telecommunications with regard to ensuring universal service and interoperability through the application of the principles of Open Network Provision (ONP).

one of the most open telecom markets. It was also timely in the context of the WTO agreement on basic telecommunication services, concluded in 1997.[4]

The Commission had also proposed an EU-wide authorisation scheme, but this was a step too far for the member states (and still is). Similarly, we probed whether member states could warm up to a European Regulator. No, they could not. The argument against this was that national markets differed, so regulation needed national implementation. Commissioner Bangemann decided to drop the idea. However, we sponsored a group of independent regulators to keep integration moving forward.

Thus, the 1998 liberalisation package resulted in a liberalised but fragmented European market. National regulators were left with a wide margin on how to implement the Directives. Mobile communications were subject to roaming charges, and spectrum allocation, despite closer coordination, remained a national competence. When clearing merger cases, the relevant markets were still defined as national. Would the following review, which was already underway in 1999, fix these shortcomings?

Data Protection

What connects the German 1987 population census to the GDPR, the 2016 General Data Protection Regulation? Mindset. The decision in 1983 to conduct a country-wide census sparked massive protests in Germany. It ultimately led to a landmark ruling by the constitutional court, which introduced the concept of 'informational self-determination'. These extreme anxieties had their roots in the country's fascist past, although they were also influenced by anti-capitalist and, ironically, pro-Soviet movements. The increasing prevalence of computerisation and data storage rekindled fears reminiscent of Orwell's *1984*. A German data protection law aiming to protect the individual against state power came into effect soon after. This created an almost 'religious' mindset towards privacy, subtly influencing the Commission.

During the late 1980s, the initial concept of a Data Protection Directive began to take shape within DG XIII. However, DG III, responsible for the Internal Market, along with its German privacy experts, found the approach insufficient and not protective enough. After an internal power struggle, a compromise was struck: DG III would develop a 'general' Directive, while DG XIII would deal with data issues specific to telecommunications. This is why there are two regulations: GDPR and ePrivacy. The segregation of these regulations, which never truly made sense, should have been rectified at long last by integrating the specifics of ePrivacy into the GDPR, but the separation reflects a form of organisational inertia that has persisted over time on this issue.

[4]Directive 97/13/EC of 10 April 1997 on a common framework for general authorisations and individual licences in the field of telecommunications services.

In 1990, the Commission proposed these two Directives. It would take 5 years to adopt the general Directive and seven for that on electronic communications. Privacy concerns were not equally shared among member states, and substantial resistance emerged. For some, it was seen as Europe meddling with national security, as unlike today, the protection of privacy was predominantly not against companies but governments. Another reason was that the Maastricht Treaty established the principle of co-decision by the European Parliament and Council for most legal acts, making a political agreement for a disputed topic even more complex.

The Data Protection Directive of 1995 laid the groundwork for privacy regulations in the EU for the decades to come. The Directive provided definitions for critical terms, such as 'personal data', 'data subject', 'data controller', and 'processing'. It established core principles, for example, that data should only be collected for specified, explicit, and legitimate purposes. People (data subjects) had to give informed and unambiguous consent for their data to be processed.[5]

Against the background of today's discussion about regulating AI, you may want to read Article 15, which states that people shall not be subject to a decision '... which is based solely on automated processing of data intended to evaluate certain personal aspects relating to him, such as his performance at work, creditworthiness, etc.'. There is nothing new under the sun, even in AI ethics.

Regarding data protection in electronic communications, DG XIII had worked out provisions addressing issues generated by ISDN and services enabled by digitalisation. The rules covered confidentiality, caller identification, traffic and billing data storage, and data minimisation. Under a different name, the Directive on ISDN privacy was finally adopted in 1997 as part of the package accompanying full telecom liberalisation. In substance, the Directive, with a neat number of only 16 articles, had been adapted in several ways compared with the original Commission proposal; for instance, rules to govern call forwarding and unsolicited calls were added. In essence, however, it was not much different.[6]

The consequences of the general privacy Directive had a global impact, particularly in relation to the international transfer of personal data from the EU. It mandated that such transfers could only occur if adequate data protection standards were guaranteed. This posed a challenge in the case of the United States, where solid economic ties existed, and American corporations held vast amounts of user data. From 1998 to 2000, the European Commission, specifically the Directorate-General established in 1993 to implement the Internal Market, engaged in extensive negotiations. In July 2000, a Commission Decision resulted in the creation of the Safe Harbour Agreement, which relied on the regulated self-governance of US companies

[5]Directive 95/46/EC of 24 October 1995 on the protection of individuals with regard to the processing of personal data and on the free movement of such data.

[6]Directive 97/66/EC of 15 December 1997 concerning the processing of personal data and the protection of privacy in the telecommunications sector.

to ensure compliance with data protection regulations relevant to trade.[7] This temporarily resolved the issue. Little did anyone suspect that the deal would unravel following the events of 9/11 and the rise of radical Islamists.

Information Security: The Encryption Debate

Today, cybersecurity is at the top of the political agenda. Cyber warfare has become an instrument in geopolitical confrontation. Given the ubiquitous presence of computers, global investment in safeguarding computer systems and networks is measured in billions of dollars, making computers tempting targets for criminals, vandals, and state actors.

However, the landscape was markedly different in the past. While cybercrime and attacks were not absent, their scale was tiny in comparison. Political discourse often revolved around the controversial practice of 'wiretapping' phone calls, particularly in the United States. Information security, back then, was primarily the domain of individual EU member states.

At the European level, security-related matters were notably absent from its research programmes. A group of senior officers known as SOGIS discussed technical aspects and security standards, playing a dual role as both a technical authority and a political safeguard against excessive EU involvement in information security. Over time, SOGIS lost its significance and was eventually absorbed and superseded by EU regulations and institutions.

EU policy and involvement in this area have changed dramatically since the process started at the end of the 1990s. Two intertwined developments characterised the beginning of a full-fledged EU information security policy.

Email and Privacy

The ascent of email communication raised privacy issues, as email servers were easy prey for hackers. The change in the threat environment generated by network connectivity surprised the IT industry, notably companies like Microsoft, Apple, and Oracle. One solution was encryption.

However, encryption requires proper management to generate, store, and process encryption keys. The most arduous task is for users to distribute the keys safely. Ensuring that the sender and receiver of a message can use the same key is manageable in small or professional groups, such as secret services or embassies,

[7] Commission Decision 2000/520/EC of 26 July 2000, pursuant to Directive 95/46/EC on the adequacy of the protection provided by the safe harbour privacy principles and related frequently asked questions issued by the US Department of Commerce.

but not for the public. The solution came with public key cryptography based on large prime numbers.

Multiplying two big prime numbers is easy, but factoring the resulting number back into the original ones is hard. An algorithm generates two keys: a private one (to be kept secret) and its public counterpart (to be published). The sender encrypts a message with the receiver's public key, who can decrypt the mail with his private key. As the encryption and decryption keys are different, the method is known as 'asymmetric'.

Three cryptographers and mathematicians, two Americans and one Israeli, Ron Rivest, Adi Shamir, and Leonard Adleman, were among the first to develop such an algorithm, tellingly named RSA key generation. RSA has become a synonym for asymmetric keys, although other methods exist, such as the Diffie-Hellman key exchange, published even earlier.

But how do I know that a public key published under your name is yours? Thus, I need a trustworthy link between your public key and you as a person. This mechanism is central to public key infrastructure (PKI) and typically relies on trusted institutions that issue digital certificates to authenticate public keys.

Keeping messages secret is good for privacy but can pose challenges for law enforcement. While in favour of cryptography helping citizens and businesses to protect themselves, authorities also feared that criminals could render legal wiretapping meaningless by encrypting their communication. Consequently, governments sought means of obtaining access to keys and devices.

In this pursuit, the US government vigorously advanced the 'clipper chip', a concept based on key escrow. This involved securing keys in hardware to which access could be granted to various government agencies and law enforcement when necessary. However, this idea failed to materialise due to opposition not only from civil libertarians but also from industry and academia, citing concerns related to both technical deficiencies and international competition. Cryptographers, who wielded considerable influence at the time, vocally highlighted the privacy and security risks of this approach.

Meanwhile, the British government introduced a more enticing yet equally contentious proposal. Rightly assuming that key management is a daunting task, their idea centred on incentivising a trusted infrastructure operated by the private sector. Under this model, Trusted Third Parties would provide encryption services with the condition of enabling key escrow capabilities for law enforcement. Recognising that the label 'trusted by the government' was not a compelling selling point, they enhanced the offering with 'digital signatures'. And this brings us to the other development that made information security so important.

e-commerce and Digital Signatures

e-commerce became the driving force for the Internet. Doing business online has many advantages: it is fast, cost-efficient, and has a global reach—in short, it is full of business opportunities. Yet, in the 1990s, it was all new, and people were demanding secure communication, safe payment services, and authentication. Who am I talking to? How can I conclude a contract? These and many more questions needed answers. One was digital signatures.

A digital signature solves two problems simultaneously. It authenticates an expression of will, commonly done through a handwritten signature, and it assures the integrity of the signed digital document to the tiniest detail of a comma. It uses asymmetric encryption but in a reverse manner. You sign a document with your private key. With the corresponding public key, everyone, for example, a judge, can verify the signature's authenticity and the document's integrity. This also means that you cannot repudiate the fact of having signed, creating trust in a business process.

Technically, a PKI for digital signatures is the same as for encryption.[8] A PKI consists of several elements and is challenging to implement. Essential elements are user registration, issuing certificates binding user information to a public key, revocation of retired keys, and time-stamping services. This was the quid pro quo the UK government offered: trust services delivering business value in exchange for key access.

In 1997, we saw a proliferation of initiatives, ranging from digital signature laws in some countries to key escrow obligations in others. We realised the increasing interest of businesses in the availability of easy-to-use cryptography. Selling information security devices from one member state to another was subject to obtaining a licence. The United States had export restrictions on both strong encryption software and hardware.

Against this backdrop, we drafted a comprehensive agenda. On 8 October 1997, the Commission adopted a policy paper entitled 'Ensuring Security and Trust in Electronic Communication. Towards a European Framework for Digital Signatures and Encryption'. Some highlights: The Commission took a pro-encryption position, voicing scepticism about key escrow or similar schemes. It launched the idea of a Directive for digital signatures. The member states should agree to a deregulation of export controls. The fifth research framework programme would provide a budget for security-related projects.

The EU became a prominent voice in the international information security and cybercrime debate. The United States and the EU gradually concluded that unduly

[8] You can find detailed descriptions of how digital signatures work online. However, you might want to look at the Annex of the 1997 Communication on encryption and digital signatures. It still serves as an instructive introduction to digital signatures.

In short, the first step is to create a 'hash' of the document you want to sign. For this, you use an algorithm that transforms text into a smaller string of letters and numbers. Using your private key, you encrypt the hash. This creates the digital signature, which is then made public or attached to the document. The relying party re-creates the received document's hash and uses your public key to decrypt your digital signature, revealing the original hash value. If both values are identical, the document is considered valid and unaltered.

limiting encryption would be counterproductive and removed export restrictions for the signatories of the Wassenaar Arrangement.[9]

Privacy advocates had anticipated widespread adoption by individuals of freely available encryption protocols, such as Pretty Good Privacy, but this did not happen. Instead, SSL (Secure Socket Layer), which out-of-the-box encrypts the traffic between the browser and server, had the most profound influence on the use of encryption for Internet security. The pivotal moment came when Taher El Gamal, a renowned cryptographer and the chief engineer at Netscape, introduced us to the algorithm and protocol. This breakthrough alleviated concerns with law enforcement (who could access data at the server with a warrant) while eliminating the need for any action on the user's part. Consequently, 'https' has become the default setting on the web today.[10]

Electronic Signature Directive

In 1998, the Commission proposed a Directive on electronic signatures. We did not use the notion of a digital signature as this is not the only way to sign documents electronically. Unfortunately, this led to rather clumsy language. For example, instead of referring to a 'public key', the legal text introduced a 'signature verification device'. The Directive, adopted a year later, prevented a patchwork of national initiatives, clarified that electronic signatures are, in principle, valid, and attempted to motivate secure signatures by linking the issuing of 'qualified' certificates to liability.[11]

During the negotiations, some member states, particularly Germany, Austria, and France, successfully pushed for the highest security standards, *de facto* requiring smart cards (for which the Directive was criticised as overly complex and costly). Signatures complying with these requirements, i.e. advanced security methods coupled with 'qualified' certificates, would 'satisfy the legal requirements of a signature in relation to data in electronic form in the same manner as a handwritten signature satisfies those requirements in relation to paper-based data'.[12] A digital signature embeds the actions of identification and authentication simultaneously in a specific document.

[9]The Wassenaar Arrangement is an international export control regime where member countries agree to maintain export controls on items with civilian and military applications to prevent the proliferation of sensitive technologies to unauthorised or potentially hostile entities.

[10]Meanwhile, the SSL protocol has been replaced by TLS (Transport Layer Security), which is designed to address the security flaws identified in SSL. TLS was standardised by the Internet Engineering Task Force (IETF).

[11]A qualified certificate must contain essential information (Annexe I of the Directive) and is issued by a service provider fulfilling a range of conditions (Annexe II of the Directive).

[12]Directive 1999/93/EC of 13 December 1999 on a Community framework for electronic signatures.

This did not prompt a digital transformation of paper-based services since member states initially had to revise form requirements for specific legal procedures to accommodate electronic documents. Only then could the principle of equivalence apply. Unfortunately, this adaptation process progressed slowly and incompletely over time, highlighting the shortcomings of top-down technical regulation. It became evident that a 'qualified signature' was not necessary for online business. Independent certification services struggled to find viable business models for qualified certificates. Nowadays, processes like tender submissions operate through secure portals, guaranteeing authenticity and integrity without the need for third-party-certified signatures in addition to TLS/SSL certificates.

At a deeper level, this teaches us something more profound: digital transformation involves more than the mere substitution of paper with electronic documents; digitisation alone does not do the trick. You need to redesign processes to fully harness the productivity-enhancing potential of digital technologies. It would take more than 20 years and two revisions of the eSignature Directive in 2014 and 2023 before progress came into view.

A Milestone Reached

As we approached the year 2000, the encryption debate appeared to have concluded. The United States adopted a fresh symmetric encryption standard, AES, crafted by Belgian cryptographers Joan Daemen and Vincent Rijmen, a technology we now employ routinely, often without even realising it. Encryption has since proliferated and plays a pivotal role in safeguarding privacy, facilitating secure transactions, and protecting communications. However, as we will discover later, the debate on encryption is far from resolved.

Copyright: The Two Faces of the Internet for Creators

> [...] may it please your Majesty that it may be enacted [...] that the author of any book or books already composed, and not printed and published, or that shall hereafter be composed [...] shall have the sole liberty of printing and reprinting such book and books for the term of fourteen years, to commence from the day of the first publishing the same, and no longer [...]
> **[Statute of Anne, 1710]**

In the middle of the 1990s, digitalisation and the vision of multimedia networks, and soon the Internet, raised the question of how to protect content when it can easily be copied and distributed. To find answers, countries worldwide had been negotiating under the auspices of the UN WIPO (World Intellectual Property Organization). Two WIPO Treaties were concluded in 1996. These treaties would pave the way for the first general European copyright law. Until that point, several legal acts on specific issues existed, such as a Directive dealing with software, *sui generis* protection for databases, and the Rental and Lending Directive.

The proponents of stronger copyright blamed digitalisation and the emerging Internet as a threat, ignoring the enabling character of these technologies for creators, at least in public discourse. In principle, nothing new. Historically, the development of copyright is a story of its adaptation to emerging technologies, which allowed new forms of expression in the first place. Yet, the Internet was arguably the biggest test for adapting the copyright framework. And so, two intertwined 'battles' unfolded.

In the first one, the interests of the content industry, such as publishers or the music and film industry, collided with the ambitions of the ICT industry to sell devices and provide services over the Internet. The latter argued that ICT and a functioning Internet are crucial for the economy. They did not question copyright but requested limitations.

The other arena of conflict, again not independent from the first one, emerged from the continental European view of copyright primarily as the protection of artists. Copyright infringements were condemned as violating personal rights and considered vital for creators to earn a living. Such a view, for instance, is typical in France, where every politician also seems to be a novelist. A libertarian perspective challenged this view, arguing that widespread knowledge enabled by the Internet would be more beneficial for society and that copyright enforcement would be invasive of privacy and potentially criminalise millions of users.

These struggles found their way inside the Commission. The copyright unit in the Internal Market DG was keen to implement the WIPO Treaties with little regard to the views of the 'digital' advocates; we in DG Information Society were eager to promote the Internet, with some of us even considering it as a sort of revolution that would require a re-think of copyright. We feared that copyright would prevent millions of users from tapping into the global knowledge pool, available at near-zero incremental costs, and restrict their creativity in mixing and altering available content.

Once created, content is a non-rival good; making millions of copies does not destroy it. Hence, economic efficiency would call for free content distribution, but this would reduce the incentive to produce, create, and invest—hence the dilemma.

International Law is on the Side of Rightsholders

In this exchange of arguments and lobbying for political approval, international law was the biggest trump card of the rightsholders. Copyright, as we know it today, goes back to the eighteenth century. In 1710, about 260 years after Gutenberg invented the printing press, the first public copyright, the Statute of Anne, came into force in England. Since then, copyright has evolved in many ways, gradually covering all kinds of exploitations of creative works, most of them enabled by technologies: music (phonograms, vinyl records, tapes, and CDs), film and video (cellulose, broadcasting, tapes, and optical discs), or developments in photography and reproduction (printing and scanning). Copyright became the subject of international law, particularly the 1886 Bern Convention, which was the first and is undoubtedly still the most important (it was last revised in 1976). The WIPO Treaties and the TRIPS (Trade-Related Aspects of Intellectual Property Rights, 1994, part of the World Trade Organisation) agreement are its more elaborate descendants, with specific legal obligations and different signatory states.

These treaties set boundaries for the work on a general copyright regulation at the European level. EU officials had a crucial role in their negotiation, so they implemented co-drafted treaties. The Commission's task was to balance the rights of content owners against the realities and economic value of the Internet. In other words, they had to redefine and fine-tune limitations and exceptions of copyright to render them viable for the Internet age.

One of the most discussed exceptions was private usage, particularly private copying. This had already become an issue with devices such as tape recorders, video recorders, photocopiers, computer disks, CD burners, and scanners. The average user has no intention of piracy and is mainly interested in making safety copies, playing music on several devices, or sharing what they legally bought with friends and families. Yet, in principle, copyright holders could limit such usage by imposing conditions to this effect when selling. Its enforcement would be complex and intrusive, risking collision with privacy laws. The initial solution was to impose a levy on devices capable of copying.

The Internet, however, distorted this balance. Hitherto, private copying was a limited issue, but the Internet allowed anyone, not only professional pirates, to distribute thousands of copies (in theory, an unlimited number) by simply publishing one version on a server. This was and still is a severe problem. The industry reacted by developing digital rights management tools (DRM) and using cryptographic methods to make copying and distributing copyrighted material difficult. Users were unhappy and sought means to circumvent DRMs. This begged the question of whether tools to break DRMs for private copying were legitimate. This issue became one of the thornier topics discussed when drafting and negotiating the European Copyright Directive.

The outcome was that private copying became an optional exception: countries could decide either way, provided they allowed the practice only in exchange for some form of levy, depending on how much copying was allowed. Tools to circumvent restrictions were illegal if they were exclusively designed to do that. However, this was impractical, as digital tools are easily designed as a 'Swiss Knife', serving different purposes.

Finally adopted in 2001, the Copyright Directive transposed the WIPO Treaties into European law.[13] It did not achieve an important goal: to create an Internal Market for content. It contained a list of limitations and exceptions other than private copying, such as quotation rights, temporary copies for technical reasons without

[13]Directive 2001/29/EC of 22 May 2001 on the harmonisation of certain aspects of copyright and related rights in the information society.

commercial intent, the purpose of caricature, parody or pastiche, or the purpose of illustration for teaching or scientific research, all of which were left to member states to apply or not. Overall, it stayed in the tradition of copyright, considering competing rights of unequal value, following the principle of *in dubio pro auctore*. The market and the Internet continued to evolve during negotiations, adoption, and entry into force of the Copyright Directive.

Technology Fills Copyright with Life

Once, in a meeting with a Hollywood executive, I asked about new business models instead of fighting market developments through lawsuits. He did not appreciate the question, pointing to the thousands of jobs at stake. And indeed, at the beginning of the Internet boom, the copyright industry had good reasons to be scared. For instance, in 1999, Shawn Fanning and his coding pals developed NAPSTER, a file-sharing system connecting the hard disks of millions of users to a virtual database containing copyrighted material. They argued that they did not copy anything, did not host content on the server, and only enabled a network of users to share all kinds of content. Nice try, but the courts had a different opinion and rendered services like NAPSTER illegal.

Sharing and distributing music and videos over the Internet was made practical by compression technologies, such as mp3 and mpeg4. In the United States, the first attempts to sell music online, for instance, (by mp3.com or emusic.com), failed. They could not secure sufficient music rights, and playing music on computers was not attractive. Steve Jobs and Apple showed the way when they introduced the iPod with the brilliant marketing of '1,000 Songs in Your Pocket'. You would have expected Sony to be the frontrunner, as they were the market leader with their Walkman, but they did not grasp the notion of disruptive technologies explained so forcefully by Clayton Christensen in his 1997 book *The Innovator's Dilemma*.

Apple did not own most of the critical technologies that went into the iPod but bought and integrated what they needed to realise their vision. Steve Jobs said that they invented the iPod because they loved music. The critical issue was convincing music labels that the iPod-iTunes combination would protect their commercial interests. This lesson is for more than just Sony: being a technology leader does not mean becoming the next innovator. The compression standard mp3 was a German invention,[14] yet no German company used it, at least not successfully. Hence, the big money was for Apple and the Americans, leaving just peanuts in royalties for Germany.

The iPod has become a thing of the past, replaced by cutting-edge video and music streaming technology. Online gaming now thrives as a billion-dollar industry, courtesy of the Internet. Social media platforms have become indispensable for

[14] https://www.iis.fraunhofer.de/en/ff/amm/mp3history.html

promoting music and videos, with TikTok users wielding significant influence over the success of songs and artists. This transformation has given birth to a diverse array of business models. The market has answered my question to the Hollywood executive.

The functioning of the internet has introduced a critical copyright-related issue: liability. As content passes through the Internet, it is temporarily stored on servers, essentially creating copies. Servers host various items uploaded by individuals who do not own them and are potentially accessible to millions of users. The pressing question arose: who bears responsibility for commercial losses and violations of criminal law if the content is illegal beyond the issue of piracy? Finding a robust answer to this question was imperative for the growth of e-commerce.

e-commerce

Video-on-demand was the elephant in the information society's room. The optimism that it could drive the information superhighway crumbled quickly, as we saw with the Orlando Project. Its time had not yet come. But the saviour was around the corner: e-commerce.

E-commerce required little bandwidth. A website on top of your traditional offline shop, and off you go. Well, not quite that easy. First, the online shop needed a payment system. Credit card companies were more than happy to provide this service. But what about security? Some banks developed an online bank transfer protocol, which was highly secure but not scalable. The solution came, as it often does, from Silicon Valley. Yes, it was Netscape's Secure Socket Layer, SSL, that we encountered earlier as becoming the default online encryption.

With secure payment out of the way (in principle), e-commerce needed good logistics, customer relationship software, online advertisement, visibility on the web, web design, and much more. Thus, selling software and services to support e-commerce boomed, but only some web shops succeeded. Some commentators quipped that it was like the gold rush. It wasn't the gold diggers who became wealthy, but the guys selling shovels.

One of the successful web shops was an online book dealer from Seattle (US). It would make little money, but the company's backers underwrote its aggressive growth strategy: Amazon (founded in 1994) launched its first website in July 1995. People here in Europe were wondering why Amazon became the darling of the stock market. This tells you a lot about American capitalism. Sure, it was risk-taking on the one hand, but Jeff Bezos convinced investors that the demand for e-commerce is global and, therefore, you had to grow quickly. They understood, and the rest is history.

European companies had a more limited view, often only national. It would be wrong to say that we at the Commission knew better. Not at all. We were still busy with telecom regulation, data protection, and so on, but towards the end of the 1990s, the penny dropped.

How could we promote e-commerce on a European scale? One idea was to exempt cross-border online trade from value-added taxes, but this idea died faster than it emerged. We included e-commerce technologies in our research programmes, but this did not deliver measurable results. At the very least, we concluded that Europe needs an Internal Market for e-commerce—an aspiration that would emerge again 20 years later with the Digital Single Market initiative.

A unit in the DG responsible for the Internal Market, headed by German lawyer Margot Fröhlinger, drafted the e-Commerce Directive, adopted in 2000, one year before the Copyright Directive.[15] It enacted the 'country of origin' principle for online business (termed 'information society services'), ensuring that a website legally established in one member state could sell across the EU without further formalities.

The most contested aspect of the Directive was its liability provisions regarding illegal (digitalised) content, which could transit through networks and be hosted on servers without the approval and knowledge of providers. Rightsholders claimed that operators and hosting services should be responsible for actively guarding against piracy and be held liable for any damage. The discussion within and outside the Commission was intense.

The solution was a 'notice and takedown' provision. Hosting providers would not be liable if they removed illegal content after being notified. Implementing this provision gave rise to various interpretations and court rulings. When is a takedown request legitimate, how swiftly must a response be, etc.? Mere conduits, caching providers, and other online intermediaries would be subject to injunctive relief under the Copyright Directive.

The e-Commerce Directive, because of its 'country of origin' and 'notice and takedown' provisions, was widely praised, though not necessarily by the content industry. As this Directive was considered a cornerstone to enable online business, the Commission never attempted to re-open it until recently, when the Digital Services Act amended it. Rightsholders lost fierce battles at the time over intermediary liability in both the e-Commerce Directive and the Copyright Directive but would eventually get their 'revenge' 20 years later with the 2019 revision of the latter.

Jurassic Park and Convergence

In 1994, we visited the computer company Silicon Graphics in California. In front of their headquarters stood a dinosaur, and the entry hall was full of posters of Steven Spielberg's Jurassic Park movie, a stark contrast to the old-fashioned Siemens building in Munich, where we had held meetings shortly before. Silicon Graphics

[15] Directive 2000/31/EC of 8 June 2000 on certain legal aspects of information society services, in particular electronic commerce, within the Internal Market (Directive on electronic commerce).

had provided the computers for animating the film. For my colleagues Michael Niebel, Jack Metthey, and me, this was the true spirit of the information age; in yesterday's language, it was simply cool.

Computers had changed the way movies were made and TV studios operated. In the analogue world, broadcasting, telecommunications, and IT were distinct. You did not watch TV on a computer. Digitalisation changed this, allowing us to consume the same content on different devices and deliver the same service over several networks. Suddenly, we had web TV, set-top boxes, a telecom back-channel to request a video via satellite, pay TV, multimedia computers, and more.

This process was called 'convergence' and is still ongoing, both in producing content and in devices and networks glued together by services. Artificial intelligence, for instance, is augmenting and replacing human-directed computer animation, as in Jurassic Park. People watch TV via the Internet and on any device. TV sets have become smart and directly connected to the Internet. Convergence is indeed one of the concepts in digital policy that has proven to correctly reflect what is happening.

In the 1990s, digital pay TV was the new kid on the block and raised unprecedented questions. Pay TV required a set-top box for signal descrambling and handling customer relationships. As consumers did not want to pile up boxes, the question of how to foster interoperability arose. One idea was to mandate a common interface to promote competition between service providers. After a long debate, the Commission did not go down this route.

The Commission's competition department forbade joint ventures of content, broadcasting, and network providers to preserve platform competition [1]. An attempt by the German pay TV Kirch Group, Bertelsmann, and Deutsche Telecom to form an alliance did not obtain the green light.[16] Commissioner Bangemann considered this joint venture a potential global actor and the focus on a national market as short-sighted. Over time, the Commission has shifted. For example, Vivendi (majority stakeholder of Canal+) was allowed to buy Seagram (owner of Hollywood studio Universal) under certain conditions.

In 1997, the Commission published a Green Paper on convergence, describing the state of the art, highlighting opportunities, and sketching regulatory avenues.[17] Yet, the paper was a bit of a tragedy. It was ahead of its time. True convergence was still to come. Besides semantically using the term in various initiatives, no significant initiative followed, as we will see with the 2002 telecom package. Its main conclusion was that the respective regulations of content and networks should be kept separate.

[16] Commission Decision 94/922/EC of 9 November 1994 relating to a proceeding pursuant to Council Regulation (EEC) No 4064/89 (IV/M.469—MSG Media Service).

[17] Green Paper on the Convergence of the telecommunications, media and information technology sectors, and the implications for regulation. Towards an information society approach. COM (97) 623 of 3 December 1997.

This conclusion was a politically motivated tranquiliser for media regulators and public broadcasters who feared being swept away by telecom-inspired deregulation. The fallacy was that content regulation was linked to specific services, but now, these could run on any network. Teleshopping was one example: it was handled differently than e-commerce. Video-on-demand rendered time-dependent protection of minors less effective, as well as restrictions on commercials. Some national regulators stepped in and created (or perhaps I should say, invented) a legal base for media regulators, such as Germany and its 16 *Länder* media agencies. Until today, this (*Telemediengesetz*) is still in force, and nobody knows what they should regulate besides defending their turf, such as state monopolies on gambling. The obligation to carry public broadcaster channels on satellite and cable TV was another example of media and telecom regulation overlapping.

Private broadcasters hoped for deregulation. Instead, they got a revision of the Television without Frontiers Directive, albeit adopted before the Green Paper. The adapted Directive codified the 'country of origin' principle. It regulated teleshopping and strengthened the protection of minors.[18]

Interestingly, it added a provision that countries could mark certain events, sports, or other cultural events as so important to society that they had to be aired on free TV. This possibility is still in place. For example, in 2012, I chaired a relevant committee meeting when Lithuania sought a positive opinion on putting the European Championship for men's basketball (the number one sport in Lithuania) on the list. There were no objections or comments; only the female Turkish representative (remember the Directive applies beyond the EU), who asked: 'Why only for men?'. The face of the Lithuanian delegate was priceless.

This legislation would last for the next 10 years. Although its review process started in 2001, it was only amended in 2007.

Consolidation of the ICT Research Programmes

The forthcoming fifth Framework Programme (FP5) was an opportunity to reflect on how to restructure ICT research given the information society narrative. FP5 was organised along four thematic priorities, one of which was 'a user-friendly information society'.[19] However, fairly spontaneously and simply ignoring the legal text, we came up with the notion of an Information Society Technology (IST) programme.

---

[18] Directive 97/36/EC of 30 June 1997 amending Council Directive 89/552/EEC on the coordination of certain provisions laid down by law, regulation or administrative action in Member States concerning the pursuit of television broadcasting activities.

[19] Decision 182/1999/EC of 22 December 1998 concerning the fifth framework programme of the European Community for research, technological development and demonstration activities (1998 to 2002).

This would become the working name for ICT research in FP5 and the official name in FP6.[20]

Our idea was to unify ICT research and integrate the three distinct programmes, ESPRIT, RACE/ACTS, and Telematics, into one, namely the IST programme (which obtained 3.6 billion euros, about 25% of the total budget). We wanted to achieve more consistency and generate synergies amongst the various stakeholders, or to put it differently, to reduce the rivalry between the programme managers. This only worked to some degree because the programmes were community-driven with an inertia resisting radical changes.

Each thematic priority of FP5 had a substructure composed of 16 Key Actions, four of which covered IST.[21] Apart from integration, three novelties stood out.

First, a significant change was the introduction of information and network security as a separate topic and the creation of a dedicated team. This was only possible after the Commission and the member states found common ground on information security. As you will see further on, it has been a success story over the years.

Second, the 'new methods of work' part revolved around the practical implementation of telework, collaborative networking, and mobile work environments. It sought to explore the prerequisites for successful execution, encompassing aspects such as ergonomics and organisational dynamics. This endeavour transpired two decades before the onset of the COVID-19 pandemic, during which the significance of these work arrangements became starkly evident. Certain ideas require the right moment to flourish. While the foundational technology existed, it had not yet achieved widespread adoption.

Third, the introduction of long-term and experimental research (FET) was supposed to act as a pathfinder, exploring new technologies, supporting outliers, and finding the seeds for innovation. FET would stay as a permanent programme element until the recently established Horizon Europe.

In addition, we established the IST Advisory Group (ISTAG), comprising industry and academic representatives. It was a revival of the Round Table of Twelve from the earlier ESPRIT era but with broader participation and technological scope. ISTAG's primary role was to provide the Commission with strategic direction and assistance in formulating the Work Programmes.

In the early 2000s, they came up with the concept of 'ambient intelligence', envisioning a future in which digital technologies would seamlessly integrate into

---

[20]Council Decision 1999/168/EC of 25 January 1999 adopting a specific programme for research, technological development and demonstration of a user-friendly information society (1998 to 2002).

[21]The Key Action 'systems and services for the citizens' was largely identical to the previous telematics programmes.

The Key Action 'information and network technologies' combined ESPRIT and ACTS research areas.

The Key Action, 'new methods of work and electronic commerce', was a novelty.

The Key Action for 'future and emerging technologies' (FET) replaced the basic research section of ESPRIT.

every facet of our lives. Household devices would become interconnected and intelligent, sensors would optimise traffic management, and the Internet of Things would take shape. We championed this narrative for nearly a decade, but the vision was once again ahead of its time. The successor to GSM, 3G, fell short of expectations; Internet access remained too sluggish, the business case for connected devices lacked allure, and smart cities remained elusive.

Fast forward more than two decades, and elements of these visionary ideas have materialised while others have not. Many of these technologies and even more advanced innovations have been brought to fruition, for example, AI in the United States and smart cities in China. One could also argue that the notion of the metaverse is, in essence, a reimagining of the ambient intelligence concept. Both envisage the fusion of the physical and digital realms; however, today's technology, particularly virtual reality and AI, affords us a much more vivid apprehension of this convergence.

Can We Promote the Information Society?

Our prevailing sentiment was that the information society required heightened awareness and a catalyst to dispel apprehensions. While acknowledging the role of private investments, we recognised the public sector's potential to lead by example. In a collaborative effort, the DG for Industry and our DG joined forces to establish the Information Society Project Office (ISPO). This initiative, entirely forgotten, carried a compelling narrative.

ISPO was not a mere communications or public relations entity, nor did it manage a substantial budget. With the IST programme already funding numerous projects, ISPO's mission was to amplify emerging political interests and channel innovative ideas towards the appropriate programmes.

Governments and corporations alike aspired to contribute to bringing the information society vision into existence, yet the primary financial support programme, telematics, operated sluggishly. The bureaucratic journey from work programme to call for proposals to project funding could extend to a daunting 18 months. Consequently, ISPO played a pivotal role in providing political recognition to these initiatives, facilitating the formation of alliances and securing essential financing. Many EU member states also established promotion offices in tandem.

ISPO pioneered the very first website of the European Commission. It served as the primary source for information on digital initiatives, later becoming an integral part of the Commission's online presence. Regrettably, the concept lost momentum over time, hampered by a lack of funding and its unconventional structure. ISPO was, in essence, a unique and autonomous undertaking—a free-spirited initiative originating from within a Commission department—a rarity in today's landscape. Its existence marked an era of genuine belief in the 'information technology revolution' instead of one where the phrase has become a perpetual motif in countless policy papers.

The 1990s: A Foundational Decade

By the end of the 1990s, most of the policies that make up today's digital policy landscape were in place: competitive telecommunication markets, an integrated ICT research programme, and an internal market for broadcasting, copyright, information security, e-commerce, and data protection.

The growth of the Internet triggered anxieties about its societal impact, leading to the principle that 'what is illegal offline is illegal online'. You can hear the same mantra proclaimed by contemporary policymakers as if it were a new revelation. Regulation served as protection against the perceived unlawfulness of the Internet, an attitude that has characterised Europe's approach to digital technologies in general, as demonstrated by the AI Act.

The information society narrative served as an umbrella for the next 10 to 15 years without, however, overcoming policy fragmentation. Each policy owner sought an extension of their regulatory approach. For example, broadcasting regulation was extended to Internet-based audio-visual content. This trend of intensifying domain-specific regulation has persisted up until today.

In Europe, many ideas arose about how to harness the potential of ICT. An impressive number of projects were launched and envisioned. Unfortunately, the state of technology was not ready for many of them, and overall, European entrepreneurship culture was less prone to bridging risky periods. For example, the dot-com crash of the year 2000 was sobering on both sides of the Atlantic, but it stifled European ambitions much more than in North America.

The RACE vision of IBC did not materialise and was replaced by the Internet. Yet, the IST programme eventually embraced the Internet and emphasised the quality of service and IPv6. The goal was to support telecom companies in developing premium Internet services, an idea soon contested by the concept of net neutrality.

The notion of 'ambient intelligence' could have become a guide to a focused and long-term research agenda. However, EU programmes must serve many stakeholders and balance the interests of member states. The ambient intelligence vision could have led to ambitious AI projects if the momentum had been sustained. Who knows, the AI revolution could have started in Europe.

Reference

1. Konstantina Bania, "European merger control in the broadcasting sector: Does media pluralism fit?", *The Competition Law Review*, Volume 9 Issue 1, pp. 49-80, March 2013.

Chapter 4
The Lisbon Agenda

The 1990s were an exciting decade filled with promise for all things related to digital technologies, and the 2000s seemed poised to pursue this momentum. Telecommunication tariffs were decreasing due to increased competition, and the advent of the third generation of mobile communication (UMTS) signalled Europe's confidence in leading the world into the mobile Internet era.

The euphoria about a 'new economy', where market share was paramount, fuelled the notorious dot-com boom but vanished quickly when the stock market crashed. However, although the crash sounded a warning, it did not dampen the optimism or alter the fundamentals of the Internet economy. Market forces did their job, clearing the deadwood and providing space for successful companies, notably Amazon, Google, and Facebook. Tragically, no European Internet giant emerged during this period.

In 2003, the website Second Life created a virtual world with avatars of real people and conquered the attention of a broad audience. Over time, it lost its appeal, but the idea lives on with the metaverse.

Globalisation was growing fast. International trade and foreign direct investment as a percentage of global GDP increased to around 60% and 5%, respectively, from below 40% and 1% in the 1980s. China's accession to the WTO further propelled this trend.

Former Italian Prime Minister Romano Prodi became President of the European Commission. Erkki Liikanen, former Finnish Finance Minister and Budget Commissioner in the Santer Commission, took charge of DG Information Society.

For Europe, the decade began with great optimism, starting with a forward-looking meeting of its leaders: the 2000 Lisbon Council.

D. Eckert, *40 Years of European Digital Policies*, Professional Practice in Governance and Public Organizations,
https://doi.org/10.1007/978-3-031-61641-9_4

Productivity Growth Matters

It was during one of our staff meetings in the middle of 1999. We were a small team attached to Robert Verrue, who had followed Michel Carpentier as Director General in 1996. Our mission was strategy development and gestation of new policies. One of my colleagues, Alain Stekke, brought up a paper published by the US Federal Reserve Bank, authored by Fed Chairman Alan Greenspan. It stated that despite the economic boom and low unemployment rate, the Fed could keep the interest rate down because of a productivity increase driven by information technology, which was behind the economic expansion. The Fed had no inflation fears.[1]

This was a revelation, a big thing. Why? Empirical evidence had been presented by a top political institution that went against the Solow Paradox. In a book review he wrote in the New York Times on 27 July 1987, Nobel Prize winner Robert Solow stated: 'You can see the computer age everywhere but in the productivity statistics.'[2] Behind this paradox was a conflict between the experience at the microeconomic level, where computers mattered, and statistics at the macroeconomic level, which did not reveal measurable productivity effects. As it turned out, celebrating the death of the Solow Paradox was premature, and Chap. 8 and the Epilogue will come back to this. But then, in our minds, it helped shift digital policy from an industrial approach to a macroeconomic level based on evidence and statistics and not merely hyped up by media and industry public relations campaigns—a big step.

In the team, we said, let's turn it into a policy proposal. So, we drafted a short paper entitled the Digital Initiative. The moment was perfect as a new Commission was about to take office. The former Jacques Santer Commission had already resigned over a dispute with the European Parliament about alleged budget irregularities. The new Commission President was Romano Prodi, who, we thought, would remember his participation in the Bangemann Group 5 years earlier. We knew someone in his preparation team who would put the paper in the hands of the incoming President.

President Prodi took the paper to the Tampere Special European Council on 15 and 16 October 1999, showed it to Finnish Prime Minister Paavo Lipponen, and proposed discussing the approach at the forthcoming Helsinki European Council in December. Yet, Portuguese Prime Minister Guterres, now the UN Secretary-General, intervened and thought this would be perfect for his special Lisbon Council in March 2000. Thus, we were asked to prepare the paper for Helsinki, which would

[1] Alan Greenspan described his thinking at that time in his book, *The Age of Turbulence. Adventures in a New World*, Penguin Books 2007, pp. 166–174. On page 167, he writes: 'My idea was that as the world absorbed information technology and learned to put it to work, we had entered what would prove to be a protracted period of lower inflation, lower interest rates, increased productivity, and full employment.'

[2] The book he evaluated delved into the decline of US manufacturing and strategies to counter it. Solow voiced his critique of the unsupported solutions proposed, particularly the idea of treating technology as a universal remedy. The resemblance to today's discourse on strategic sovereignty is quite remarkable.

be welcomed in its Conclusions and then referred to in Lisbon. Remember, in the EU, everything is a process.

As planned, the Commission presented the paper 'eEurope—An Information Society for All' to the leaders, who concluded:

> The European Council invites the Commission, together with the Council, to prepare the eEurope Action Plan, to provide a progress report to the Lisbon Special European Council on 23/24 March 2000 and to conclude the Action Plan by June 2000.[3]

The writing of the progress report was unique at the time and probably still to this day. Member states directly contributed to the drafting instead of waiting for the Commission to submit a full-fledged proposal. The new Information Society Commissioner Liikanen engaged personally: the notion of an information society for all, an inclusivity objective, was one of his political priorities. On 31 January 2000 in Lisbon, in a meeting chaired by the Portuguese Minister for Science and Technology, José Mariano Gago, officials from the member states and the Commission ran through the draft, discussed details, and decided together on the approach.[4]

The 2000 Lisbon European Council

The Lisbon Council became famous for setting the objective that the EU should become the most competitive region in the world by 2010.[5] The 'new economy', driven by e-commerce, fast Internet, and mobile communications, was a natural focal point of the discussion. The leaders intensively discussed the proposals of the eEurope progress report. Director General Robert Verrue, who was standing by for questions, said he never believed leaders would discuss such details, down to encryption export controls and local loop unbundling. Some commentators even called that Council meeting a Dotcom Summit, which was ironic in the face of the imminent stock market crash.

The Lisbon Agenda aimed to set up a comprehensive reform process, for which the information society was essential. The agenda encompassed research, employment, social affairs, education, and vocational training. The Open Method of Coordination was the way to proceed. This method consisted of benchmarking, monitoring, guidelines, and multilateral surveillance. The idea behind the latter was that member states would analyse each other's performance and comment on

[3] See point 45: https://www.consilium.europa.eu/media/21046/helsinki-european-council-presidency-conclusions.pdf

[4] Commission Communication COM (2000) 130 of 8 March 2000 on eEurope. An Information Society for All. Progress Report for the Special European Council on Employment, Economic Reforms and Social Cohesion—Towards a Europe based on Innovation and Knowledge, Lisbon, 23 and 24 March 2000.

[5] https://www.consilium.europa.eu/media/21038/lisbon-european-council-presidency-conclusions.pdf

mutual progress. So-called multilateral surveillance became a standard process, particularly for employment and macroeconomic policy, and is still current today.

Household Internet penetration stood at 12% on average across Europe, with the Nordic countries way ahead of everybody else. The worrying figure for us was that the United States had reached almost 40%. What calmed us down was mobile phone penetration: it was approaching 50% in Europe, while the United States, with 30%, was behind.[6] Thus, the expectation was that 3G-UMTS would put us ahead in mobile Internet. We were right to assume that mobile access to the Internet would become a driver for the digital economy, only it would be 4G and not 3G and not Nokia but Apple.

The UMTS Disaster

eEurope coincided with the launch of the Universal Mobile Technology System (UMTS) or 3G. In 1998, the spectrum for 3G was harmonised, and the member states were busy preparing for auctions.[7] The frequencies for GSM had been handed out in return for a relatively small fee, if any at all. Now that operators were making profits, the prospect of a mobile Internet boom stimulated stock market fantasies, and governments wanted their share. Why hand out scarce resources for free?

Economists argued that spectrum should be allotted to its most efficient use, and a bandwidth auction is the best way to ensure this. It would also solve problems linked to a 'beauty contest', which can become subject to litigation and not give fair chances to new players. So, a great deal, offering both efficiency and money for governments.

The first problem, however, is that this auction would not decide on the best use—because the application for the spectrum, namely 3G with well-defined parameters—was already signed and sealed, and it was only about which operators would win the licence. Thus, one of the economic textbook arguments could be discarded.

The economists also claimed that, as high as they might end up, auction fees would not negatively impact investment and mobile tariffs, as they are sunk costs. However, these advisers ignored or dismissed the problem of the 'winner's curse' [1]. First, all incumbents had no choice but to pay any price as they had to become a 3G operator; otherwise, this would have ended their mobile business. Thus, potential entrants could tactically increase the cost to astronomical levels, and in some countries, the incumbent offered compensation for them to stop bidding. This was pure gambling and had nothing to do with the efficient allocation of resources. Second, all bidders had the same value assessment attached to the spectrum, as it was

[6] See Annexe of Progress Report.

[7] CEPT report. "Auctions and Beauty Contests in CEPT Administrations". Brijuni, May 2005. https://docdb.cept.org/download/361

about 3G and nothing else. Both effects led to everyone paying too much. Europe-wide, the auction raised more than 150 billion euros. The German government could sell the 3G spectrum for 50 billion euros [2]; 20 years later, it 'only' raised 6.6 billion euros for the 5G spectrum.

The high spectrum prices had two consequences. First, the roll-out of 3G and complementary investments was slowed. The competitive advantage of an early 3G launch was gone. Second, Europe's operators had a financial burden to carry, and if they ever had a chance to compete with the emerging US Internet giants, this chance was gone.

Investment decisions are not only governed by expected returns but also by what the financial market expects. Since then, and indeed for other reasons such as regulation, Europe's operators have suffered from relatively low market capitalisation, and this began with the UMTS disaster.

What are the alternatives to a beauty contest, as used by, for example, Finland? Most importantly, one should design spectrum auctions not to maximise government revenues but to hand bandwidth to operators that will roll out the network quickly and efficiently. Furthermore, one could invest the auction money in passive infrastructure, like renting space for towers or digging trenches to connect these towers with fibre cables. Governments could also pay back parts of the fees in relation to roll-out performance. One could also discourage tactical bidding by asking for a higher entry fee.

This lesson has only been partially learned. The regulators are more careful in designing the process, and the operators know better how to avoid running into a disaster. Yet, the 4G and 5G spectrum auctions still led to valuable investments being taken out of the market.

eEurope 2002 Action Plan

After the Lisbon Council, we finally drafted, again with direct input from the member states, the eEurope 2002 Action Plan. Why 2002? The idea was to launch an initiative with actions to be accomplished by the end of 2002. The stakes were so high that it should be linked to a critical date, as with the Internal Market 1992 objective. Europe had no time to lose; the United States was pushing ahead at 'Internet' speed.

On a personal note, during that time, I developed a close working relationship and friendship with the Portuguese Minister for Science and Higher Education, Mariano Gago, and his team, which lasted for many years until his premature death on 17 April 2015.

The eEurope Action Plan became lengthy, with more than 60 measures to be completed by the end of 2002. Its structure and design became a model for many initiatives that followed, even until today. We most visibly introduced the 'who does what, how, by when' boxes and the formula 'The Commission will/intends' and 'Member States are invited to', which have become standard in such strategy documents. The initiative contained quantitative indicators to measure progress, a practice that persisted until the recent Digital Compass.

The Commission adopted just a draft as it had to be reviewed and endorsed by the European Council in Feira on 19/20 June 2000.[8] And this is what happened:

> The European Council endorses the comprehensive eEurope 2002 Action Plan and requests the institutions, the Member States and all other actors to ensure its full and timely implementation by 2002. . . .[9]

Bingo. Since then, digital action plans and strategies have become indispensable in every Commission and European Parliament cycle.

Achievements

The initial impetus behind eEurope stemmed from the perceived increase in productivity attributed to ICT. In the annexe to the eEurope progress report of March 2000, you will find a macroeconomic analysis of what was termed the 'e-economy' or the 'new economy'. The main instrument for increasing productivity centred on the rapid proliferation of the Internet premised on the principles of being 'cheaper, safer, faster'. The productivity narrative waned as time passed and never resurfaced in subsequent strategies. It seems you cannot sell productivity as a policy goal.[10]

eEurope encompassed numerous measures tailored to specific applications and technologies, such as healthcare, skill development, and transportation. This approach followed the tradition of earlier initiatives like the Information Society Action Plan and the ambitions of telematics programmes. While these measures may have had a limited direct impact, their role in stimulating the development of ecosystems should not be underestimated—two examples illustrate this well.

We initiated a Smart Card programme supported by European stakeholders. These smart cards were designed to enhance the security of digital transactions, with a particular emphasis on their implicit role in advanced electronic signatures. While the initiative did not immediately lead to widespread adoption of smart cards, it did lay the foundation for electronic Identity Cards (eID). Estonia took the lead in Europe by issuing the first eID cards in late 2002.[11]

---

[8]Draft Action Plan COM (2000) 330 final of 24 May 2000 on eEurope 2002. An Information Society for All. Prepared by the European Commission for the European Council in Feira, 19–20 June 2000.

[9]See point 22: https://www.consilium.europa.eu/media/21027/santa-maria-da-feira-european-council-presidency-conclusions.pdf

[10]The Lisbon process and eEurope encouraged our colleagues from the DG dealing with economic affairs to launch the KLEMS project, aimed at collecting productivity and growth statistics. This data set is still being updated. https://www.rug.nl/ggdc/productivity/eu-klems/

The project has been extended to global cooperation: https://www.worldklems.net/wkhome

[11]https://e-estonia.com/the-making-of-a-giant-estonia-and-its-digital-identity-infrastructure/

Another initiative involved 'grid technology', a concept originating from CERN, which envisioned distributed computing to manage the vast volumes of data they needed to process. Unfortunately, as an extension of the web, the Worldwide Grid never materialised. Federated computing, while valuable, has remained a specialised application, as the prevailing solution today is cloud computing.

Interestingly, many may not be aware that the Galileo project, Europe's satellite navigation system intended as an alternative to GPS, was a component of the eEurope strategy. It received a significant boost through political elevation to the European Council, which kick-started its development.

And then, there was the dot-eu domain. Commissioner Liikanen discussed creating this domain during one of our internal meetings.[12] Wonderful. The idea was to bolster the Internal Market for e-commerce, providing companies with a European presence. However, acquiring this domain name presented challenges, primarily because the EU is not a traditional nation-state. With the assistance of RIPE, we managed to persuade ICANN that, from an Internet perspective, the EU functioned as a *de facto* country. Initially, European institutions used the dot-int domain name but transitioned to dot-eu once it became operational. So, dear reader, when you utilise dot-eu, you now know where it came from.

Finally, the Action Plan lent political momentum to the adoption of the 2002 telecom package, which was still pending at that time. In addition, the Commission increased competition for Internet access by mandating 'local loop unbundling'. Let's examine these two measures.

Local Loop Unbundling

In the late 1980s, AT&T in the United States explored ways to deliver high-quality media, particularly video on demand, through the copper telephone network to compete with cable companies. Cable companies and satellite providers were employing cumbersome methods for video on demand, involving the establishment of a telephone backchannel and downstream media products.

Meanwhile, at Bellcore, the renowned Bell Labs, Joseph Lechleider developed Asymmetric Digital Subscriber Line (ADSL) technology, offering more download bandwidth and effectively eliminating copper wire noise.[13] As a commercial application, it did not gain traction; even cable companies struggled to provide a profitable video-on-demand service.

However, a team from the French company Alcatel witnessed a demonstration of ADSL technology at Bellcore and was highly impressed. Alcatel invested in this

[12] In his memoir *The Commissioner*, as yet only published in Finnish, Liikanen attributed the idea to Christopher Wilkinson, a manager at DG INFSO who lived in his neighbourhood and who never made the proposal to the drafting team internally.

[13] https://gizmodo.com/joseph-lechleider-inventor-of-early-dsl-internet-tech-1701997663

technology, a decision that would prove prescient. ADSL was a solution that met the growing demand for fast Internet access. Before this, the dominant access method was via an ordinary telephone line with dial-up modems, which was both slow (Broadband ISDN modems could only provide up to 144 Kbps) and expensive. In contrast, ADSL offered speeds of up to 6 Mbps, representing a significant leap forward. Alcatel maintained a leading position in the ADSL market for many years and continued to develop more advanced solutions, including VDSL and Vectoring.[14]

What makes ADSL interesting for regulators is its ability to unbundle Internet access from ordinary telephone service. Competition to provide phone services mainly consisted of a competitor reselling the incumbent's capacity, particularly for long-distance and international calls. With the increasing demand for fast Internet access, the 'local loop', the last mile from the street cabinet to the home, became the battleground. Competitors were interested in 'renting' the ADSL part, excluding the less attractive phone service.

Local loop unbundling emerged as a cornerstone of the eEurope initiative. It initially garnered political consensus at the Lisbon Council and received subsequent confirmation at the Feira European Council. Commissioner Erkki Liikanen was an early advocate of this legal measure.[15] He insisted on mandating unbundling through a Regulation. Remarkable inter-institutional cooperation facilitated the swift adoption of the Regulation in December 2000.[16] Including it in a Directive of the revised telecom framework, which was adopted in 2002, would have resulted in a delay of roughly 4 years (considering transposition time). Consequently, DSL broadband access rapidly increased, and the vision of an Information Society for All began to take shape.

The 2002 *ex ante* Competition Framework for Electronic Communications

The liberalisation of telecommunications allowed competition but did not guarantee it. The 1998 framework aimed to stimulate competition through regulation, mainly through mandating Open Network Provision (ONP). Colleagues from the competition department thought measures against abusing dominant positions would suffice.

[14] https://ieeemilestones.ethw.org/Milestone-Proposal:ADSL

[15] In *The Commissioner* (quoted above), Liikanen recalled how he was inspired by a research paper authored by three French academics: J.J. Laffont, P. Rey, and J Tirole, "Network competition: I. Overview and nondiscriminatory pricing", *RAND Journal of Economics*, 1998 29(1), 1–37. https://doi.org/10.2307/2555814In this paper, the authors write: '...freely negotiated access charges may prevent effective competition in the mature phase of the industry'. The reference to the 'mature phase' is crucial, as the question of whether regulated access should also apply to new markets, like fibre cables, has remained a controversy until today.

[16] Regulation (EC) No 2887/2000 of 18 December 2000 on unbundled access to the local loop.

The option to withdraw the ONP regulation and replace it with the application of *ex post* competition law was included in Recital 25 of the 1997 Interconnection Directive. Yet, as anti-trust cases take time and might not deter subtle anti-competitive behaviour, the Commission and the member states eventually dismissed this approach. Instead, the telecom units in both DGs worked out a detailed regulatory regime modelled on competition law.

The methodology consisted of defining adequate markets for, among others, leased lines or call termination, followed by an analysis to determine whether these markets were competitive. The main criterion for competition was the absence of a player with Significant Market Power (SMP), defined as a market share of more than 25%. National regulators would use Commission Recommendations and Guidelines to do this job and take appropriate measures from an impressive arsenal. For example, regulators could mandate transparency, co-location of equipment, facility sharing and even impose price controls. The expectation was that competitive markets would predominate over time and regulation would gradually scale back. Twenty-plus years later, the picture is mixed.

The idea of establishing a European regulatory authority had been discussed with member states since the 1998 package. As mentioned in the previous chapter, member states consistently argued that their national regulators were best positioned to implement these rules. As a result, the Commission again did not put forth any proposal in this regard.

Considering convergence, the framework replaced the term 'telecommunications' with 'electronic communications', which has become the established terminology. It notably clarified that cable TV network operators are subject to telecom regulations unless operating under those relating specifically to TV broadcasting. For the sake of practicality, I will continue to use the term 'telecommunications' or 'telecom' as it is more concise.

The comprehensive reform package was officially adopted in March 2002, comprising four Directives: one establishing the framework, another outlining access obligations, a third defining the authorisation authority of member states, and a fourth adapting universal service provisions. The Framework Directive laid the foundation for a sophisticated regulatory structure and culture, focusing on fostering competition, safeguarding consumer interests, and upholding user rights.[17] Alongside the 2002 package, there was a revised ePrivacy Directive, often humorously referred to as the *Cookie Directive*, which will be discussed in the following section.

[17] Directive 2002/21/EC of 7 March 2002 on a common regulatory framework for electronic communications networks and services.

Directive 2002/22/EC of 7 March 2002 on universal service and users' rights relating to electronic communications networks and services (Universal Service Directive).

Directive 2002/20/EC of 7 March 2002 on the authorisation of electronic communications networks and services (Authorisation Directive).

Directive 2002/19/EC of 7 March 2002 on access to, and interconnection of, electronic communications networks and associated facilities (Access Directive).

The political yardstick of success was falling price levels, increasingly focusing on Internet access. Politicians like celebrating consumer benefits. However, incumbents voiced concerns that the regulatory burden would stifle their ability to invest in enhancing networks. Regulators argued the opposite and referred to the 'ladder of investment' hypothesis, according to which new entrants would use the networks of the incumbent operator as a hub. After establishing a customer base, they would build their physical network elements step by step, including fibre deployment. This prediction was contested by incumbents arguing that competitors would be satisfied with offering services based on guaranteed network access [3]. The empirical evidence is mixed as market developments and regulatory approaches differ between countries. The issue of service-based versus facility-based competition remains unsolved.

The *Cookie Directive*

Why are cookies called 'cookies' on the Internet, even though we cannot eat them? Wikipedia tells us this term derives from 'fortune cookies', which contain a message. In 1994, a software engineer from Netscape (what a fantastic company that was!) developed how a website stores information on a user's browser, improving the shopping experience. In practice, if you visit a site to make a purchase, fill your virtual shopping cart with items, but leave the site to think about it, then, upon your return, without a cookie, you will have to start all over again. Thus, cookies are helpful and often indispensable for a comfortable web experience. But not all cookies are equal.

Almost routinely, websites also set 'third-party' cookies in addition to their own cookies in a browser (or at least do not prevent their being set). These mainly stem from advertisers' interest in finding out users' preferences. Various methods allow these cookies to find their way to your browser, often through arrangements between websites. Even if you never visit the advertiser's site, these cookies can (to some extent) track your web browsing and display commercials that might interest you. This service is not inherently a vulnerability; many users appreciate relevant advertisements. However, it was considered that people would prefer to be asked for permission first.

This is what the 2002 ePrivacy Directive aimed to achieve.[18] It replaced the 1997 Directive and addressed, amongst other things, the cookie issue. Service providers must inform users about cookies and offer an opt-out option. Only in 2009, when the Directive was amended, did the cookie rule change to opt-in. Websites must now obtain explicit user consent for cookies (and similar methods) that are not technically

[18] Directive 2002/58/EC of 12 July 2002 concerning the processing of personal data and the protection of privacy in the electronic communications sector (Directive on privacy and electronic communications).

necessary but enhance functionality. As the State of California issued a similar regulation, worldwide websites have adopted the practice of displaying a pop-up banner to ask for consent.

Over time, many people have grown weary of constantly being prompted to click on something to dismiss these banners. Who wants to try and grasp all the implications? So, browsers are increasingly blocking third-party cookies by default. However, this is not the end of tracking, as alternative methods exist to achieve this goal. This illustrates that general privacy rules are more appropriate than technology-oriented regulations.

eEurope 2005

The eEurope initiative struck a chord with the zeitgeist, capitalising on the public's fascination with the Internet. However, the Action Plan's philosophy of 'quick implementation, then it's done' was politically and practically unfeasible. Occasionally, visionaries must confront the harsh realities of the situation. Consequently, policymakers in Brussels called for the development of a follow-up programme. Commissioner Erkki Liikanen entrusted us with preparing eEurope 2005.

At the end of 2002, the Seville European Council endorsed the eEurope 2005 programme.[19] Its logic was to simultaneously address both the demand and supply sides of the digital landscape. Central to this strategy was promoting broadband Internet access while focusing on digitalising public services, creating a positive feedback loop. The succinct action list featured 22 action points alongside proposals for benchmarking and governance.

Broadband was only slowly making its way into homes. The original vision of the RACE programme to build country-wide fibre optical networks was notably absent from the action items. The infrastructure build-out was deliberately left to the private sector. Leveraging local loop unbundling, we had already harvested the low-hanging fruit of stimulating competition. eEurope 2005 proposed that member states reduce costs for rolling out fibre through their town and country planning. Combining road construction efforts with fibre installation could result in significant cost savings. A decade later, this recommendation would evolve into a Directive. Two decades later, the Commission would propose the Gigabit Infrastructure Act to provide more robust regulatory support for this concept. Nevertheless, this begs the question: why is regulatory intervention necessary when member states have been aware of this approach for two decades?

eEurope 2005 emphasised spectrum allocation, expecting that the switchover of terrestrial TV to digital would free resources for fast mobile communications. Yet, it

[19] Commission Communication COM (2002) 263 final of 28 May 2002 on eEurope 2005: An information society for all. An Action Plan to be presented in view of the Sevilla European Council, 21/22 June 2002.

said nothing about how to reap the digital dividend. The strategy did not prepare for 4G, which was a serious oversight.

The Action Plan referred to IPv6 as the foundation for a new Internet, which is misleading. While IPv6 offered a significantly larger address space, it did not promise to revolutionise the Internet or enhance its speed or security. IPsec, which enabled package encryption, had already been integrated into the existing IPv4 architecture. Nevertheless, a few years later, unrelated to eEurope, we devised an action plan to promote IPv6 because the problem of IPv4 address shortage had become pressing.[20]

Despite its strong narrative about broadband, eEurope 2005 did not establish specific targets for download speeds, as would become standard in later strategies. Yet, it was the first initiative that explicitly formulated a broadband policy for the Internet.

On the demand side, proposals were more familiar and more to the point. Support for eHealth, eLearning, and eGovernment had been on the agenda since the Bangemann Report. We agreed with the member states that 20 government services should be digitalised as a priority—12 for citizens, such as birth certificates, car registration, or tax declarations and 8 for businesses, such as planning permissions, VAT declarations, or public procurement. The IST and IDA (Interchange of Data between Administrations) programmes supported projects to add a cross-border dimension.[21]

Despite political enthusiasm, the digitalisation of government services has remained a slow-moving train. Initially, the problem of deploying telematics solutions stemmed from immature technology. Meanwhile, it has become evident that organisational inertia was and remains the main obstacle. Public administrations often settle for specific service levels and established processes, particularly cross-border services.

The eEurope 2005 Action Plan also addressed the issue of information security. Vandals and professional hackers had been plaguing the Internet with viruses and self-propagating worms, resulting in significant damage. Microsoft's software was a frequent target; some may recall the Slammer worm that wreaked havoc on ATMs worldwide. While Internet Explorer, the dominant browser at the time, featured an in-built firewall, it was not activated by default. As many users overlooked it, the Slammer worm was able to spread unchecked. Consequently, the political focus shifted from confidentiality to ensuring the availability of services. It became evident that we needed to consider multiple aspects beyond encryption.

[20]Commission Communication COM (2008) 313 final of 27 May 2008 on Advancing the Internet, Action Plan for the deployment of Internet Protocol version 6 (IPv6) in Europe.

[21]The IDA programme became the ISA programme, Interoperability Solutions for European Public Administrations, which ended in 2021. The Digital Europe Programme now finances projects.

Information Security: The Story of ENISA

Since the establishment of cybersecurity as a European policy, both in terms of research and regulation, we have been discussing related issues in the Council, leading to several policy conclusions. Member states committed to establishing or strengthening computer security emergency response teams or centres (Certs) tasked with raising awareness and providing practical advice.

So far, so good. However, when we reviewed progress in the Council formation, it appeared that not much had been done—lots of papers and declarations, but no action was taken on the ground. Our conclusion was to propose setting up a Task Force at the Council level to assist member states. This became part of the eEurope 2005 programme.

But when we got into the nitty-gritty with the Council, it emerged that they did not have a budget or resources. This was a cold shower—time for plan B. We wrote up the whole concept, thinking we could slide it into a budget managed by the Commission. Our budget colleagues clarified that the Commission could not fund a Council action of this kind. The shower became icy. But then it got interesting. One of the budget experts chimed in and said our document made sense as an advisory agency. Suddenly, the water got warmer. After an internal discussion, Commissioner Liikanen gave us the green light, and we transformed the concept paper into a formal legislative proposal.

The member states were receptive. It helped that the draft proposal contained a sunset clause, signifying that the Regulation establishing the agency would not only be reviewed but also subject to renewal—a significant distinction. This provision gave sufficient assurances to the member states, especially since the idea of creating an agency had come as somewhat of a surprise. Moreover, member states retain significant influence on ENISA's activities through the management board.

In 2004, the European Network and Information Security Agency (ENISA) was established in Heraklion, Greece.[22] While our initial proposal had favoured Stockholm, the European Council decided otherwise. Heraklion was not the ideal location, being somewhat remote, and the agency had a difficult start, including some management issues. Yet, with time, ENISA found its purpose and mission. Its role was upgraded with the Cyber Security Act of 2019, and a year later, its official seat was relocated to Athens while retaining some presence in Heraklion. ENISA's mandate has become permanent, and today, it stands as a cornerstone of European cybersecurity policy.

[22]Regulation (EC) No 460/2004 of 10 March 2004 establishing the European Network and Information Security Agency.

European Research Area

In national politics, research and technology rarely figure among election-winning topics. Still, at the EU level, they are core instruments of making politics and have steadily grown in importance.

Research and technology figured highly on the Lisbon Agenda, where a new concept emerged, the European Research Area (ERA), which became a leitmotif for the sixth Framework Programme (FP6) from 2002 to 2006.[23] The ERA follows Internal Market logic to overcome fragmentation. In practice, it meant more mobility of researchers, a European Patent, and better-synchronised member-state programmes, although the latter never quite came to fruition.

The ERA would remain a mantra of every incoming Commissioner responsible for research up to this day. While attempts to fill this concept with new life have shown only modest success, at least the budget for research programmes at the EU level has increased.

FP6 introduced three instruments that would help make the programme more effective. First, networks of excellence strengthened the value of EU programmes as a driver for ecosystems. Second, integrated projects supported the 'critical mass' idea by supporting more significant initiatives. Third, European Technology Platforms (ETPs) gathered stakeholders around strategic technologies such as nanoelectronics, which integrated projects would implement. The ETPs were the frontrunners of the various public-private partnerships that would become crucial for future FPs.

On 15 and 16 March 2002, the Barcelona European Council enhanced the Lisbon Agenda by setting the objective that the EU should spend 3% of its GDP on R&D by 2010.[24] The EU started with an average of about 1.8% in 2000, half public and half private, and did not reach this goal in 2010, and not even in 2023. The Bruegel Institute ironically remarked that the EU was missing the wrong target [4]. The point here is that private research investments are a function of industry structure and company profiles. For instance, if a country's economy is based on tourism, banking, or agriculture, its research needs are lower than in a country with automobile, electronic, and airspace industries. The EU was setting a target that did not correspond to the structure of its economy. Nevertheless, it would stick to this target with its Europe2020 strategy during the second Barroso Commission.

[23] Decision No 1513/2002/EC of 27 June 2002 concerning the sixth framework programme of the European Community for research, technological development and demonstration activities, contributing to the creation of the European Research Area and to innovation (2002 to 2006). The IST programme supported about 1100 projects, and 5000 organisations participated.

[24] See point 47: https://www.consilium.europa.eu/media/20939/71025.pdf

The Information Society Technology Programme

> The activities . . . are intended to stimulate the development in Europe of both hardware and software technologies and applications at the heart of the creation of the information society in order to increase the competitiveness of European industry and allow European citizens in all Union regions the possibility of benefiting fully from the development of the knowledge-based society.
>
> Decision of the European Parliament and the Council to establish the sixth framework programme, Annex 1, 27 June 2002.

It is hard to believe we penned such a verbose piece. This quote illustrates how grand policy ambitions tied to research programmes can sometimes lose touch with the practical realities of what these programmes can or cannot achieve. I have included it because this overly wordy drafting remains a common feature in digital policy documents.[25]

The IST programme was allocated 3.6 billion euros, which accounted for approximately 22% of the total FP6 budget of 16.3 billion euros. In relative terms, the budget allocated to ICT was on the decline, having previously constituted around 30%, and in FP5, it still represented approximately 25%. This divergence from earlier levels contradicted the notion that ICT would play a pivotal role in achieving the Lisbon objective.

The ISTAG continued to serve as a strategic adviser and renewed its vision of ambient intelligence. As said earlier, this vision could have been the narrative for shaping the IST programme and beyond, but this was not the case. It merely found sporadic mentions in the bi-annual work programmes.

The IST component of FP6 broadly encompassed the same technologies as in FP5, albeit with a different packaging. In FP5, they were organised as Key Actions, while in FP6, they were framed as Technological Priorities,[26] and in the ensuing work programmes, sub-categories were labelled as Strategic Objectives, which is perplexing, as the Framework Programme should ideally be the arena for defining strategic objectives.

In December 2009, an impact study lauded the programme's effectiveness in achieving its objectives.[27] However, this assessment relied solely on interviews with programme participants. Such evaluations tend to accentuate the positive aspects and often narrow their focus to specific goals rather than considering the broader

[25] Article 3.1 (a) (general objectives) of Decision (EU) 2022/2481 of 14 December 2022 establishing the Digital Decade Policy Programme 2030 reads: 'promoting a human-centred, fundamental-rights-based, inclusive, transparent and open digital environment where secure and interoperable digital technologies and services observe and enhance Union principles, rights and values and are accessible to all, everywhere in the Union'. All 11 objectives in this Article are written more or less in this style.

[26] These covered citizen and business applications, communication and computing infrastructure, components and microsystems, information management and interfaces, and FET (Future and Emerging Technologies).

[27] WING Watching IST Innovation and Knowledge, FP6 IST Impact Analysis Study, December 2009.

perspective. The gold standard for evaluation is a counterfactual impact assessment, a challenging endeavour that necessitates identifying a control group that did not participate in the programme. Our internal review of what we had accomplished with FP6 and previous Framework Programmes differed from the findings of this study.

A View from Inside the Machine Room

In 2007, the management of DG INFSO took a day out to discuss where we stood and where we wanted to go. The meeting focused on the *raison d'être* of the IST programme and research policy in general. Is it about technology, innovation, science, or industry? Our meeting was timely as we were starting the ICT part of FP7.

Most participants believed we should aim at an active industry policy, becoming a pathfinder anticipating opportunities and problems. One example put forward was developing or influencing standards at a pre-competitive stage. Could we have better promoted Hyper LAN, the European alternative to the American Wi-Fi standard? Probably not, but in any case, we conceded that technology was moving too fast for our research programmes. One colleague stated that 2 years would pass from designing a call for proposals until projects might start. So, in many cases, leaving things alone would deliver better results.

Nevertheless, ever since ESPRIT, the Commission has retained the ambition of growing a competitive European industry, which, by design, research programmes are not sufficient to achieve. As another colleague concluded: 'We can only scale up if the industry scales up.' However, the lack of global digital players has become a systemic problem for Europe's ambitions. The Commission acknowledged this with the 2023 Chips Act and mobilised resources to bolster production facilities.

We asked ourselves how we picked topics for the research programmes. This simple question led us to delve deep into policymaking. This is worth taking a closer look at.

At a high level, and setting aside the fundamentals of basic science, research topics tend to be industry- and technology-specific, displaying a remarkable degree of consistency. Foundational components of the ICT industry, such as semiconductors, computers, and software, were as relevant in the ESPRIT programme as they are in Horizon Europe today. The fundamental changes occur within the sub-areas, mirroring specific technologies' evolving economic and social significance. Such topics can be integrated effectively into the research programme only by a collaborative constituency.

Engaging with this constituency demands an open and fair approach that respects various interests. It entails personal interactions, public consultations, workshops, thorough analysis, and the acquisition of independent advice. European research programmes excel in organising and maintaining this well-structured and transparent process. However, this process is heavily influenced by 'public perceptions'. The ICT industry is adept at creating hype, attracting significant media attention to which a political entity like the Commission is not immune. This is why politically irrelevant issues like RFID (radio frequency identification) chips came onto the agenda. Furthermore, striving for openness and fairness can lead to a tendency to try to please everyone. For instance, we supported 3D TV sets because the consumer electronics industry held considerable sway, even though our research funding was not a decisive factor in this commercial endeavour—which has only enjoyed limited success thanks to the so-far-unbridged gap between business hype and reality.

This last example hints at a paradox. Once a constituency is established, it tends to dictate the selection of research topics along a path-dependent trajectory. However, this does not necessarily translate into projects building upon each other to form a coherent long-term strategy. Projects within the same field, from one Framework Programme to another or one work programme to the next, often stand alone and are soon forgotten once the new programme commences. This phenomenon also results from the day-to-day realities faced by project officers. The obligation to manage and conclude a project according to a complex rulebook without incurring issues with the Court of Auditors often takes precedence over effectively exploiting the project's outcomes.

As a result, the chain of projects within a specific field does not necessarily contribute to a growing knowledge and technology base. A lack of institutional memory can hinder the development of a more impactful research agenda. However, a word of caution, as we have witnessed, RACE I and II pursued the philosophy of a cumulative research agenda but failed to achieve their goals. FP7, as discussed in the next chapter, introduced some innovative approaches to obtaining a more streamlined research agenda.

References

1. Martin Bennett and Matthijs Canoy: "Auctions and Precautions: Overbidding in Spectrum Auctions and its Possible Impact", *Working Paper 127, CPB*, June 2000.
2. Veronika Grimm and Frank Riedel and Elmar G. Wolfstetter, "The Third Generation (Umts) Spectrum Auction in Germany", October 2001. https://ssrn.com/abstract=287846 or https://doi.org/10.2139/ssrn.287846
3. Marc Bourreau, Doğan Pinar and Manant Matthieu, "A Critical Review of the 'Ladder Investment' Approach", *Telecommunications Policy*, 2010, 34(11):683-696.
4. Bruno van Pottelsberghe, "Europe's R&D: Missing the wrong targets?", *Bruegel Policy Brief*, Issue 2008/03, February 2008.

Chapter 5
Reform of the Reform Agenda

In 2004, the EU expanded by eight new member states, from the Baltic countries to Malta. Bulgaria and Romania would follow 3 years later.

A new Commission under the leadership of former Portuguese Prime Minister José Manuel Durão Barroso took office in 2005. Viviane Reding from Luxembourg became Commissioner for The Information Society and brought media policy with her, a responsibility she had assumed in the Prodi Commission.

In the meantime, it became clear that the Lisbon objectives would not be reached, and the strategy needed overall improvement. A report by former Dutch Prime Minister Wim Kok lamented the member states' lack of will and determination to act. The deeper explanation, however, is that Europeans at the time had and to this day still have no desire to live in the world's most competitive region, which requires more competition, more deregulation, and fiscal discipline, all of which remain deeply unpopular.

On 25 and 26 March 2005, the European Council agreed on a revised strategy based on suggestions prepared by the Commission. At the heart of Lisbon Reloaded was economic growth and employment. 'We must deliver jobs and growth by making Europe an attractive place to invest and work, placing knowledge and innovation at the heart of European growth,' President Barroso told the European Parliament. The similarity to the Delors White Paper was glaringly obvious, but nobody asked what could be learned from its fate.

The new approach emphasised research, innovation, infrastructure, and human capital. ICT became one industrial policy, amongst others. As the successor to eEurope, the Commission launched 'i2010—A European Information Society for Growth and Employment'.[1]

[1] Commission Communication COM (2005) 229 of 1 June 2005 on i2010—A European Information Society for growth and employment.

D. Eckert, *40 Years of European Digital Policies*, Professional Practice in Governance and Public Organizations,
https://doi.org/10.1007/978-3-031-61641-9_5

i2010

Why was it labelled i2010 instead of e2010? It was about being different. However, the resemblance to Apple's product line looked awkward.

i2010, which encompassed 17 measures, maintained the Information Society narrative but shifted its focus towards growth and competitiveness, aligning with the updated Lisbon Agenda. It also gave more prominence to themes related to the media. Unlike the two eEurope Action Plans, i2010 explicitly emphasised the research programme. Two years later, the Commission revisited i2010, adding more actions to the mix.[2]

That pretty much sums up the process. One of the most intriguing concepts within i2020 was the 'single European information space'. Regrettably, it did not delve into its deeper meaning. Nevertheless, i2010 deserves recognition for introducing a fundamental element of digital policy that remains relevant today, albeit under the name of the Digital Single Market.

Ironically, the most visible and popular action contributing to the Single Market vision was not part of i2010—addressing exorbitant roaming charges within the European Union. In 2007, a regulation capping roaming tariffs for voice communication was adopted, and over time, it gradually extended to cover data.[3] This proved a resounding success. Citizens could see the benefits of a genuinely European market in terms of convenience and savings.

This was a top-down political decision. Commissioner Reding made the call. It ran counter to the instincts of DG INFSO; after all, mobile communication markets were competitive, operators had invested heavily in spectrum, and price controls appeared overly interventionist. But in this case, political intuition prevailed, unlike in many episodes of *Yes, Minister*.

Among the various measures envisaged by i2010, three actions deserve closer examination: The revision of the Television Directive, the Telecom Framework, and the development of the ICT part of FP7.

Convergence Reloaded: The Second Revision of the Television Without Frontiers Directive

Ten years after the Convergence Green Paper, the rules for television were due for review. The critical question was how to deal with audio-visual on-demand (VoD) services. In the 1990s, VoD was in its infancy, not convincing enough for a mass market. Ten years later, this had changed. Faster Internet and advanced compression

[2]Commission Communication COM (2007) 146 of 30 March 2007 on i2010—Annual Information Society Report 2007.

[3]Regulation (EC) No 717/2007 of 27 June 2007 on roaming on public mobile telephone networks within the Community and amending Directive 2002/21/EC.

technologies rendered on-demand video distribution qualitatively better and more affordable. And this was before video platforms like Netflix, HBO, Hulu, or Disney+ became available. For example, Netflix only started its online service in 2006.

Should on-demand services become part of a television-inspired rule set? The motivation to regulate broadcasting in the first place was that video content can be distortive, manipulative, and harmful to minors. It was also considered an essential carrier for cultural content. As television reached the entire population, politicians wanted regulatory oversight in the public interest. The argument for the extension of regulation from linear to non-linear audio-visual services television was that the impact of video content on people would be the same. In addition, as both services would compete for the audience and advertising revenues, different rules would distort competition. This was the 'level playing field' argument.

Telcos, cable operators and digital service providers contested these assumptions. They argued that users could choose from a spectrum of content and generate their own programmes. Rules for broadcasting would, therefore, not be justified. They would also not be enforceable, as users could tap into a global content pool not subject to European rules. Ironically, the best shield against unlimited video content entering the EU is copyright, which has a territorial scope. Rightsholders can enforce copyright rules country by country. For an ordinary user, accessing protected content abroad is no simple matter.

In 2007, the legislators amended the Television without Frontiers Directive.[4] The title of the Directive changed to Audio-visual Media Services (AVMS). Non-linear services became subject to specific rules of linear broadcasting, such as editorial information and various restrictions on advertisement, sponsoring, and product placements. The law obliged the member states to take measures so that service providers would, for example, protect minors against targeted commercials promoting alcohol. And yes, the providers had an obligation to promote European content, but without a quota.

The law confirmed the country-of-origin principle. It left the member states leeway on whether and how to implement specific rules. The Directive applied to service providers under the jurisdiction of the member states, so it had no extra-territorial scope. Three years later, the legislator brought all the bits and pieces of the twice-amended original Directive together—lawyers call this codification—which simplified interpretation and future amendments.[5]

[4]Directive 2007/65/EC of 11 December 2007 amending Council Directive 89/552/EEC on the coordination of certain provisions laid down by law, regulation or administrative action in Member States concerning the pursuit of television broadcasting activities.

[5]Directive 2010/13/EU of 10 March 2010 on the coordination of certain provisions laid down by law, regulation or administrative action in Member States concerning the provision of audiovisual media services (Audiovisual Media Services Directive).

Telecommunications: 'More Europe'

The ambition behind revising the legal texts governing telecommunications was 'More Europe', meaning more harmonisation.[6] Essentially, this aspiration involved just two areas. The first was to give Brussels more power in allocating and assigning spectrum. The second one was to improve consistency in the application of rules, for which the Commission revived the old idea of a European regulator. In retrospect, this was the beginning of a journey leading to the current discussion about the future of telecommunications and gigabit connectivity.

As if these two issues were not head-scratching enough, two complex themes triggered by the proliferation of the Internet also emerged: one was related to copyright and the other was net neutrality.

Let's take these four issues individually, starting with the spectrum.

Spectrum

The spectrum available for electronic communications is a limited and valuable resource. Member states regard this spectrum as an element of their national sovereignty and, as such, closely safeguard it. Within this spectrum, multiple stakeholders, including broadcasters and mobile operators, vie for access to the same frequency bands. Additionally, international coordination of spectrum is essential. Notably, at the ITU World Radiocommunication Conference (WRC), the EU participates solely as an observer, not a full member.

The success of GSM paved the way for increased coordination at the EU level. A policy group comprising national and EU officials leads the reservation of specific bands for mobile communications.[7] The Commission collaborates closely with this group to establish shared positions for international events like the WRC, as exemplified by the 2023 conference in Dubai. However, it remains the prerogative of member states to decide independently on methods for allocating spectrum to operators and setting usage conditions.

The Commission wanted more influence and achieved some of its goals, although not everything it desired. Revised provisions mandated member states to establish an inventory to streamline coordination efforts. They also encouraged member states to permit operators to engage in spectrum trading and transfer activities. Furthermore, operators were entitled to employ newly acquired spectrum for innovative

[6]Directive 2009/140/EC of 25 November 2009 amending Directives 2002/21/EC on a common regulatory framework for electronic communications networks and services, 2002/19/EC on access to, and interconnection of, electronic communications networks and associated facilities, and 2002/20/EC on the authorisation of electronic communications networks and services.

[7]Commission Decision 2002/622/EC of 26 July 2002 establishing a Radio Spectrum Policy Group.

technologies, a practice referred to as 'refarming'. The revised set-up helped, if only a little, towards ensuring a coordinated launch of the successor of 3G-UMTS.

A European Telecom Agency

A decade ago, the concept of a European regulator did not make it into a legal proposal. The European telecom market remained a collection of national markets. Regulators had formed a group for cooperation rather than for synchronising their decisions. The framework review presented an opportunity to introduce consistency and encourage market analysis with a broader, more European perspective. This included defining relevant markets, establishing criteria to determine market competitiveness, and selecting the best regulatory remedies for specific situations.

The revised Directives modified several processes for addressing these questions with a standardised approach.[8] They granted the Commission a more significant role in shaping these answers. A separate Regulation also established two institutions: BEREC—the Body of European Regulators for Electronic Communications, and an Office.[9]

DG Information Society and its Director-General, Fabio Colasanti, invested enormous effort in developing a proposal agreeable to member states. Firstly, the Regulation established the function of a European regulator as a hybrid solution. The national regulators would collectively constitute an official body known as BEREC, serving as an advisory institution to the EU and the member states, entrusted with several well-defined tasks. These tasks include delivering opinions on market definitions, designating operators with significant market power, and identifying transnational markets. BEREC would operate independently, elect a Chair and a Vice-Chair, and the Commission would have an observer role. An office, legally designated as a European agency located in Riga, Lithuania, would support BEREC's work.

This was not the regulator we had longed for, but it represented a significant step in moving beyond a focus on national circumstances and towards a broader perspective.

---

[8]Directive 2009/140/EC of 25 November 2009 amending Directives 2002/21/EC on a common regulatory framework for electronic communications networks and services, 2002/19/EC on access to, and interconnection of, electronic communications networks and associated facilities, and 2002/20/EC on the authorisation of electronic communications networks and services.

[9]Regulation (EC) 1211/2009 of 25 November 2009 establishing the Body of European Regulators for Electronic Communications (BEREC) and the Office.

Copyright

The rightsholders wanted more than the Copyright Directive. They criticised the law for not adequately preventing illegal downloads of copyrighted material. The revision of the telecom framework was an opportunity to fix this gap.

They lobbied Brussels. Our DG was not too keen to burden the telecom package with copyright issues. However, the Commission, as a college, decided to include relevant clauses in its proposals for amending the Universal Service and User's Rights and Authorisation Directives. One provision would have obliged operators '. . .to inform subscribers of the most common acts of infringements and their legal consequences'.[10] At first glance, this did not look dramatic, but the member states would have to specify what 'legal consequences' meant.

The intention behind this clause was the active participation of the operators in enforcing copyright. Operators would be mandated by national law to help identify users that infringed copyright and, in a 'graduated response', warn them, throttle traffic, and finally cut them off from the network. Known as the 'Three Strikes' proposal, it generated a heated debate and more stakeholder lobbying. It raised privacy concerns, and operators worried about the costs. Critics pointed to enforcement problems: what happens, for example, when a user's Wi-Fi network is hijacked and abused for illegal downloading?

A majority in the European Parliament was against this provision but eventually agreed to a compromise whereby the member states were entitled to request such contract clauses from operators. Still, they were not obliged, yet again watering down an attempt for greater harmonisation. Anyway, the Parliament introduced Recitals into the Universal Service Directive, *de facto* a disclaimer saying that implementing this provision must respect people's *fundamental rights* and privacy and be subject to a due judicial process.[11]

By and large, this provision was enacted only in a few countries—in France, but also in the United Kingdom and Belgium. Yet nowhere were users cut off. The national laws mainly served as a basis for enforcing cooperation between operators and rightsholders.

---

[10] Proposal COM (2007) 698 of 13 November 2007 for a Directive amending Directive 2002/22/EC on universal service and users' rights relating to electronic communications networks. Directive 2002/58/EC concerning the processing of personal data and the protection of privacy in the electronic communications sector and Regulation (EC) No 2006/2004 on consumer protection cooperation, Article 20(6).

[11] Directive 2009/136/EC of 25 November 2009 amending Directive 2002/22/EC on universal service and users' rights relating to electronic communications networks and services, Directive 2002/58/EC concerning the processing of personal data and the protection of privacy in the electronic communications sector and Regulation (EC) No 2006/2004 on cooperation between national authorities responsible for the enforcement of consumer protection laws. Recitals 29, 30, and 31.

The debate revealed that the Internet was considered an indispensable window to the world. People should not be deprived of access to it. This brings us to net neutrality.

Net Neutrality: The First Attempt

The reader may recall that the costs and benefits of the Internet are not symmetrical. Broadband roll-out requires substantial investments with modest margins and is subject to regulatory oversight. Offering applications and services (over the top) on the Internet is usually less expensive, quick and easy to do, and the profit for those who succeed (we only see the winners) can be staggering.

Both mobile and fixed network operators did not find this burden-sharing fair, and they still don't. They were and are looking for ways to generate revenue beyond merely offering connectivity. One idea was to prioritise the traffic of service providers who pay a premium for their service offerings. Critics feared this could lead to a two-tiered Internet, one slow and one fast, favouring big players. It could also hamper innovative applications if users could not access them at adequate speeds.

This brings us to the net neutrality debate that emerged in the United States—how could it be different—in the early 2000s [1]. Net neutrality is a non-discrimination concept: operators should treat all content, technically all packets, equally. Its foundation was the end-to-end Internet architecture, and it was conceived as a network design principle, but whether it should lead to a regulatory principle was the subject of debate.[12] The American network regulator, FCC, issued several non-discrimination rulings, all contested in court. The Bush administration was not overly keen on intervening too strongly in the communication markets. The view in Brussels was in favour of a strict net neutrality provision. The political motivation was the perception of preserving the Internet as an open platform for innovation and free expression. You can sense the positive framing in this formulation, although the argument was not and is still not shared by everyone. Operators argued that net neutrality prevents them from competing with powerful Internet companies. The net neutrality proposal by the European Commission did not find approval in the Council. The Commission added a Declaration on net neutrality to the Framework Directive in favour of 'an open Internet'. Concrete provisions had to wait a few years until everyone understood what was technically feasible. Not a bad strategy: do not regulate prematurely.

---

[12]The WIRED Guide to Net Neutrality, 2020: "ISPs shouldn't be able to block some sorts of data and prioritize others. Here's what to know about the struggle to treat all information on the internet the same." https://www.wired.com/story/guide-net-neutrality/

FP7: More Money for ICT

Framework Programme 7 (FP7) covered the period from 2007 until 2013.[13] Compared with the previous ones, the extension to 7 years was to align the programme with the EU's Multiannual Financial Framework (MFF). The MFF, always the subject of intense debate among European leaders (to be polite), provides the EU with a 7-year budget structure for policy development and guidance for its annual budgeting.

The overall FP7 budget was nearly 56 billion euros; the ICT part received around 9 billion euros (16%). This jump from about 19 billion euros in FP6 was due to an EU with ten new member states needing more money and the revised Lisbon Agenda having identified research and technology as priorities. The annual budget for ICT more than doubled compared with FP6. True, the relative share of digital had gone down again, but this was a consequence of the rise of other areas such as energy and transport. In addition, these areas included much ICT-related research for their specific needs.

Let's Deviate for a Moment

Speaking of finances, the MFF included a relatively modest policy support initiative known as the Competitiveness and Innovation Programme (CIP). Part of the CIP, 730 million euros, was allocated to support Information and Communication Technologies. This allocation laid the foundation for what would later become the Digital Europe Programme.[14]

In preceding years, digital policy initiatives also received funding from sources other than research programmes, often insufficient to create a significant impact. It is worth noting these initiatives for historical reference. These included Modinis,[15] the predecessor of CIP designed to support the implementation of eEurope 2005; eContentplus,[16] which focused on developing digital content; and eTEN,[17] which provided funding for the digital aspects of trans-European networks. The underlying

---

[13] Decision No 1982/2006/EC of 18 December 2006 concerning the Seventh Framework Programme of the European Community for research, technological development and demonstration activities (2007–2013).

[14] Decision No 1639/2006/EC of 24 October 2006 establishing a Competitiveness and Innovation Framework Programme (2007 to 2013).

[15] Decision No 2256/2003/EC of 17 November 2003 adopting a multiannual programme (2003–2005) for the monitoring of the eEurope 2005 action plan, dissemination of good practices and the improvement of network and information security (MODINIS).

[16] Decision No 456/2005/EC of 9 March 2005 establishing a multiannual Community programme to make digital content in Europe more accessible, usable and exploitable.

[17] Decision No 1376/2002/EC of 12 July 2002 amending Decision No 1336/97/EC on a series of guidelines for trans-European telecommunications networks.

idea of eTEN, supported by a legal basis in the Treaty, was to facilitate connecting transport, energy, and digital infrastructures across national borders.

The ICT component of the new CIP was designed to promote various application areas, including eGovernment, eHealth, and intelligent transportation. While the initial budget may have seemed modest, if cleverly applied, even a smaller budget could yield significant results when used wisely.

Consider self-driving cars, also known as intelligent vehicles. You might recall the DARPA Grand Challenge, an event that set the stage for autonomous vehicles. Launched in 2004, back when the technology was far from mainstream, this competition ran not once but twice more. The winning team was rewarded with a modest prize of just two million dollars; most participants came from academic institutions. Despite the relatively small purse, the challenge ignited a significant wave of enthusiasm, forming a dedicated community of technology enthusiasts committed to advancing the self-driving car vision.

In Europe, among the pioneers was Ernst Dickmanns, a German engineer and professor at the German Army University in Munich.[18] He collaborated with Mercedes, and his project received support from the EUREKA Prometheus initiative. In a remarkable feat in 1987, his Mercedes Van (with a nominal price tag of 100,000 euros) autonomously covered 20 kilometres on a test road, reaching speeds of 97 kph. The team would have won the DARPA Grand Challenge easily. In 1995, they achieved another milestone by driving from Munich to Copenhagen autonomously, with only occasional driver interventions, and notably, without GPS assistance.[19]

Regrettably, the project ended, as Mercedes chose not to pursue it further. Nonetheless, Dickmanns' groundbreaking concept of predictive driving remains unmatched. The technology was deemed too expensive then, and the available computer chips lacked the necessary processing power. Curiously, this was a period when people were well aware of Moore's Law, which predicted rapid advancements in computing power over time. In hindsight, it would have been a tremendous opportunity for Europe to establish leadership in this transformative field.

FP7's Confusing Terminology

Returning to FP7, if you want to assess how framework programmes have shifted their priorities and orientations over time, you will likely encounter some perplexing terminology.

Within FP7, the section dedicated to cooperative research projects, which represented a significant portion of the budget, defined ten themes with Information

[18] https://www.politico.eu/article/delf-driving-car-born-1986-ernst-dickmanns-mercedes/

[19] https://youtu.be/I39sxwYKlEE

and Communication Technologies among them: ICT had replaced the notion of IST.[20]

The cooperative research activities of ICT were organised into activities encompassing technology pillars, applications research, and technology integration. These activities were the foundation for constructing work programmes around seven ICT Challenges. Among these challenges, three pertained to technological building blocks, and four focused on applications. This configuration was, at times, presented as a 3-to-4 matrix, with technology integration conceptually woven into it. This was far from clear, as this arrangement diverged from the classification used in the ICT programme.

If this nomenclature labyrinth was not sufficiently bewildering, consider the evolution of terminology across the two preceding framework programmes. We encountered Key Actions in FP5, which evolved into Technology Priorities in FP6. In FP7, we refer to them as Activities, which may or may not align with their predecessors. On the work programme level, what were once Clusters in FP5 transformed into Strategic Objectives in FP6 and have now taken on the moniker of Challenges.

So, is it worth paying attention to this nomenclature quagmire? Absolutely. Altering the terminology and structure of a programme from one period to the next complicates comparisons with previous iterations. It obscures what has evolved and what has remained consistent. A uniform format would render evaluations more meaningful, allowing for longitudinal analyses. Moreover, it would be sensible to centre the narrative, objectives, and rationale on new instruments and rules while communicating to stakeholders why changes are occurring. Potential participants need to understand how the Commission will run the programme. And indeed, FP7 introduced some intriguing novelties in this regard, and I'd like to highlight two of them.

Joint Technology Initiatives

The first is the concept of the Joint Technology Initiative (JTI). It addresses critical questions: How much should we invest in a particular technology to make a meaningful impact? How can we leverage our funds through private investments? How do we secure the participation of member states? JTIs also represent the fusion of research and industrial policy.

A JTI is managed by a legal entity known as a Joint Undertaking (JU), in which the Commission, participating member states, and the private sector, typically represented by industry associations, have a stake. A JU has a legal foundation in

[20] Council Decision of 19 December 2006 concerning the specific programme 'Cooperation' implementing the Seventh Framework Programme of the European Community for research, technological development and demonstration activities (2007 to 2013).

the Treaty (Articles 187 and 188.1), making its establishment straightforward. A Regulation defines its governance structure, through which a JU manages the budget, establishes a research agenda, selects projects, and negotiates grant agreements. Despite its club-like nature, it must consider project proposals from non-members and treat them equally. The expectation is that the budget to which participating member states contribute will be substantial enough, and the research will be sufficiently relevant to have a positive impact on the competitiveness of the European industry.

Two ICT-related JUs were established: ARTEMIS (embedded systems) and ENIAC (nanoelectronics). In Horizon 2020, the successor of FP7, these two, along with the Technology Platform EPoSS (Smart Systems Integration), were merged into the JU ECSEL (Electronic Components and Systems for European Leadership).

JTIs (JUs) are now firmly entrenched in the European research architecture. They align with Europe's industrial strengths and seek to bolster them.[21] Participants follow a technological trajectory, solve problems, and validate concepts. However, JTIs do not venture into uncharted territory, and scientific breakthroughs are not their primary aim. This ambition belongs to the second novelty, FET (Future and Emerging Technologies) Flagships.

FET Flagships

Since FP6, the FET instrument has been part of our toolkit. It occupies a space between basic and applied research, supporting experimental projects with a clear technology orientation. The credit for the Flagship approach belongs to Wolfgang Boch, a research manager at DG INFSO, who recalled that the idea emerged during discussions within the FET Advisory Group. These experts recommended adopting a longer-term perspective than the typical 2-year work programme cycles. And so, the concept was born: to commit 10 years of funding to a specific research direction. The envisioned budget for each project was approximately 1 billion euros, with roughly 50% from the EU budget.

The concept of Flagships can be understood in two ways. One approach is to define an ambitious, visionary goal, akin to a 'moon shot' mission, and provide the necessary time and resources to work towards it. For example, the Human Brain

[21] *ARTEMIS, in particular, was recognised by several stakeholders consulted as helping to keep the competitive position of Europe because of its capacity to involve several key industry players in drafting a common research agenda.*

ARTEMIS received 410 million euros and ENIAC 440 million euros in EU funding, leveraging member states and private investments to reach total budgets of 2.8 billion euros and 2.6 billion euros, respectively.

Ex-post evaluation of ICT research in the Seventh Framework Programme. Final report prepared by DG CONNECT, January 2015.

Project, which originated from the University of Lausanne and was selected as one of the two Flagships for a ramp-up phase in 2011, falls into this category.

Managing a project of this magnitude is complex and carries the risk of selecting an incorrect path. Yet, how can you determine if a project is not progressing towards its objectives when it spans a decade? This dilemma came to the forefront with the Human Brain Project, which sparked disagreements within the research community regarding the project's direction. Following its official launch in 2013, the orientations changed, transforming it into a funding mechanism that supported various avenues related to the fundamental concept of comprehending the brain through computerisation. In September 2023, the project concluded with a final conference, and its website details the achievements, which are interesting in scope. Its main legacy seems to be a research infrastructure known as EBRAINS, 'which offers access to digital tools, models, data and services, facilitating the integration of brain science across disciplines and national borders'.[22]

Another approach to implementing the Flagship concept involves defining a long-term research agenda centred around a specific theme. The Graphene project, the second Flagship, exemplified this approach. The project website describes graphene in simple terms as 'a one-atom-thick layer of carbon atoms arranged in a hexagonal lattice'.[23] Graphene has great versatility as a material, which the Flagship aimed to exploit. Researchers successfully developed industrial-scale methods for graphene production and demonstrated its diverse applications, including in batteries, autonomous driving, and aviation. The project concluded in 2023, and its website contains extensive information about its outcomes and achievements.

Lessons

What can we learn from JTIs and FET Flagships? They pooled resources around specific technology and science fields, thereby contributing to the European Research Area (ERA). However, this needs to be kept in perspective. The funding amounts were relatively modest; we are talking about total annual funding ranging from 50 million euros to 100 million euros for each project. Substantial? Yes, but not revolutionary.

The Flagships were primarily geared towards achieving scientific and technological breakthroughs, while JTIs were centred on boosting the competitiveness of their industrial participants. Interestingly, these two concepts shared more similarities than initially apparent, aside from being long-term and focused. Over time, the Flagships broadened their industrial participation and, with a growing technology focus, increasingly resembled JTIs. The fundamental distinction between them

[22] https://www.humanbrainproject.eu/en/follow-hbp/news/2023/09/28/human-brain-project-ends-what-has-been-achieved/

[23] https://graphene-flagship.eu/graphene/understand/

continued to lie in their organisational structure and the roles played by the member states. In the case of JTIs, this involvement entailed a direct financial contribution, while member states were involved indirectly with Flagships through their national mirror initiatives.

Both concepts have remained relevant. In 2021, the Quantum Technology Flagship was launched, and several JTIs, such as the one for smart networks and services, now constitute a major element of Horizon Europe. JTIs and FET Flagships helped strengthen Europe's competitive position in their fields. Nevertheless, Europe's digital industry had lost its competitive edge in other, economically more significant areas.

Losing the Competitive Edge

> Europe remains a global force in advanced information and communication technologies (ICT). The World Wide Web, the mobile GSM standard, the MPEG standard for digital content and ADSL technology were all invented in Europe. Maintaining this leadership position and turning it into a competitive advantage is an important policy goal.
>
> Europe's Digital Competitiveness Report. Main achievements of the i2010 strategy 2005–2009, 4 August 2009.

Yes, Europe was successful with ADSL and GSM. Yet, it fell behind in fibre deployment and was late with 4G-LTE. Yes, the WWW was developed at CERN, but the browser came from the United States. And the MPEG standard helped Hollywood more than European filmmakers. And worse was still to come.

The combination of three innovations has cemented the dominance of the US digital industry: the iPhone (and the iPad), cloud computing, and social media. 4G/LTE became the glue between them, creating a digital ecosystem dominated by a few US companies, sometimes called Big Tech.

The iPhone

Europe's aspirations for digital leadership ended on 9 January 2007 in San Francisco.

On that day, Steve Jobs unveiled the iPhone with a captivating stage performance. Little did he know that his 'gadget' would evolve into a groundbreaking innovation permeating every facet of our lives. Allegedly, Jobs' initial goal was to create a 'cool' phone to counter the competition the iPod faced from phone companies.

Ironically, the iPhone's initial phone capabilities were not impressive, causing many, including rivals like Microsoft and Nokia, and us in the Commission, to underestimate its potential. We failed to grasp that people were more interested in the apps it offered than in making traditional phone calls. Within 5 years, Apple had sold around 200 million iPhones.

On the other hand, Google played its cards wisely and had a stroke of luck. They had already positioned themselves for entry into the mobile device market by acquiring a company called Android.[24] The Android team developed an operating system based on Linux and, in November 2007, introduced a beta version in collaboration with manufacturers and network operators. The first Android phone hit the market in September 2008 (courtesy of T-Mobile, a German subsidiary). Today, Google's Android and Apple's iOS dominate the smartphone market by a wide margin.

The lesson here is striking. As with the iPod, Apple integrated various technologies to create a product that resonated with consumers. Despite having a smaller research budget than Nokia, Apple managed to dethrone the market leader with a brilliant concept. Some may recall Nokia's Communicator, which was undoubtedly an engineering marvel but lacked the appeal and user-friendliness of Apple's offerings. Consumer-oriented innovation, rather than sheer technology, made the difference. This had profound implications for Europe, which became evident relatively quickly.

Cloud Computing

If you search for cloud computing, you will discover that the concept dates back to the 1960s and is closely related to the ARPANET. Yet, the innovators of modern cloud computing were Salesforce in 1999 and Amazon in 2002. Microsoft joined in 2010 and rapidly gained momentum, ultimately reshaping the industry.

In Europe, cloud adoption initially faced scepticism. Concerns centred around security and interoperability. Users sought guarantees they could seamlessly combine cloud services from various providers and transfer data as needed.

The Commission launched its cloud computing initiative in 2012 to foster the adoption of cloud services and bolster European providers. This initiative prioritised technical standards, data portability, trustworthy certification, and the formulation of equitable contract terms. Numerous research projects supported these efforts, focusing on cloud services tailored to the scientific community.[25]

However, the outcome of this strategy has been underwhelming. Nearly a decade later, on 21 January 2021, Eurostat published a statistic with the headline 'Cloud computing for business yet to go mainstream in the EU'.[26] Eurostat surveys reveal that cloud service usage among businesses in the EU27 had slowly grown from 18% in 2014 to 36% in 2020, 41% in 2021, and 45.2% in 2023. These figures masked substantial variations between member states, ranging from Finland at 78.3% to

[24] https://www.androidauthority.com/google-android-acquisition-884194/

[25] Commission Communication COM (2012) 529 final of 27.9.2012 on Unleashing the Potential of Cloud Computing in Europe.

[26] https://ec.europa.eu/eurostat/web/products-eurostat-news/-/ddn-20210121-1

Bulgaria at 17.5% in 2023. The positive aspect is that about three-quarters of enterprises using public clouds, regardless of size, had already embraced advanced services like security applications, database hosting, and application testing.[27]

The initiative had little discernible impact on the evolution of the European cloud market. Globally and within Europe, three major cloud providers dominate: Amazon Web Services, Microsoft Azure, and the Google Cloud Platform. In Europe, these three are followed by Alibaba and IBM. European cloud providers have remained niche players. While their revenues have increased in response to rising demand, their market share has dwindled from 27% to 13%. Among the Europeans, SAP and Deutsche Telekom emerged as the leaders, each accounting for 2% of the European market.[28]

This development has raised concerns among European policymakers. GAIA-X represents one reaction to the overwhelming presence of American cloud giants. In a broader context, the Commission proposed a data strategy encompassing two legislative acts. Although these measures are conceptually related, they do not draw on the lessons from the earlier cloud initiative. This recurrence is not unprecedented: digital initiatives are often launched without due consideration for the insights gained by their predecessors.

Social Media

The i2010 assessment paper mentioned social networks as a promising way for users to interact and be creative. I would not characterise this as particularly visionary.

Among the early social media platforms, MySpace emerged in 2003 but eventually faded into obscurity. Initially designed for Harvard students in 2004, Facebook swiftly became the dominant player in online personal connections. YouTube launched in 2005 and was later acquired by Google in 2006, while Twitter (now X) began in 2006 and evolved into a powerful communication tool. Other platforms, including WhatsApp and Instagram (now under Meta's ownership), followed suit. Some, like Snapchat, enjoyed remarkable beginnings but gradually lost appeal.

A common thread persisted: in each service segment, one platform reigned supreme. This phenomenon can be attributed to the network effect, which wields substantial influence in social media. The more users a network accumulates, the more enticing it becomes, drawing in additional users, thus perpetuating a virtuous cycle that often leads to quasi-monopolies.

---

[27] https://ec.europa.eu/eurostat/statistics-explained/index.php?title=Cloud_computing_-_statistics_on_the_use_by_enterprises

[28] Depending on the data source, the European market size in 2022 is estimated to be between $40 billion and $60 billion.

https://www.srgresearch.com/articles/european-cloud-providers-continue-to-grow-but-still-lose-market-share

https://www.gminsights.com/industry-analysis/europe-cloud-computing-market

None of the major social media companies are of European origin. While one might argue that Europe was sluggish and that it is too late to catch up now, examples like Telegram in 2013 and TikTok in 2016 demonstrate that it is possible to compete through innovation. This supports my belief that policy measures seldom drive innovation unless closely linked to public procurement.

Certain voices have contended that stringent data protection regulations could stifle European social media growth. This argument, however, might oversimplify the issue. Conversely, claims by proponents of robust online privacy protections that this could provide European companies with an advantage due to greater trustworthiness are not substantiated by market realities.

The Political Narrative Became Decoupled from Market Realities

At the end of the Lisbon decade, several regulations had been successfully enacted, with the roaming regulation being a notable success story. FP7 also had promise regarding available funds and instruments, filling us with optimism as we prepared for the Digital Agenda and contemplated the future.

Yet, none of the three transformative developments—smartphones, cloud computing, and social media—had fully registered on our radar screen. Our focus for the 2010 decade revolved around broadband expansion, eGovernment, high-performance computing, embedded systems, and establishing the digital single market. Even 4G technology was mainly an issue in relation to the allocation of the necessary spectrum.

In retrospect, this period marks a juncture where the political agenda became detached from the rapidly evolving market dynamics. This does not imply that the policy measures, including eEurope and i2010, were inherently flawed. Rather, it signified that technology and global market forces had gained dominance. Policy measures could not decisively shape the course of international markets or ensure the competitive edge of European companies. Digital policies need to be conceived with a broader approach if they hope to exert a more profound influence. However, the Digital Agenda merely followed the paths laid out by its predecessors.

Reference

1. Tim Wu, "Network Neutrality, Broadband Discrimination", 2003. https://scholarship.law.columbia.edu/faculty_scholarship/1281

Chapter 6
A Digital Agenda

We are in 2010. President Barroso had obtained a second mandate. Former competition Commissioner Neelie Kroes took over responsibility for digital and renamed DG Information Society as DG Communication Networks, Content, and Technology, DG Connect for short. Robert Madelin, a senior British official, became its Director-General.

The Barroso II Commission adopted a 10-year growth and jobs strategy, Europe2020, as an answer to the recession caused by the banking collapse that started in 2008.[1] It aimed to create 'a smart, sustainable, and inclusive economy with high levels of employment, productivity, and social cohesion'. The strategy had five headline targets to be achieved by 2020: to increase employment, improve education, reduce poverty, reduce greenhouse gas emissions, and increase research and development spending. Digital was notably absent.

The financial crisis eventually turned into a Eurozone crisis, during which the EU rescued Greece, Spain, Portugal, and Ireland from fiscal collapse through specific programmes of credit guarantees against reforms. The EU established a complex legal framework to prevent macroeconomic imbalances and ensure fiscal stability.

The mechanism put in place was an annual cycle starting with an economic analysis, followed by country-by-country analyses by the Commission, which finally led to 'country-specific recommendations' adopted by the European Council. The EU managed to drive several reforms in member states through this process (called the European Semester, although it turned out to be 12 months instead of 6).[2] None of these were aimed at digital transformation. Priorities were fiscal stability, labour market reforms, and social cohesion. Unlike 10 years earlier, policymakers did not consider digital policies macroeconomically relevant.

[1] Commission Communication COM (2010) 2020 of 3 March 2010. Europe 2020: A strategy for smart, sustainable and inclusive growth.

[2] https://www.consilium.europa.eu/en/policies/european-semester/

D. Eckert, *40 Years of European Digital Policies*, Professional Practice in Governance and Public Organizations,
https://doi.org/10.1007/978-3-031-61641-9_6

The Making of the Digital Agenda

In the DG, we had wished to be more visible in the core policy. Nevertheless, the Digital Agenda was one of seven flagship projects underpinning the Europe 2020 strategy. These flagships were a collection of existing work programmes in various policy domains, so our work had begun even before the new Commission took office: drafting a Digital Agenda for Europe.[3]

Commissioner Kroes and her team had in mind an eight-action-area structure for the Agenda, comprising research, standards, broadband, social, skills, digital single market, international, and cybersecurity. Our task was to fill this structure with content. Based on the experience with eEurope and i2010, we would have preferred a streamlined initiative, one that aimed at a few significant objectives. Yet, we ended up with more than 100 individual actions.

These actions aimed at the wider deployment and effective use of digital technologies. Commissioner Kroes introduced the notion of 'Every European Digital' as a motto, continuing the tradition of eEurope's 'Information Society for All' theme. Establishing a convincing leitmotif can be a catalyst for the success of a strategy. However, most policy headlines were more slogans on top of an action list rather than reflecting an inherently concise paradigm.

Like i2010, the Digital Agenda initially did not impress with ambitious legislative initiatives. One of the few Directives concerned an adjustment to copyright to address 'orphan works' for which no rightsholder could be found. However, you could not call this a game changer. Another exception was the revision of the eSignature Directive.

Cross-border Authentication

Since the adoption of the eSignature Directive, social media and e-commerce had changed the digital landscape. Secure but simple authentication to a plethora of services, not signatures, was needed. Authentication attests to an identity, such as a person or an arbitrary username, and grants access to a service. Rising cybercrime made it necessary to augment password-only authentication with one or two additional verification steps, for example, using a smart card or a fingerprint. And here we are back to the eSignature realm.

Although the qualified signature concept was not meant as a user identification tool, but to transpose the legal meaning of a handwritten signature into the digital world, it can be used for secure authentication because of the underlying PKI. However, it used to be too complex and cumbersome for most applications. This changed when governments issued Electronic Identity (eID) Cards based on a national PKI, covering the exorbitant costs of operating a Certification Authority

[3]Commission Communication COM (2010)245 of 19 May 2010 on A Digital Agenda for Europe.

(CA). After paper IDs had become plastic cards, it was easy to 'glue' a chip on them. Countries, to different degrees, used these eID cards as carriers for qualified-like signatures usable as authentication tools for public services. Estonia became an early adopter of eID cards to underpin online public services and widen their scope.

Yet, many EU countries did not establish eID systems; when they did, these were national islands. Cross-border authentication to access online public services was generally limited and not based on national eIDs. This was the starting point of the eSignature revision, leading to the eIDAS Regulation in 2014.[4]

The eIDAS Regulation encouraged member states to open their eID systems to users from other member states' systems, for example, to apply for a job or submit a document. This required detailed notification of the eID scheme to the Commission, which had to fulfil specific criteria. These were similar but not identical to those for qualified signatures.

The eIDAS Regulation extended the eSignature scope to other trust services, providing electronic seals, time stamps, and registered delivery services. The provisions follow the eSignature approach by granting, in principle, these electronic services and documents a legal effect.[5] The requirements for trusted services were similar to those for qualified signatures. Although formulated in a technology-neutral way, the implication was that these services had to be built on a PKI. By the way, you could achieve all this with a qualified signature integrated into appropriately designed services. The advantage of the Regulation was to make the validity of such documents explicit.

The success of eIDAS was modest. By 2022, 14 member states had notified 19 systems, covering about 60% of EU citizens. These schemes were not always interoperable and needed gateways (eIDAS nodes) for interaction. The number of services using national eIDs remained limited and hardly ever included private services—sufficient justification for a further revision.

So, let's fast forward to 2023, when the EU became more decisive. On 8 November 2023, the co-legislators reached a political agreement on the Commission's proposal to amend the eIDAS Regulation.[6] The core novelty is the introduction of a European Digital Identity Wallet (EDIW). Member states must provide at least one to their citizens and legal entities, who are free to take up the offer; the wallet will be voluntary.

The wallets are designed, issued, and managed nationally—not necessarily by public administrations, but always under their supervision. They can be linked to existing national eID schemes or developed as identity systems in their own right. The idea is a common platform to interconnect national eID schemes and broaden

[4]Regulation (EU) No 910/2014 of 23 July 2014 on electronic identification and trust services for electronic transactions in the internal market and repealing Directive 1999/93/EC.

[5]The formula of the eSignature Directive is that an electronic 'something' should not be denied legal effect solely on the grounds that it is electronic.

[6]Commission proposal COM (2021) 281 of 3 June 2021 for a Regulation amending Regulation (EU) No 910/2014 as regards establishing a framework for a European Digital Identity.

their applications. The wallet will be most useful as a smartphone app. The Commission will provide technical harmonisation for cross-border use, security, and common functionalities. It would have been a powerful move if the EU had agreed on one common wallet. The way this concept is implemented reflects the reality of many policy actions. Member states insist on the importance of their national circumstances even if they accept being more or less coordinated by the EU. The accumulation of these partly harmonised measures cements fragmentation, admittedly less than without Europe, but nevertheless, digital policies do not scale.

Citizens should be able to authenticate their interactions with public and private services, create digital signatures, store documents (driver's licence, diploma, birth certificate, etc.), log transactions, and request the deletion of data. The EU envisages a wide range of applications: requesting birth certificates, reporting a change of address, opening a bank account, filing tax returns, applying for a university, age verification, storing a medical prescription that can be used anywhere in Europe, and renting a car using a digital driving licence. The EDIW resembles a Swiss Army Knife, and the designer needs to pay attention to its usability. Moreover, if the government opens its authentication methods to use by the private sector, privacy should be substantially strengthened. It does not make sense to force the industry to ask for consent for third-party cookies and then deliver them a perfect tracing tool implemented as an EDIW.

Very large online platforms (as defined by the Digital Services Act) and private services requesting strong authentication (undefined, but probably meaning two-factor authentication) must accept EDIW as an access method. This is peculiar because attractive EDIWs should not need an obligation to find adoption, and unconvincing ones would be a burden. This was the experience following the 1999 eSignature Directive. The best way to promote the EDIW platform is to redesign public services so that their online usage becomes a productivity boost. The pilot projects the Commission supports are promising, but widespread implementation must follow. This will determine the success of the EDIW. It is instructive to refer back to the eGovernment section in Chap. 4. After 20 years, citizens and businesses might finally obtain easy-to-use access to public sector online services.

The 2023 eIDAS Regulation also went into the realm of website authentication, which caused angry reactions from browser vendors, net and privacy activists, and predominantly American certification authorities. I need to get a bit technical now, but this serves as a good illustration of a culture clash over how the Internet should be governed.

The revised eIDAS Regulation obliges browser vendors to accept so-called Qualified Website Authentication Certificates (QWAC) as root certificates (Article 45): 'Qualified certificates for website authentication ... shall be recognised by web-browsers. Web-browsers shall ensure that the identity data attested in the certificate and additional attested attributes are displayed in a user-friendly manner.'

Recall the SSL/TLS encryption of communication between a browser and a website's server, introduced in the 1990s (Chap. 2). Setting up an encrypted channel and verifying the domain identity rely on a certificate provided to the browser by the server. The domain owner obtains the certificate from a certification authority,[7] a trusted service provider, choosing between two options.[8] A domain-validated (DV) certificate is issued following an automated check that the entity applying for the certificate controls the domain.[9] An extended-validated (EV) certificate is based on more background verification and allows the browser to display a full name. DV certificates are by far the most common certificates as they are cheap and work well. EVs are more expensive and are about to disappear.[10] Europe would not be Europe if it were happy with 'good-enough' solutions and if it did not know better than the industry, thus the eIDAS-enforced QWACs are a particularly sophisticated EV certificate.[11]

A CA digitally signs certificates it issues with its private key, allowing the browser to verify its validity with the CA's public key. For this to work, the CA's certificate must be accessible by the browser, thereby becoming a root certificate. Who decides about root certificates? As with so many things on the Internet, it is community-driven, with a vital role for the dominant browser vendors, all US-based.[12] This dependency contradicts the European philosophy of digital sovereignty, which might explain the provision in the eIDAS Regulation to enforce QWACs as the root for authentication. As certificates not only authenticate the domain but also the public key used for SSL/TLS encryption, the alarm bells of browser vendors and privacy advocates went off.

The critiques voiced by browser vendors and others were alarming about the threat to the safety of users worldwide. However, they did not bother to detail these scenarios. You need to read expert group discussions to get a sense. A compromised certificate, linking a valid domain name to the wrong SSL/TLS key, allows a man-in-the-middle attack when the attacker can intercept the communication.[13] The Internet

---

[7] These are private or semi-private entities. For the global forum, see https://cabforum.org European organisations also work together: https://www.european-signature-dialog.eu/

[8] Self-authentication is possible, but browsers might not trust those certificates.

[9] This is usually done through checks on WHOIS information and DNS records or by confirming that the applicant can make specific changes to the domain configuration.

[10] Most browser vendors have been removing EV UIs.

https://www.troyhunt.com/extended-validation-certificates-are-really-really-dead/

For example, a Google team writes: 'Through our own research as well as a survey of prior academic work, the Chrome Security UX team has determined that the EV UI does not protect users as intended (see Further Reading below). Users do not appear to make secure choices (such as not entering password or credit card information) when the UI is altered or removed, as would be necessary for EV UI to provide meaningful protection.'

https://chromium.googlesource.com/chromium/src/+/HEAD/docs/security/ev-to-page-info.md

[11] The requirements for a qualified web certificate are laid down in Annex V of the eIDAS Regulation and resemble the qualified certificates for signatures.

[12] The browser vendors have a root store policy supervised by a community-driven transparency mechanism. Rogue or careless certification authorities, for example, those who hand out unauthorised certificates or do not check identity properly, will be blocked, and their root certificates will be revoked. https://certificate.transparency.dev/

[13] https://www.enisa.europa.eu/topics/incident-response/glossary/man-in-the-middle

community rejected the idea of being forced to accept certificates (under government oversight, which they distrust by default) without checks and without the option to revoke them on account of the Regulation stipulating that 'Qualified certificates for website authentication shall not be subject to any mandatory requirements'. This was the core of the concerns, and they are justified.

The final text of the Regulation somewhat mitigated the critical core of the criticism: '... in case of substantiated concerns ... web-browsers may take precautionary measures...'. However, browser vendors must subsequently notify the Commission, trust provider, and national authority of the details of their concerns. After investigation, they might be told to end the preventative measures. This provision is not designed to please the browser-certificate community.

Ultimately, it is about governance, which goes beyond the specificities of this dispute. The Internet works because it does not depend on governments agreeing to standards and procedures. The EU might have set a precedent for other countries to impose their root certificates on browsers. Europe should defend the community-driven Internet and tackle dominance with competition policy.

Let's go back to the year 2010 and the Digital Agenda.

How Do You Define Success?

Measuring progress is a headache for policymakers as the impact of policy measures is usually influenced by external factors, making it difficult to isolate the policy effect. Only occasionally are these effects relatively straightforward; for example, telecom liberalisation enhanced competition, and roaming regulation directly capped tariffs.

With the Agenda, we established a Digital Scoreboard, which includes a set of key performance targets. These targets defined the EU's quantitative ambitions for 2020 regarding broadband, public service, digital single market, research, and inclusion. My colleagues meticulously compiled a comprehensive dataset and substantially improved its visual presentation. Subsequently, DG Connect calculated the DESI index, which is used to rank member states based on their level of digitalisation.

Indices possess the advantage of being easily communicable, a quality appreciated by politicians for its simplicity. Yet, indices can be susceptible to statistical biases such as autocorrelation, arbitrary aggregation, and random assignment of weights to individual indicators. Nonetheless, the Scoreboard and its collection of indicators are of high quality and have become an asset for evidence-based digital policymaking.[14]

The broadband targets turned out to be the most influential: by 2020, 100% of households should be covered by 30 Mbps (download), and 50% should have a

[14] https://digital-strategy.ec.europa.eu/en/policies/desi

100 Mbps subscription. The 30 Mbps target became a relevant threshold to qualify for state aid, and 100 Mbps set an orientation for the definition of very fast broadband.

The problem with the underlying statistic is that speed and technology are not entirely congruent. For example, VDSL typically supports 30 Mbps, while VDSL-2 Vectoring may or may not produce around 100 Mbps, depending on distance and line quality. Moreover, it is not trivial to calculate take-up figures from coverage statistics. This is why the Commission relies on special studies to obtain more detailed insights, for example, to single out rural and remote areas.

According to the Scoreboard, the EU missed the 100 Mbps take-up target. In 2020, its average stood at 33.4%, though up from 15.5% in 2017. Sweden, Spain, Portugal, Hungary, Belgium, Luxembourg, and Romania had already passed the mark. Heavyweight Germany was trailing with 27.6%. However, in 2022, the EU average had increased to 55.1%, and the Digital Agenda team could relax. After all, a 2-year delay does not appear too bad.[15] The coverage figures, which were not a target, looked already better in 2020 when 76% of households could subscribe to download speeds of at least 100 Mbps.[16]

The 30 Mbps target was not achieved either. In 2020, 85% of households were covered by networks that could deliver that speed.[17] The gap of about ten percentage points is relevant as it mainly stems from rural areas and is, therefore, difficult to close. You could say that this was disappointing with respect to the *Every European Digital* slogan of the Digital Agenda, which motivated this universal broadband target. However, given almost universal mobile and satellite broadband coverage, this goal is superseded.

Modesty is not part of digital strategies, so the Commission already upgraded the coverage objective in 2016: by 2025, all European households, rural or urban, should have access to networks offering a download speed of at least 100 Mbps, which could be upgraded to 1 Gbps.[18] A few years later, the Digital Decade programme—as we will see—extended this target further to full gigabit coverage by 2030.

With hindsight, the initial Digital Agenda did not contain convincing actions that would lead to its ambitious connectivity objectives. However, this would change shortly after its launch. Two kinds of measures stood out: money and regulations.

[15] https://digital-decade-desi.digital-strategy.ec.europa.eu/datasets/desi/charts/ (accessed on 2 March 2024).

[16] HIS Markit, OMDIA, Point Topic (2022) Broadband Coverage in Europe 2021. Mapping progress towards the coverage objectives of the Digital Decade. A study prepared for the European Commission, p. 48.

[17] Ibid.

[18] Commission Communication COM (2016) 587 final of 14 September 2016 on Connectivity for a Competitive Digital Single Market - Towards a European Gigabit Society.

Money for Broadband

First, money. At the MFF 2014–2020, President Barroso proposed establishing a programme to finance trans-European energy, transport, and digital projects: the Connecting Europe Facility (CEF). The difference with the existing Trans-European Network (TEN) programmes was the move from shared to centralised management. The Commission would select the projects to ensure they corresponded to European priorities and not to the taste of local politicians, a common problem with decentralised European programmes. Member states were dragging their feet; notably, CEF would support projects on merit and not via national quotas.

The Commission proposed 9.3 billion euros for the CEF Digital programme, covering networks and services. The inclusion of services was crucial as they drive digitalisation across borders, but they were more difficult to 'sell' to member states. MFF negotiations are lengthy, complex, and unpredictable as the member states and European Parliament have different priorities. Sadly, we came out with just 1 billion euros over 7 years, which was underwhelming.[19] Critics of CEF Digital, such as the German government, argued that broadband was for the market to solve. A year later, in a twist of political irony, a new government set up a national budget for investments in fibre networks, acknowledging that many areas would remain uncovered. Yet the country continued to underperform,[20] but this is a different story.

A much bigger pot of money than CEF was and is available through the Structural Funds.[21] As it is costly to roll out broadband networks in rural areas, grants can be helpful. Member states are responsible for planning and spending these Funds according to programme and financial regulations, including state aid rules. The Commission issued guidelines that clarified rules but did not ease processes.[22] Furthermore, several public actors are often involved at national, regional, and local levels, leading to coordination tasks. Even for well-equipped administrations, the complexity of managing this process is a challenge.

From 2013 to 2018, member states notified the Commission of 157 projects with a combined budget of about 39 billion euros, among which one from France accounted for 13 billion euros alone.[23] This was too little to have a significant

[19]Regulation (EU) No 1316/2013 of 11 December 2013 establishing the Connecting Europe Facility, amending Regulation (EU) No 913/2010 and repealing Regulations (EC) No 680/2007 and (EC) No 67/2010.

[20]Fibre coverage was a meagre 7.1% in 2017, and in 2022, not much better with 15.4%.

[21]https://ec.europa.eu/information_society/newsroom/image/document/2017-33/european_funding_for_broadband_CAC9F47E-BA2A-1424-044BE071D91F4335_46275.pdf

[22]EU Guidelines (2013/C 25/01) for the application of State aid rules in relation to the rapid deployment of broadband networks.

[23]Richard Feasey, Marc Bourreau, and Antoine Nicolle, "State Aid for Broadband Infrastructure in Europe", Report November 2018, Centre on Regulation in Europe (CERRE).

Richard Feasey, Marc Bourreau, and Antoine Nicolle, "Assessing Fifteen Years of State Aid for Broadband in the European Union: A Quantitative Analysis", in *Telecommunication Policy*, Vol. 44, Issue 7, August 2020.

impact, mainly because not all the money was spent. Data about the final spending are difficult to ascertain because they depend on the reporting of the member states. This makes it nearly impossible to include the Structural Funds in a consistent broadband strategy at the European level.

Alternatives to subsidies are loans and guarantees, which are less sensitive to state aid rules. The European Investment Bank established programmes to ease the financing of broadband networks. Yet, as operators were usually creditworthy, there were limited incremental benefits compared with loans from the financial markets.

In these ways, public money did help trigger investments, notably in rural areas, but it was never a game changer. The development of fast Internet connectivity remained a market-driven process, as intended, since the liberalisation of telecommunications. However, the wish to provide all citizens with Internet access changed the perception that the market was sufficient. Policymakers have manoeuvred themselves into a situation where they set objectives and are held responsible for achieving them while depending on private actors to make the necessary investments, which are subject to profitability considerations and uncertainty. And here, regulation comes into play.

Could Regulation Help?

This is still an ongoing discussion. Operators, subject to Significant Market Power (SMP) rules, give one chief explanation for the investment gap: lack of return on investment due to over-regulation and bureaucratic obstacles to infrastructure roll-out. They also mention the overly strict application of competition law, which prevents them from gaining closer cooperation and setting up joint ventures.

Investments in networks are expensive, with a long pay-back time. Europe's established regulatory framework obliges the dominant operators to grant access even to new networks at regulated prices. This reduces, so goes the argument, not only profitability but also increases uncertainty. Through their organisation ETNO, the former incumbents point to the stark differences in market capitalisation between them and their US counterparts. Thus, they claim that at least 'regulatory holidays', which means that access regulation should be suspended for a certain time, would help. Competitors organised in ECTA object to this and argue that only competition guarantees investments. Recall that ADSL local loop unbundling ensured competition on the legacy copper networks; here, we are dealing with investments in greenfield networks or significant upgrades.

DG Connect's experts had been scratching their heads for years about balancing competition (let's drive tariffs down) with investments (returns are needed). One action they took was to issue a Commission Recommendation to the National

Regulatory Authorities (NRA) on regulated access to Next Generation Access Networks (NGA), which aimed to even out the two positions.[24]

This Recommendation was the cornerstone of the Digital Agenda's broadband strategy. It did not entail regulatory holidays but endorsed a risk premium that regulators should consider when determining wholesale access prices. NRAs should distinguish between competitive situations; for example, obligations could be less demanding if intense competition exists in a region—typically in a larger city. Also, co-investment arrangements should be encouraged; for example, new entrants could obtain attractive access prices in return for a commitment to buy a specific traffic volume over a more extended period.

Such a Recommendation is not legally binding, but the NRAs must take utmost account of it.[25] However, the details make all the difference. Regulatory principles are one thing; deciding on obligations in concrete cases is another. Did the Recommendation accelerate the deployment of broadband? This cannot be answered with certainty, as many factors influence the observed connectivity trends. However, it articulated the insight that regulating fibre networks would need to be different from how legacy copper networks were dealt with.

A rule of thumb says that about 80% of the outlay for rolling out a fibre network consists of civil engineering, particularly digging trenches. Therefore, it is a no-brainer to reduce these costs through better coordination. Operators could piggyback on roadworks or projects of other utilities like energy or water. However, town and country planning falls under national and local competence.

The NGA Recommendation already contained a provision to enhance transparency on the available infrastructure and help competitors deploy their cables alongside those of the dominant operator (multiple fibre competition). In 2012, colleagues initiated the idea of targeting cost reduction for all players through a Directive. The Broadband Cost Reduction Directive was adopted in May 2014.[26]

The Directive called for simplifying and accelerating administrative procedures, allowing operators to access existing physical infrastructure, such as ducts and masts, improving transparency and coordination in civil engineering, and establishing reasonable prices for rights of way. However, member states' obligations were limited to 'best effort' requirements. Not all administrations felt the urgency to adapt their infrastructure planning to the needs of telecom operators, and the latter do not plan their investments according to others' preferences.

Beyond money, regulation, and costs, we also suspected that the fragmented European telecom market was a factor in the slow broadband roll-out. In the network industry, size matters. The telecom regulatory scheme was and remains based on

---

[24] Commission Recommendation (2010/572/EU) of 20 September 2010 on regulated access to Next Generation Access Networks (NGA).

[25] Directive 2002/21/EC on a common regulatory framework for electronic communications networks and services, Article 19.1.

[26] Directive 2014/61/EU of 15 May 2014 on measures to reduce the cost of deploying high-speed electronic communications networks.

national markets. At the start of the Digital Agenda, we did not have a clear plan, and only in 2013 was the proposal for a Single Market Directive for telecoms made. It mainly aimed at a common authorisation scheme, including mobile communication. The proposal was late in the legislative cycle, too ambitious, and did not fulfil expectations. What remained was a Regulation that extended the roaming provisions and encoded net neutrality in European law.[27]

Net Neutrality

The net neutrality debate had moved on since 2009. The revised telecom framework required operators to provide customers with information about the quality and speed of their connections. The Commission stated the fundamental nature of guaranteeing Internet access. This time, member states were receptive to fully legislating net neutrality.

Operators were also interested in clarification. They wanted to broaden their business by developing managed or specialised services, for example, guaranteeing bandwidth and latency for video-on-demand, online gaming, or telemedicine applications. This would also be a vehicle to compete with digital providers offering such services via the Internet, so-called Over-the-Top (OTT) players, mainly from the United States. This term has gradually been replaced by Big Tech.

The Regulation, which came into force in 2016, rules that 'Providers of internet access services shall treat all traffic equally' (Article 3.3). Yet, it also says that this provision shall not prevent them from implementing reasonable traffic management measures, such as maintaining network integrity and security. They are entitled to offer specialised services on the same network as the Internet but should not degrade the performance of the public Internet. This is a fine example of striking a balance.

Operators' hopes for a profitable telecom-like service business alongside public Internet access have not materialised. Every year, the Internet has become better for bandwidth-demanding services like video streaming. Its backbone grew exponentially, and together with compression algorithms, the need to manage capacity diminished. Proxy servers and content delivery services overcame latency problems.

Initially, the United States and the EU agreed to some degree on the need to ensure net neutrality, but in 2017, under the Trump administration, the US regulator, the FCC, repealed these provisions. Internet service providers were no longer classified as common carriers, allowing them to block, throttle, and prioritise traffic. The US regulator believes competition forces are sufficient to ensure Internet access.

---

[27] Regulation (EU) 2015/2120 of 25 November 2015 laying down measures concerning open Internet access and amending Directive 2002/22/EC on universal service and users' rights relating to electronic communications networks and services and Regulation (EU) No 531/2012 on roaming on public mobile communications networks within the Union.

However, the FCC mandated transparency about operators' network management practices.[28]

The Internet economy has continued its expansion, and net neutrality has lost much of its relevance, but the question of burden sharing is still on the table.

4G Was a Game Changer

3G-UMTS did not meet expectations for a mobile Internet revolution. It did not extend the lead Europe had built up with 2G-GSM. During the 2000s, video began to account for the most Internet traffic in volume, and with smartphones turning into miniature computers, people wanted to use them to watch videos, live TV, and play data-hungry online games. The demand for speed, data capacity, and latency grew beyond the capability of 3G-UMTS. Work was underway to introduce a significantly faster mobile technology: LTE and 4G. The meaning behind these terms tells us something interesting about the mobile industry.

As consumers, we have become used to the constant progress of mobile communications. The annual cycle of new smartphones attracts our attention. In contrast, a new generation of networks appears in a 10-year cycle, and without much fanfare, our latest phones just connect to them. However, this only happens because of impressive international cooperation in which two organisations play a decisive role.

First is the third Generation Partnership Project (3GPP), a consortium comprising seven standardisation organisations from Japan, the United States, China, South Korea, India, Europe, and hundreds of contributing companies. It was founded on the initiative of ETSI in 1998. The founding idea was to foster a global 3G standard (UMTS) based on the success of GSM. This triggered a competing initiative in the United States, but eventually, both converged towards one basic technology.

3GPP agrees on specifications by consensus, which are published as Releases relatively infrequently; Release 18 is scheduled for 2024. Enormous work goes into each one. These Releases are transposed into standards by the participating organisations. Building on the initial design of a particular technology, 3GPP publishes a series of specifications, enhancing its performance and adding features.

Globally, work on 4G started around 2004. 3GPP was not the only actor; two competing institutions also aimed at 4G but ultimately failed.[29] 3GPP started Long Term Evolution, LTE; as the name suggests, it was an evolution building on UMTS. The LTE specifications were published as Release 8 in 2008.

Second, there is the International Telecommunications Union (ITU), under whose aegis the World Radio Conference takes place. The ITU publishes specifications of

[28] https://www.fcc.gov/document/fcc-releases-restoring-internet-freedom-order

[29] One was a US consortium (3GPP2), initially founded to develop 3G standards based on CDMA 2000 and promoted Ultra Mobile Broadband. The other one was the WiMAX technology building on Wi-Fi that came out of IEEE.

new mobile technologies that would qualify for designated spectrum bands. Industry and standardisation organisations assume the task of further refinement and implementation. The ITU finally endorses such standards.[30]

The initial LTE Release 8 did not reach all the performance targets set by the ITU, but this would be fixed with LTE-Advanced (Releases 10 and 12). 3GPP has constantly worked on feature upgrades for 4G, even with 5G in the pipeline. For example, it added specifications for vehicle-to-everything communication or enhanced machine-type communication (eMTC) to support industrial applications. This is important as mobile networks are crucial for industry and productivity.

In 2009, TeliaSonera Sweden launched the first LTE network in Stockholm and Oslo, with equipment from Ericsson and Huawei. However, no mobile phone was available, and customers had to use a computer dongle to connect. But finally, in September 2010, Samsung put the first LTE mobile phone on the market. Since then, 4G-LTE has become a major success.[31].

4G-LTE brought broadband to mobile phones. The average speed of 4G-LTE for a user is about five times faster than 3G. It has other advantages, for example, more efficient use of spectrum, easier-to-manage networks, and shorter latency (about 50 milliseconds). It was crucial for the rise of social media and made smartphones a must-have device. Increasingly, the life of a modern citizen worldwide takes place on the smartphone. In some countries, it has become extreme. Life without a smartphone and WeChat is almost impossible for an average Chinese citizen. Maybe one day, we will say the same about the EDIW.

Astonishingly, neither i2010 nor the Digital Agenda had an explicit 4G strategy. The focus was on harmonised spectrum allocation. Sure, FP7 supported the development of 4G technologies and applications with about 300 million euros. However, there was no European Technology Platform and no Joint Technology Initiative. 4G was a wake-up call. It significantly impacted the digital economy so much that 5G became a political priority. Horizon 2020 would pay more attention.[32]

---

[30]The ITU manages a global platform for mobile technology called 'International Mobile Technology' IMT. This platform describes the specifications of the forthcoming technology. IMT-2000 was for 3G, IMT-2010 for 4G, and IMT-2020 for 5G.

[31]By 2015, there were 560 million subscriptions; by 2018, there were 3.6 billion; and by 2023, the world would count 5.2 billion. Interestingly, Asia consistently showed the highest numbers. 4G-LTE subscriptions will decline from 2024 onwards as users move to 5G (already 1.5 billion in 2023). https://www.statista.com/statistics/521572/4g-5g-mobile-subscriptions-worldwide/

When reading mobile communication statistics, subscriptions or connections (typically, the number of active SIM cards) must be distinguished from subscribers, as people and organisations often have several SIM cards.

[32]https://5g-ppp.eu/projects/

Call Me by My Name: Horizon 2020

Horizon 2020 was the first research framework programme with a name. In addition, its full title replaced the word technology with innovation, which became the eighth Framework Programme for Research and Innovation. This was consistent with the Europe 2020 strategy, which included the flagship project of the Innovation Union.

Placing innovation at the forefront was a reaction to recurring criticism that Europe is good at developing technologies but underperforms when bringing them to market. However, whether public subsidies for projects can make companies more innovative is questionable. Innovations are hard to predict, let alone plan. They result from talent, risk-taking, and luck. Innovators must be fast and flexible, requirements ill-suited to the rigid structure of a public funding programme.

Nevertheless, Horizon 2020 contained some innovation-friendly measures. A fundamental assumption was that support for SMEs equals support for innovation. Thus, Horizon 2020 had an action exclusively aimed at SMEs, yet it was with a 600 million euros budget for 7 years. More straightforward participation rules, such as applying flat rates or reducing reporting obligations, facilitated the involvement of SMEs in the programme. New forms of funding helped innovative companies: for example, pre-commercial procurement, inducement prizes, and dedicated loan and equity instruments. Beyond SME support, more public–private partnerships, either as a Joint Technology Initiative (JTI) or through contractual arrangements, were supposed to make the research fields more relevant to the industry.

The designers of Horizon 2020 continued the practice of inventing a new structure and vocabulary for the framework programme. But as an added benefit, a clearer design emerged. The top structure consisted of three pillars: Scientific Excellence, Industrial Leadership, and Societal Challenges.[33]

ICT in Horizon 2020

Three programme features distinguished ICT integration in Horizon 2020 from that in FP7.

The first concerns ICT for societal challenges, the former telematics programmes. They were moved to vertical policy areas. Digital has become mainstream, and to be effective, it must be integrated into the business processes of the healthcare, transport, or energy sectors. The disadvantage of this integration is that conservatism may hold back digital transformation. However, digital projects were still managed alongside other technologies, and divergent views about which direction to take would persist.

---

[33] Horizon 2020's budget of nearly €80 billion was decided as part of the MFF 2007–2013 with the same duration.

For instance, some preferred Wi-Fi as the radio technology for cooperative, assisted, and autonomous driving. This technology had already undergone safety scenario testing. DG Connect leaned towards cellular radio technologies, specifically LTE and 5G, which the 3GPP had standardised for vehicle-to-everything (V2X) applications. The decision on which technology to adopt now lies in the hands of market forces. This example underscores how research programmes can present choices, but sector policies and market dynamics determine the course of action.

Second, although artificial intelligence had existed for decades, it remained a relatively novel concept for many. It often existed as a subtheme in previous programmes, sometimes concealed within broader categories like information management. Even at the outset of Horizon 2020, it remained embedded within the realm of Big Data. The potential of neural networks, which had been on the horizon for over a decade, essentially went unnoticed. This situation lasted until 2018 when AI was formally incorporated with the introduction of the last ICT work programme and the publication of a policy paper. We will delve deeper into AI in Chap. 8.

Lastly, the ICT segment of Horizon 2020 experienced a notable increase in the prevalence of public–private partnerships (PPPs). As we explored in the preceding chapter, these partnerships had gained popularity during FP7 in two distinct forms: JTIs (JUs) and contractual arrangements. Contractual PPPs, compared to JTIs, had a more straightforward set-up process. They were designed to foster a collaborative ecosystem around specific topics. A financial commitment memorandum was typically established between the Commission and participating industries to generate critical mass. Private sector participants would then formulate a strategic research agenda. However, unlike JTIs, the Commission's services remained responsible for crafting the work programme, issuing calls for proposals, and selecting projects. Horizon 2020 witnessed the establishment of several contractual PPPs (cPPPs) covering areas such as 5G, big data, and photonics. I will briefly delve into one already initiated during FP7: Future Internet, known as FI-PPP. It offers us valuable insights into the disparity between narrative and reality.

The Illusion of a Future Internet

> The objective is to reinforce the competitiveness of European industry in developing, mastering and shaping the next generation Internet that will gradually replace and surpass the current Web, fixed and mobile networks and service infrastructures, and enable the interconnection of trillions of devices (IoT) across multiple operators and domains that will change the way we communicate, access and use knowledge.
>
> Council Decision of 3 December 2013 establishing the specific programme implementing Horizon 2020.

DG Connect has always had an ambivalent relationship with the Internet. On the one hand, promoting Internet uptake has been a priority since eEurope 2002. On the other hand, there was a constant feeling that the Internet was not good enough for various use cases. However, time and again, the Internet improved and supported scenarios sceptics did not expect it could; in areas from voice to music to video-on-demand, the Internet excelled. Two factors explain the origin of this European scepticism. First, traditional telecommunications networks guarantee a 'quality of service' as opposed to the 'best effort' of the Internet. Second, in telecommunications, Europe has a competitive edge. In contrast, the United States dominates Internet technologies.

This is the background for the above quote, which reveals a tremendous amount of wishful thinking. The Internet and the web are not the same, and neither will be replaced anytime soon. Yet, there was a strong wish for Internet technologies made in Europe. And so, in FP7, the Future Internet public–private partnership, FI-PPP, was launched and renewed in Horizon 2020. With 300 million euros in EU funding, it ran in three phases from 2011 until 2016. What was it about?

It aimed to develop technologies for edge networks in the private and public sectors, particularly 'enabling components'. These are called smart infrastructures in the initiative, such as smart cities, smart energy, smart industry, and just about everything smart. Participants developed software, data models, and authentication methods and designed business processes. Through an open-source platform, FI-Ware, these components were made freely accessible. They launched experimental use cases in various innovative infrastructure domains that could use these components. An accelerator programme supported start-ups with money and expertise (mimicking the 'business angel' tradition in the United States).

The initiative's results might prove useful; however, this was not about a next-generation Internet. One could refer to it as a collection of projects advancing the industrial applications of Internet technologies. To a certain degree, we are talking about the Internet of Things (IoT). It fostered an ecosystem of companies designing and building smart networks at the edge of the Internet. As data and cloud computing played an increasing role in the FI-PPP, we can draw a logical line to GAIA-X, conceptually a similar initiative of the present day.

GAIA-X was proposed by France and Germany in 2019. Their governments were unnerved by the dominance of US cloud providers and saw a risk that European data would be exploited overseas and could not be shared between European actors. GAIA-X defines its mission as 'to create an open, transparent, and secure federated digital ecosystem, where data and services respond to common rules and can be securely built, collated, and shared'.[34] The similarity to the FI-PPP is obvious, yet it seems that GAIA-X fails to take advantage of its achievements, for example, the FI-Ware repository. Maybe this does happen beneath the surface at a project level, but it is not visible as a strategic component.

The makers of GAIA-X are realistic enough not to have the ambition to compete against the big cloud providers (hyper-scalers). GAIA-X does not offer a cloud. Their main goal is to force the dominant cloud platforms to adjust their business practices to European culture and improve business opportunities for European players.

[34] https://gaia-x.eu/what-is-gaia-x/vision-and-mission/

A Final Point on Horizon 2020

President Barroso came to office with the idea of setting up a European MIT, creating a centre of excellence known as the European Institute of Technology (EIT). That was a neat idea, particularly relevant for ICT, precisely because MIT has been a leading force in advancing digital technologies, such as the web, as I mentioned earlier. It is also an example of how to grow talented scientists.

Replicating the US university system in Europe is difficult. Europe's traditions differ and vary among member states. The EU research programme would not be able to match the endowment system of the United States. The top US universities have multi-billion capital stocks accumulated over two centuries.

Nevertheless, the project moved ahead and quickly hit a problem common in Europe. Which country would host the EIT? Countries other than the host country would be reluctant to co-finance it through the EU budget. The solution was a decentralised EIT with a coordinating agency in Budapest (Hungary). Its funding structure would be around Knowledge and Innovation Centres, linking research and higher education. It is a valuable concept, but the initial idea was much more intriguing.

The Digital Agenda Had a Transitional Effect

The Digital Agenda played a role in charting the course for upcoming initiatives. As mentioned above, it led to the development of a scoreboard that tracks progress through various indicators. Among these indicators, the broadband targets emerged as the primary benchmark for evaluating digital policies, also serving as criteria for assessing state aid in the broadband sector.

The scoreboard unveiled noticeable disparities among member states. Hopes were initially pinned on regional Structural Funds to address these differences. However, their impact was predominantly local and had less influence on national progress, which depended on broader country-specific circumstances. Unfortunately, one of the EU's most potent tools for promoting structural reforms, the country-specific recommendations of the European Semester, did not address these conditions. For instance, it would have been advantageous if several countries had been compelled to assign spectrum for 4G-LTE earlier and at a more affordable cost for operators.

Since the Lisbon Process, one priority for the Commission had been to align EU policies with national initiatives, achieve critical mass, and avoid conflicting measures. This was the motivation for an annual Digital Assembly, organised by the country holding the EU presidency, bringing stakeholders from the public and private sectors together to discuss progress and generate ideas. This institution has remained in place and has taken the form of a conference discussing the latest digital policies and technologies.[35]

Towards the end of the second Barroso-led Commission, it became evident that Europe was lagging in vital digital advances, including cloud services, social media, smartphones, digital platforms, AI, and chip production. A Chinese competitor, Huawei, even posed a challenge to one of Europe's strongholds: mobile communication networks.

Nevertheless, the most pressing concern remained the slow progress in establishing the Digital Single Market (DSM). Undoubtedly, a larger domestic market facilitates global competitiveness, prompting the prioritisation of the DSM in the latter half of the 2010s. One legislative initiative, initiated in 2015 and spanning two Commissions and two digital strategies, stood out as globally influential: the GDPR, considered one of Europe's most impactful regulations ever.

[35] The Digital Assembly 2023 took place in Arlanda, Sweden, on 15/16 June 2023.

Chapter 7
A Digital Single Market

In 2015, Jean-Claude Juncker, the former Prime Minister of Luxembourg, assumed leadership at the European Commission. He introduced the concept of Vice-Presidents, who were tasked with coordination without specific Directorate-Generals under their direct command. Andrus Ansip, an Estonian, was designated Vice-President responsible for digital affairs, and Günther Oettinger, a German, was appointed Commissioner in charge of DG Connect. Later, Oettinger transitioned to the budget portfolio, and Mariya Gabriel, a Bulgarian, took his place.

President Juncker strengthened the role of DG Connect by transferring the responsibilities for e-commerce and copyright to it.

The Euro crisis had stabilised, and growth had come back. Yet mass migration, mainly from Syria, inflicted significant strain. Donald Trump became US President. The British people voted in favour of leaving the EU. These events highlighted the darker side of social media, with disinformation campaigns exacerbating polarisation within Western societies. In addition, geopolitical tensions reshaped the West's relationship with China, marking initial signs of technological decoupling.

The Europe 2020 strategy continued with a heightened emphasis on social issues. Under the Juncker Commission, the Digital Single Market (DSM) emerged as one of its ten core priorities. The aspiration for a DSM had roots in initiatives like i2010, the Digital Agenda, and even earlier, with measures such as the e-Commerce Directive. However, unlike these previous initiatives, the DSM encompassed steps that extended beyond the confines of digital policy but were vital to achieving its objective.

D. Eckert, *40 Years of European Digital Policies*, Professional Practice in Governance and Public Organizations,
https://doi.org/10.1007/978-3-031-61641-9_7

Ambitions

The idea behind the DSM looks straightforward: if I am in the EU, it should not matter where I buy or sell within it. Consumers should enjoy a uniform online experience, from accessing a website to selecting delivery and payment options. Companies should be able to harness the benefits of a large market, allowing them to expand globally, an aspiration that, until today, has remained unfulfilled. The DSM aimed to eliminate barriers to online consumption and business.

However, translating this idea into reality is far from straightforward, primarily due to the diverse nature of these obstacles. Some, like payment and delivery services, fall beyond the scope of digital policy. Others partially lie outside the EU's jurisdiction, such as taxation and civil law. Several other aspects, such as copyright and spectrum harmonisation, had previously encountered political resistance. Perhaps even more influential are subtle factors like language barriers (despite translation technology), cultural nuances (how business is conducted), and institutional intricacies (which administration is responsible for what). These factors are challenging to address solely through legal instruments.

Practical Improvements

Nonetheless, the Commission's legislative programme has brought tangible improvements for consumers and businesses. To start with, roaming charges for mobile telephony were eventually abolished in 2017, bringing significant relief to tourists and business travellers. Another example is that subscribers to audio-visual streaming services can now enjoy their content across all EU countries without encountering restrictions, provided their stay outside their home country is temporary (this is to avoid abuse).[1]

The DSM initiative has simplified cross-border shopping. Consumers often grappled with geo-blocking, a method that prevents users from accessing certain services or websites in other countries. Moreover, some retailers discriminated against consumers and businesses from different EU countries regarding access to prices and payment conditions. A Regulation adopted in 2018 was helpful in making progress on this, although copyright-protected content was excluded, and access problems persist.[2]

[1]Regulation (EU) 2017/1128 of 14 June 2017 on cross-border portability of online content services in the internal market.

[2]Regulation (EU) 2018/302 of 28 February 2018 on addressing unjustified geo-blocking and other forms of discrimination based on customers' nationality, place of residence or place of establishment within the internal market and amending Regulations (EC) No 2006/2004 and (EU) 2017/2394 and Directive 2009/22/EC.

Uncertainty about the recourse available in case of issues with foreign suppliers has led many to favour domestic companies. To address this, two Directives have been introduced to harmonise contractual matters when purchasing goods and services, whether physical or digital, from another member state. However, several sectors, including transport, finance, health, and audio-visual services, are exempted from these provisions.[3] Despite efforts to better coordinate between consumer protection authorities, many consumers may not be aware of these improvements.

The smooth operation of cross-border parcel services is vital for Europe-wide e-commerce. A Regulation tackled this issue.[4] It emphasises transparency by compelling providers to furnish clear and readily accessible information concerning their pricing structures, terms, and conditions. National regulatory authorities are tasked with enforcing the Regulation, including the power to intervene in cases of excessive pricing. Furthermore, the law promotes access to essential postal infrastructure, such as post offices, parcel lockers, and collection points. Efficient complaints handling and dispute resolution mechanisms are also enshrined in the Regulation. These measures benefit consumers and businesses alike.

I have not yet mentioned the younger sibling of the Television without Frontiers Directive. It goes by the name of the Cable and Satellite Directive, and it was adopted back in 1993. This Directive stipulates that operators and service providers can secure copyright clearance for content in their own country, a common country-of-origin provision essential for the smooth functioning of the Single Market. These two Directives now have a little brother, a Directive about ancillary audio-visual services. Essentially, it extended the country-of-origin provision to ancillary online transmission channels.[5] This represents a valuable incremental adjustment to the copyright regime.

More than e-commerce

The above provisions form the core of what would directly promote cross-border e-commerce in Europe, a DSM in a narrow sense. Yet, strategies at the European level are seldom narrowly focused, and the DSM was no exception. It encompassed actions that addressed a broader spectrum of digital issues reminiscent of its predecessors, notably the Digital Agenda.

---

[3] Directive (EU) 2019/770 of 20 May 2019 on certain aspects concerning contracts for the supply of digital content and digital services.

Directive (EU) 2019/771 of 20 May 2019 on certain aspects concerning contracts for the sale of goods, amending Regulation (EU) 2017/2394 and Directive 2009/22/EC, and repealing Directive 1999/44/EC.

[4] Regulation (EU) 2018/644 of 18 April 2018 on cross-border parcel delivery services.

[5] Directive (EU) 2019/789 of 17 April 2019 laying down rules on the exercise of copyright and related rights applicable to certain online transmissions of broadcasting organisations and retransmissions of television and radio programmes, and amending Council Directive 93/83/EEC.

Among the regulatory initiatives were familiar ones, covering telecommunications, copyright, audio-visual content, and privacy. However, that was not all; initiatives targeting cybersecurity, digital skills, e-government, and IT standardisation, all elements seen in previous strategies, were also incorporated into the DSM initiative. The DSM strategy did not explicitly reference the ICT research programmes, as Horizon 2020 had just begun.

Privacy played a particular role insofar as the General Data Protection Regulation (GDPR) was neither part of the Digital Agenda nor the Digital Single Market strategy. The revision of data protection law became necessary as the Internet was in its infancy in 1995. Thus, one might have expected it to be integrated into a coherent digital strategy.

Instead, only the revision of the 2002 ePrivacy Directive became the privacy component of the Digital Single Market strategy; a proposal for an ePrivacy Regulation introduced in 2017 is still under discussion. This represents a missed opportunity for regulatory simplification. Integrating e-privacy provisions into the GDPR would have been a logical approach, with implementing acts addressing specific issues. Hence, a decision made in 1990 to separate ISDN privacy from general data protection continues to endure.

GDPR: A Model for the World?

Maybe, but keep it in perspective.

The GDPR, adopted on 27 April 2016, replaced the 1995 Data Protection Directive. It took 4 years of negotiations. Agreements on privacy laws are complicated; it took 5 years to agree to the 1995 Directive. In May 2018, the GDPR came into force.[6]

Europe's privacy laws have achieved worldwide fame, even before the GDPR, arguably the most quoted piece of EU legislation. EU representatives proudly point out that many countries, including Brazil, Japan, and South Africa, have used the GDPR as a blueprint or at least as an inspiration. However, one should not exaggerate. Many countries used similar terminology but also tailored their privacy law to national traditions and circumstances.[7]

---

[6]Regulation (EU) 2016/679 of 27 April 2016 on the protection of natural persons with regard to the processing of personal data and on the free movement of such data, and repealing Directive 95/46/EC (General Data Protection Regulation).

[7]For example, India adopted a new privacy law in August 2023. While inspired by the GDPR, it differs in many aspects.

https://www.huntonprivacyblog.com/2023/08/22/india-passes-digital-personal-data-protection-act/

https://www.linklaters.com/en/insights/blogs/digilinks/2023/august/india-the-digital-personal-data-protection-act

Trading partners complain about the GDPR's extra-territorial reach. This challenge is twofold. First, it is hard to compare legal systems. The United States, for example, tried to accommodate European legal concerns by introducing the concept of 'proportionality' in its national security practices. This concept, however, is more of a guide for the administration, whereas, in Europe, it is a fundamental principle of law. Second, there are cases where data transfer is needed in the interest of humanity, for example, to fight a global pandemic, support international humanitarian actions, assist international organisations, underpin global research cooperation or address migration issues [1].[8]

Rules for international data transfer cannot be set unilaterally if they are to be effective globally. The EU has a legalistic approach to international data transfers, which sometimes runs up against political realities. In 2022, several countries, including Japan, South Korea, Canada, and the United States, launched a Global Cross-Border Privacy Rules initiative as an alternative to the GDPR adequacy regime. For now, the initiative has limited impact, and there are questions about whether it is a serious initiative to increase protection; however, it is still in the early stages, and things could change. Other countries and regions, such as ASEAN, have also begun to establish model contractual clauses for such transfers.[9]

Europe considers privacy a fundamental right that must be balanced with other competing rights or interests. The rulings of the European Court to invalidate both the first 'Safe Harbour' agreement with the United States and its 'Privacy Shield' follow-up, for instance, show that it does not recognise privacy rights as being able to be regulated in classical trade agreements. The GDPR is based on Article 8(1) of the Charter of Fundamental Rights of the European Union and Article 16(1) of the TEU, not Single Market provisions.

What Are the Main Differences Compared with the 1995 Directive?

The GDPR enlarged the scope of the 1995 Directive.[10] It covers the personal data of EU residents independent of geography. Hence, it applies to organisations outside the EU that process EU residents' data by offering them goods or services or monitoring their behaviour within the EU. The Regulation introduced significantly

[8]Christopher Kuner, "International Data Transfers after Five Years of the GDPR: Postmodern Anxieties" in *5 Candles for the GDPR, Symposium EU Law Live,* May 2023, edited by Dominik Düsterhaus.

[9]https://www.allenovery.com/en-gb/global/blogs/data-hub/global-cross-border-privacy-rules-and-the-new-initiatives-to-support-data-free-flow-with-trust

[10]It also enlarged the volume of the legal text from 34 Articles to 99 Articles. The privacy world has become more complicated.

higher penalties for serious breaches, of up to 4% of global turnover. It imposed stricter requirements for obtaining valid consent.

The GDPR also aims to overcome one shortcoming of the 1995 Directive, namely the 'fragmentation in the implementation of data protection across the Union' (GDPR, Recital 9). For over 20 years, the so-called Article 29 Working Party (comprised of the data protection authorities from the member states) tried to overcome the patchwork of privacy practices. It published many guidelines that contributed to a more harmonised interpretation of the Directive, but these were non-binding and failed to produce true harmonisation.

The GDPR now provides a higher degree of harmonisation. However, enforcement practices across countries still diverge. One of the notable areas is the interpretation of consent. What exactly constitutes valid consent has been subject to differing interpretations by member state authorities. This has led to inconsistencies in how organisations seek and obtain consent from individuals, creating challenges for businesses operating across borders. Another example is the interpretation of what constitutes a legitimate interest that justifies the processing of data. One member state may consider direct marketing a legitimate interest, while another may require stricter justification. Additionally, there are differences in the thresholds triggering data protection impact assessments and the processes involved in their execution. Finally, the GDPR contains exemptions for national matters and specific sectors, such as the public sector, employment, or health care, which are subject to less harmonisation. In these cases, organisations may need to deal with multiple authorities, depending on the nature of the data processing.

The laudable 'one-stop shop' concept in the GDPR aims to streamline the regulatory process by allowing organisations to deal with a single data protection authority (DPA) or supervisory authority (SA) in the EU member state where they have their main establishment. This SA would then act as the lead authority responsible for cross-border cases. However, these processes can be complex, leading to delays and difficulties in reaching a consensus. In the latter case, a consistency mechanism could be invoked. In case of disagreement, the European Data Protection Board (EDPB), which replaced the Article 29 Group, can issue a binding decision. For instance, in December 2022, the EDPB ruled that the Irish regulator must issue a fine against Meta. Several data protection authorities had not agreed with the Irish regulator's draft decision, so the consistency mechanism was invoked.[11]

Critics often view the GDPR as a hindrance to innovation, citing instances where business models, policy measures, or research appeared unfeasible due to data protection constraints. Yet, the GDPR defines legitimate data usage scenarios and endorses privacy-enhancing technologies like pseudonymisation for data protection in business contexts. Thus, these activities can often proceed, albeit with added effort

[11]https://edpb.europa.eu/system/files/2023-01/edpb_bindingdecision_202203_ie_sa_meta_facebookservice_redacted_en.pdf

The issue was about the way Meta sought consensus for personalised advertising.

and legal expertise. In addition, there is increasingly a business case to be made for privacy, as customers and individuals expect companies to protect their data. However, organisations may take a precautionary approach, exacerbated by the stringent practices of authorities. For example, anonymisation, a tool for balancing data utility with privacy protection and particularly important in healthcare-related research, is sometimes met with apprehension, as authorities have doubts about its effectiveness.

The Social Media Reality

Privacy advocates might hope that the GDPR will curb the business of social media platforms. While these platforms had to adapt several practices, and most recently, some had to pay significant fines (which may be appealed), the GDPR will not stop the further ascent of companies like Meta and Google. It has not been designed or intended to thwart certain business models. The core tenet of European data protection is 'specificity'. Organisations obtain consent to utilise private data for a precise purpose and are not authorised to exercise unrestricted control, such as merging data at will or trading them without permission.

When the GDPR is reviewed by the Commission, how the system can become less bureaucratic and more harmonised should be investigated. Ensuring that its enforcement across borders becomes more predictable is crucial. On the global stage, the current practice of unilateral adequacy decisions made by the Commission, which are then challenged before the European Court of Justice, is becoming increasingly unsustainable. However, there appears to be no clear concept of how to reconcile an approach rooted in fundamental rights with the practical demands of international trade and the necessity to collaborate with foreign legal systems.

The Copyright Reform

It was a sunny and pleasant summer day just outside Brussels in 2009. We, the management team of then DG INFSO, met for our third brainstorming meeting about the direction of digital policies. I reported in a previous section about our first one in 2007.

One issue was the digitisation of European cultural heritage, a topic close to the heart of our Commissioner, Viviane Reding. We had just launched Europeana, a platform to make European art and literature available to everyone and to foster tourism.[12] At the same time, Google initiated an ambitious project to digitise vast volumes of books in public libraries. Thus, our idea was a kind of 'European culture

[12] Visit this website and enjoy European culture. https://www.europeana.eu/en

at your fingertips' to paraphrase Al Gore's 1995 vision of the information superhighway.

But then there was copyright. One colleague presented the issue of 'orphan' works, particularly books, where the rightsholders were unknown. As copyright does not need to be registered, institutions interested in making available a digital copy must find the rights owner or otherwise risk being sued. Nobody undertook this effort because of the low economic value of digitising orphan books. 'Wealthy' Google was an exception but could only digitise a part of this body of work, the part covered by the US principle of 'fair use'.

Disillusioned, we triggered a discussion with our copyright colleagues from the Internal Market department. The result was a 2012 Directive that allowed public (not private) institutions to digitise presumably orphan works after making a diligent effort to find the rightsholders and publishing these works on a dedicated list so that a potential rightsholder could subsequently receive adequate remuneration. Ten years later, this measure is yet to have much impact, as it has proved too complicated and too risky for institutions. It is simply not trivial to reconcile the way copyright works with the digital age, even if it only concerns the practical question of rights clearing.[13]

However, regarding commercially available books, the situation improved remarkably through innovation. The most important came from Seattle in 2007 with Amazon's e-reader, Kindle, which made e-books popular. So-called e-readers were not new but were too clumsy and not embedded into a value chain. The Kindle changed the market, similar to the effect generated by the iPod. Other prominent players, such as Barnes & Noble and Sony, followed. The way to ensure copyright was linked to the digital rights management embedded in devices and later by software—an ecosystem enabled by the 2001 Copyright Directive's provisions on technological protection measures. It is the same for music, film, and video games—beyond social media.

The Reform Proposal

In 2019, after a lengthy negotiation characterised by several clashes of cultures, the Council and Parliament adopted a Directive broadening and amending the 2001 InfoSoc Directive.[14] The underlying idea of the Directive was to modernise copyright, taking into consideration market developments and technical progress over the previous decade. It was another attempt to build an Internal Market for content, which, given the territorial nature of copyright, comes close to squaring the circle.

---

[13]Directive 2012/28/EU of 25 October 2012 on certain permitted uses of orphan works.

[14]Directive (EU) 2019/790 of 17 April 2019 on copyright and related rights in the Digital Single Market and amending Directives 96/9/EC and 2001/29/EC.

The Directive gave many stakeholders what they wanted. The music industry sought a way to make online platforms pay for uploaded user content. Book publishers needed a fix for some levy issues. Newspaper publishers requested their rights. Composers wanted mandatory contract law. And technology companies needed text and data mining. Though neither of them wanted much of what the others wanted—the art of EU law-making can ultimately make all stakeholders equally happy and unhappy. Let's unpack it a bit.

The thorniest issue of the Directive concerned the introduction of new obligations for online content-sharing service providers such as YouTube, Facebook, or Twitter (now X). Rightsholders considered the 'notice and takedown' rule insufficient because of the sheer volume of uploaded content and growing piracy. The new rules stipulated that platforms had to seek authorisation before allowing protected content to be uploaded and were, in principle, liable for infringements by their users, thereby overruling the e-Commerce Directive. Provisions of this sort always come with many caveats and conditions, introduced with formulas such as 'provided that' or 'unless they'. This Directive is no exception, and relevant Article 17 contains a number of these twists and tweaks.

The one that managed to trigger protests in the streets across Europe concerned a provision for platforms to avoid liability if they can demonstrate having tried to block unauthorised content with state-of-the-art technology, expeditiously remove it and prevent further uploads. Technically, this requires upload filters, which created fear of 'censorship' and raised strong opposition from so-called civil society. The legislator tried to mitigate these concerns with several provisions; for instance, users should not be prevented from uploading content under certain copyright exceptions, platforms should establish a complaint resolution mechanism for content unduly blocked, and general monitoring should not occur. Concerns remained. The mere existence of filtering created uneasiness, although platforms already routinely carried out content moderation, which is another word for filtering.

How on earth can all of this be implemented? Well, big platforms have the means to operate efficient, targeted filters and blocking mechanisms, but smaller competitors might face disproportionate costs [2].[15] Very small platforms are exempt from deploying such techniques, although they still must follow specific rules. At least, nobody can accuse the EU of favouring domestic platforms, which are all smaller than their US competitors.

Beyond this contentious issue, the Directive contains an assembly of provisions without a discernible philosophy. It addresses, for example, 'out of commerce' work (same idea as with orphan works but different provisions), clarifies that reproducing visual art, which is no longer under copyright, is legitimate (thereby preventing a

[15] Thomas Spoerri, "On Upload-Filters and other Competitive Advantages for Big Tech Companies under Article 17 of the Directive on Copyright in the Digital Single Market", *Journal of Intellectual Property, Information Technology and E-Commerce Law*, 10(2019)2.

common practice among museums of restricting such copies), and introduces a remuneration scheme for the printed press if their journalistic work is exploited more by online news aggregators than through hyperlinks such as Google does. The latter rule also gave rise to an animated discussion, and its practicability remains to be seen. Meanwhile, the press sector is busy furthering its repertoire of legal claims against the platforms via *ex ante* competition law, the Digital Markets Act, to make their new copyright work.

The legislator introduced three mandatory exceptions, thereby, unlike the 2001 Directive, ensuring the approximation of national regulations in line with the DSM objective: text and data mining, cross-border e-learning, and preservation of cultural heritage. Let's zoom in on the first one, as it could be more significant than the negotiators initially thought.

Unexpected Implications for AI

The legislation contains a 'text and data mining' exception for research and cultural institutions, which rightsholders can only limit through security and integrity measures. A second exception applies to private actors and commercial usage but does not include storage for verification and gives rightsholders the option of a machine-readable opt-out.

Technically, text and data mining require making temporary copies of content to extract data with no intention to reproduce or distribute the original material. One could argue that such an activity should be excluded from a copyright regime altogether. Yet, the legislator took the view that making any copy, even if only for a fraction of a second, is a copyright-relevant act but could then be exempted from copyright as an exception.

The opt-out clause could hamper services linked to data analytics, and here, AI comes into play. AI was not on the political agenda when the Directive was concluded. Now, it is. The problem is twofold. First, European companies will be disadvantaged when they can use less data than their global competitors. Second, as they are not allowed to keep copyrighted training data for documentary purposes, they might not be able to fulfil the requirements of the AI Act, which will mandate data storage for verification purposes. Thus, legislation seems to squeeze European players in their ability to use sufficient data. However, the copyright discussion has also been gaining pace in the United States, and therefore, American AI companies may face similar, or even more rigid, restrictions.

Indeed, the possibility of AI generating art (music, pictures, paintings, books, and soon movies), which already sells well and wins prizes, brings copyright concerns to the forefront. Take, for instance, the creation of graphics for books, games, music, or film covers. AI 'text-to-image' models such as DALL-E2 or Midjourney are becoming so natural and artistic that they will no doubt undermine the business foundations of illustrators. This development will affect many domains, albeit to a different degree, such as photography, scriptwriting, news articles, etc. Some might call it 'generative copying'. The list is long and will get longer.

Against this background, artists and creators claim that these models, which only exist because of their initial work, remove them from the market without compensation. Yet, training data originate from thousands of sources worldwide; thus, the individual contribution is negligible. The collective accumulation of artwork leads to these impressive AI models. Furthermore, copyright protects pieces of artwork but not style. Only, where is the boundary?

An alternative for rightsholders and artists to generate revenue could be to offer quality databases with curation, metadata, and search filters. Another avenue is to allow data storage, which could help comply with the AI Act.

AI unleashes enormous potential by offering artists tools to create new art forms. It also allows more people to exploit their imaginations to produce artistic work. One thing is sure: this is only the beginning. 'You ain't seen nothing yet.'[16]

Outlook

Where do we go from here? We have a patchwork of copyright legislation at the European level, addressing various aspects without finding a comprehensive solution to reconcile the Internal Market with the territorial copyright regime. Progress has been made in facilitating rights clearing. User rights have been strengthened, even more than rightsholders find justified but less than consumer organisations hoped. Societal interests, such as education and cultural heritage, are no longer exceptional but have become legitimate competing interests.

Will we see a continuation of the current piecemeal approach, fixing problems at the fringes, or will we see a fundamental shift towards a European Copyright Code? Bernt Hugenholtz, a distinguished copyright law professor, published an early vision of this idea.[17] A Code would not only mean full harmonisation of exceptions and contractual laws but also an extension of the territorial scope to the entire EU. In a less ambitious version, it could follow the path of trademarks and patents, where a European title exists parallel to national regimes.

These ideas are in a drawer, waiting for better times. Therefore, you will continue to encounter the message 'this content is not available in your country' for a long time. So be patient.

---

[16] Bachman-Turner Overdrive.

[17] Bernt Hugenholtz, "Copyright territoriality in the European Union", published by the European Parliament, February 2010, PE 419.621.

Bernt Hugenholtz, "Copyright in Europe: Twenty Years Ago, Today and What the Future Holds" *Fordham Intellectual Property, Media & Entertainment Law Journal*, 2013. https://ir.lawnet.fordham.edu/iplj/vol23/iss2/4

Audio-Visual Regulation Remains Complex

The first recital of the 2018 revision of the Audio-Visual Media Service Directive (AVMSD) refers to the 'ongoing convergence of television and internet services', reminiscent of the 1997 Convergence Green Paper. Following this logic, the Directive extends its reach to video-sharing platforms (VSPs). However, including VSPs deviates from the rationale of regulating services with editorial responsibility, which these platforms do not have.[18]

Why do regulators feel so strongly about audio-visual services, and why should broadcasting regulation be extended to video platforms? The main argument remains that audio-visual content substantially impacts human perception, emotions, and opinions more than written, audio, or still image content. Is that convincing? I could think of many influential books, investigative newspaper stories, or iconic photos. Donald Trump had the most impact through Twitter, the Wall Street Journal, and Fox News, not via YouTube or Netflix. Online services are individualised, time-independent, and, in the case of VSPs, user-generated. The legislator, nevertheless, felt a responsibility to extend the scope of the AVMSD to VSPs because they attract the same audience and compete with other media. Thus, the revision may more closely reflect the desire of media regulators to remain relevant in a changing media landscape.

Provisions

In a nutshell, what does the Directive say? VSPs must take appropriate measures to protect minors and the general public from harmful and illegal content, for instance, regarding underage content 'which may impair their physical, mental or moral development'. The Directive lists measures that member states should take depending on the situation. For instance, VSPs need to provide a mechanism for users to signal advertisements in uploaded videos, a notification system for harmful and illegal content, and, if applicable, age verification tools. Here, you can see the indirect influence of a programme that DG Connect's Luxembourg division has been running for years, called Safer Internet, which promotes safety standards and voluntary commitments by companies to protect children.

The revised Directive contains various other provisions, such as commercials on broadcasting services or product placements in children's programmes. It attempts to enhance transparency about media ownership. The Directive also stipulates that media content should be delivered without interruption, altering, or commercial

[18] Directive (EU) 2018/1808 of 14 November 2018 amending Directive 2010/13/EU on the coordination of certain provisions laid down by law, regulation, or administrative action in Member States concerning the provision of audiovisual media services (Audiovisual Media Services Directive) in view of changing market realities.

overlays. This 'signal integrity' provision is addressed to intermediaries such as Smart TV manufacturers or network operators. While it protects the interests of content and service providers, it could prevent device innovations or technical features needed for navigation.

Implementing the VSP provisions is complex because a diversity of actors is involved: the platform owners, users that globally upload thousands of videos every minute, advertisers and influencers, and device manufacturers. Why divide online regulation according to types of content? These provisions could have waited for the Digital Services Act (DSA), adopted 4 years later.

The Media Reality

Despite its country-of-origin focus, the media landscape in Europe has remained noticeably disjointed. Member states differ in how they handle media concentration. The presence of public broadcasters, although financed differently depending on the country, exerts direct or indirect influence on the advertising market. This entanglement of interests and regulatory intricacies persists, with a complex interplay between 'information society services' on one hand and the traditional broadcasting milieu, encompassing video-on-demand, on the other.

The traditional media landscape remains susceptible to political influences. Against this backdrop, it is no surprise that the ascent of social media platforms is perceived as a challenge. But what, precisely, does this challenge entail? Is it the apprehension of political parties relinquishing their grip on shaping the agenda, or is it broader anxiety about the tenets of democracy itself?

Brexit, as a concrete event, precipitated the United Kingdom's de facto withdrawal from negotiations concerning the AVMSD. Without this departure, the 30% mandatory European works quota (as opposed to the previous 'wherever practicable' quota) would most likely not have been included in the revised AVMSD.

Furthermore, the Directive authorised member states to impose investment obligations on services targeting their respective jurisdictions, provided such obligations pertain to local services. Different implementations of this provision contradict the philosophy of the DSM, which aims to at least avoid further fragmentation in the regulatory landscape. It can lead to the cannibalisation of local resources being directed to global producers. It contributes to the cultural dominance of the larger EU countries as they mobilise more investments, and service providers can fill a large portion of their European catalogue with these productions, which, as you remember, is relevant for the quota system. In addition, sooner or later, Brexit will raise the question of defining European works, as the European catalogues are filled with British content.

In retrospect, media regulation had a limited impact on enhancing the global appeal of European content. Although local content retained popularity, achieving this did not necessitate a quota system. Conversely, American streaming platforms have invested substantially in European content, while European VoD providers have struggled to attain a significant market share. As a result, entertainment offerings often lean towards being either American or locally produced, with limited availability of trans-European content.

Electronic Communications: The Code

> Governments worldwide are increasingly realising that broadband access will be central to the economic development of their countries.

No, this quote is not from the DSM strategy but from eEurope2005, two decades earlier. Why does Europe, on average, still lag behind in deploying high-speed networks?

After a disappointing review of the telecom framework at the beginning of the 2010 decade, the Commission was convinced that the DSM should deliver substantial reform, leading to more investments and better connectivity. The outcome was the European Electronic Communications Code (EECC), accompanied by a revised Body of European Regulators for Electronic Communications (BEREC) Regulation.[19] This framework aimed to increase harmonisation, stimulate investment in high-speed networks, enhance consumer protection, and integrate telecom-like Internet services.[20] It amalgamated all four Directives from the last major telecom regulatory overhaul of 2009 into a single legislative piece.

The Code is complex and the result of many compromises. It has garnered extensive analysis and commentary since its adoption. Within our narrative, the key focus revolves around fibre deployment and increased integration, and for the latter, the roles of BEREC and spectrum harmonisation in particular.

---

[19] Directive (EU) 2018/1972 of 11 December 2018 establishing the European Electronic Communications Code (Recast).

Regulation (EU) 2018/1971 of 11 December 2018 establishing the Body of European Regulators for Electronic Communications (BEREC) and the Agency for Support for BEREC (BEREC Office), amending Regulation (EU) 2015/2120 and repealing Regulation (EC) No 1211/2009.

[20] The definition of electronic communication services has undergone a revision, expanding to encompass Internet-based services. The Code introduces a distinction between number-independent and number-based interpersonal communication. For example, Facebook Messenger falls under the category of number-independent, while Skype relies on numbers. The primary obligation is placed on number-based services to register for general authorisation purposes. However, being recognised as a relevant service simplifies potential future regulatory procedures, even though, with the Digital Markets Act (DMA) and the Digital Services Act (DSA) in play, the necessity for such registration appears somewhat limited.

How Do We Bolster Investment in Fibre Deployment?

The objectives of the Digital Agenda did not initially necessitate fibre connections; upgraded copper and cable networks could deliver the needed 100 Mbps (and even higher) download speeds. And indeed, average connection speeds have consistently risen over time. However, already in 2016,[21] the Commission raised the bar and aimed for gigabit connectivity, a goal reinforced by the subsequent Digital Decade strategy, as we will explore in Chaps. 9 and 10. Thus, the crux of the matter lies in the level of political ambition and the policy framework that shapes investment incentives. However, opinions diverge on how this framework should be structured.

Under the umbrella of ETNO, former incumbents complain about disincentives for fibre investments, attributing them to excessive regulation and bureaucratic hurdles in infrastructure deployment. They argue that stringent access regulation diminishes profitability and restricts flexibility in devising pricing models. ECTA, representing challengers, along with BEREC, hold a different perspective, contending that competition is the primary driver of investment incentives. Upon closer examination, the disparity in their views is not centred on the value of competition but rather on the extent of the *ex ante* regulation required to ensure it thrives.

Consequently, the member companies within ETNO had high hopes for significant deregulation, often referred to as 'regulatory holidays'. However, their hopes were ultimately dashed. But ECTA also had its grievances, which I will briefly delve into.

The Code introduced the concept of co-investment to incentivise network deployment with minimal regulatory interference. In scenarios where an incumbent operator initiates an investment project to deploy high-capacity networks alongside co-investors, this consortium would only be subjected to light regulation. This could include obligations such as negotiating access in good faith.

This provision was well-conceived and drew inspiration from existing national schemes, such as those in France. However, it risks being bogged down in regulatory micromanagement. The Code regulates various aspects of such arrangements in detail. For instance, it stipulates that the project must remain open to new participants at any time. National Regulatory Authorities (NRAs) determine whether the project qualifies for light regulation. Additionally, competition rules aimed at preventing the abuse of market power are still in effect.

Another approach incorporated into the Code is the 'wholesale-only model', where an entity solely constructs a network without offering services. The Code permits NRAs to mandate such a separation under specific conditions and can also be embraced voluntarily. In practice, significant private investments, often in collaboration with local authorities, have been directed towards developing passive

[21] Commission Communication COM (2016) 587 final of 14 September 2016 concerning Connectivity for a Competitive Digital Single Market—Towards a European Gigabit Society.

infrastructure at regional and local levels, destined to be utilised subsequently by service providers.

Competitors may have reservations about the provision requiring NRAs to consider risks when imposing access conditions for high-capacity networks. This provision, initially in the NGA Recommendation, has become a binding measure. Furthermore, access remedies should only be directed towards the wholesale market and no longer apply to retail segments. Additionally, under certain circumstances, the potential for symmetrical access regulation has been introduced, which includes sharing essential facilities, even for non-SMP (Significant Market Power) providers.

Striving for More Integration

The Commission's initial proposal contained several provisions to achieve a more integrated market. The two that would have had a significant impact concerned BEREC and spectrum allocation.

The initial idea was to transform BEREC into an agency with executive powers. Although member states did not endorse this proposal, BEREC did secure additional competencies, including a veto right to be exercised in collaboration with the Commission. The argument that telecom markets remain predominantly national, a relic of the 1990s, still holds some validity. However, maintaining the status quo in the regulatory landscape would effectively perpetuate the fragmented telecom market. We might take a page from the US playbook to address this, where authority is shared between the FCC and state regulators.

Similarly, countries continue to closely guard their competencies regarding spectrum allocation. The economic rationale for closer coordination, including full harmonisation of timing, spectrum bands, and methods to assign spectrum, is compelling. For example, some member states have earmarked 5G spectrum for private business use, primarily to facilitate industrial digital transformation. Yet not all member states followed suit, and in numerous cases, countries have allocated different frequency bands, hindering the seamless connection of sites and cross-border service provision. Despite this, the Code did manage to harmonise certain aspects, such as stipulating that licences should have a minimum duration of 20 years and permitting the trading of second-hand spectrum. Nevertheless, the allocation of frequency bands for 5G continues to resemble a disjointed process.

The 2009 framework had already established a consultation process for defining relevant markets, identifying market power, and implementing remedies. This process involved BEREC, the Commission, and all NRAs. This process has now been refined to grant more extensive veto powers to both BEREC and the Commission, which must be jointly applied (a double lock mechanism).

Outlook

The Code, proposed in 2016, adopted in 2018, and progressively transposed into national law by member states, marks the preliminary endpoint of a journey spanning over 30 years, which began with a Green Paper in 1986. This does not imply that telecom regulation will come to a standstill; there will be ongoing refinements and, eventually, another revision.

However, with the Code, telecom regulation has matured in terms of institutions, practices, court decisions, and accumulated experience, establishing a natural inclination towards continuity. As connectivity continues to improve, the urgency to resolve the investment versus competition trade-off will diminish. At that point, Europe may have attained a satisfactory level of facility-based competition, allowing for a shift towards *ex post* competition rules. Consequently, the next major revision could focus on simplification and deregulation. Chapter 10 will delve into this.

DSM Achievements

The legislative agenda of the Digital Single Market was executed as planned, marking an achievement with tangible progress in several areas. The Commission services, with DG Connect at the forefront, rightfully took pride in this accomplishment.

In many ways, the European Union's legislative process operates seamlessly. The EU institutions function as a well-coordinated machinery, demonstrating high competence in crafting intricate legislation applicable to the 27 member states and beyond. However, it can be challenging for those outside the EU's sphere to fathom the extensive efforts invested in each of these legislative endeavours.

Nonetheless, regulation alone does not guarantee enhanced competitiveness, if this is the appropriate goal at all, as I will discuss in the Epilogue. The DSM initiative aimed to boost competitiveness, assuming that a larger market inherently fosters it. However, this is not always the case. A more harmonised environment in Europe could instead make it easier for foreign companies to establish a presence. Business organisations in Brussels have consistently supported the internal market for that reason. The DSM enhances Europe's attractiveness for business and investment. It expands consumer access to a broader range of services. However, its impact on Europe's digital competitiveness remains unclear.

References

1. Christopher Kuner, "International Data Transfers after Five Years of the GDPR: Postmodern Anxieties" in *5 Candles for the GDPR, Symposium EU Law Live,* May 2023, edited by Dominik Düsterhaus.
2. Thomas Spoerri, "On Upload-Filters and other Competitive Advantages for Big Tech Companies under Article 17 of the Directive on Copyright in the Digital Single Market", *Journal of Intellectual Property, Information Technology and E-Commerce Law*, 10(2019)2.

Chapter 8
The Age of Artificial Intelligence

> There is an easy seductiveness to stories that cast a technology as brand-new, . . . seen this way, the future is a space of reinvention and possibility, rather than something intimately connected to our present and our past. . . . . Knowing the history of a technology, or the ideas it embodies, can provide better questions, reveal potential pitfalls and lessons already learned, and open a window onto the lives of those who learned them.
>
> Genevieve Bell, "The metaverse is a new word for an old idea. To understand what we are—and should be—building, we need to look beyond *Snow Crash*", *MIT Technology Review*, 8 February 2022.

On 30 November 2022, the company OpenAI released ChatGPT. GPT stands for Generative Pre-trained Transformer. 'Generative' refers to its ability to generate context; 'pre-trained' signifies that it is trained on a large dataset before being fine-tuned for specific tasks; 'Transformer' refers to the underlying neural network architecture it employs.[1] It brought AI to public attention. True, AI had made headlines before. DeepMind, a British start-up acquired by Google, developed AlphaGo, which beat the world Go champion, Ke Jie, in 2017. This marked a significant milestone, as Go is more complex than chess, with a vast number of possible moves. According to former Google executive and VC investor Kai-Fu Lee, this event served as a 'Sputnik moment' for China, sparking significant investments in AI [1].

Earlier, in 2012, AI experts celebrated a milestone when AlexNet, a deep neural network, emerged as the champion in the ImageNet Challenge, a renowned competition dedicated to computer vision tasks. Following this watershed moment, the

[1] Transformer models are a type of neural network architecture that excels at a variety of natural language processing tasks, including text generation. They are often used in generative AI applications, such as chatbots or text-to-image creation.

The Transformer concept was first published by a group of Google researchers. The paper by Ashish Vaswani et al., "Attention Is All You Need". *arXiv:1706.03762v5* of 6 December 2017, was initially presented at the Neural Information Processing Systems (NeurIPS) conference in 2017.

D. Eckert, *40 Years of European Digital Policies*, Professional Practice in Governance and Public Organizations,
https://doi.org/10.1007/978-3-031-61641-9_8

field of image recognition has witnessed significant advances, for example, the widespread adoption of facial recognition for user authentication.

However, merely reading about what AI can do differs significantly from having the opportunity to use it for one's own purposes and witnessing firsthand its capabilities. With the introduction of ChatGPT, people gained access to a system capable of performing a wide range of tasks, from generating text and answering questions to making travel plans and much more.

The Financial Times, in July 2023, and the magazine WIRED, in March 2024, published the fascinating story of Transformer models [2, 3]. While Google initially underestimated their potential, it created an environment that allowed its employees to pursue an unconventional idea: replacing recurrent neural networks with a self-attention mechanism. Remarkably, the authors of the groundbreaking paper had diverse backgrounds from Ukraine, India, Germany, Poland, Wales, Canada, and the United States. Except for one member, they all left Google and founded their own companies. Once again, Europeans played a crucial role in developing the foundations of modern AI. The paper was public, and OpenAI seized the opportunity. Nothing fundamental prevented European entrepreneurs from doing the same.

The news about AI also landed on the desks of policymakers across the world, who immediately expressed concerns, as they did when computers, industrial robots, and the Internet became popular. Many of them called for regulation. Not so in the EU—the AI Act had already been proposed in April 2021.

The AI Act

Until 2018, the EU had no AI strategy. The first two work programmes of Horizon2020 referenced big data, machine translation, and robotics but did not explicitly address AI. In 2018, the Commission reacted to the significant advances in AI. It published a policy paper that deplored a substantial investment gap between the EU on the one hand and the United States and Asia (notably China) on the other.[2]

The paper set the objective of raising Europe's annual public and private investment in AI from around 5 billion euros to 20 billion euros by the end of 2020. The expectation was to motivate member states to aggregate their efforts. The Commission committed about 1 billion euros to AI from the Horizon 2020 programme. The 20 billion euros target was not achieved; indeed, a 2020 White Paper repeated the same analysis with the target remaining, as so often, a mere aspiration.[3]

[2]Commission Communication COM(2018) 237 of 25 April 2018 on Artificial Intelligence for Europe.

[3]White Paper, COM(2020) 65 final of 19 February 2020 on Artificial Intelligence—A European approach to excellence and trust.

Following the 2018 paper, a high-level group was tasked with developing principles for AI ethics. Based on their report,[4] a second policy paper highlighted a human-centric and trustworthy AI.[5] Eventually, the incoming new Commission announced its intention to propose an AI Regulation preceded by another White Paper. Remember that everything in the EU is a process.

Ethics, human-centricity, and trustworthiness have become the dominant narrative of the EU's approach to AI. And so, after two and a half years of negotiations, a political agreement on the AI Act was achieved on 8 December 2023 and formally adopted in 2024 [4].

The AI Act is a typical product safety regulation targeting risks. Its implementation rests on the assumption that the product manufacturer best understands its technicalities and can carry out a self-assessment. The result must be registered in a public database, documented, and subject to verification. This will lead to a CE mark being required to place a product on the EU market.

The Regulation does not guarantee safety but ensures that specific AI systems have undergone a verifiable design and production process. Thus, a CE-marked system may still generate biases, but the risks of doing so are reduced. Even if an AI provider complies with the requirements of the Regulation, it could become subject to liability claims.[6]

The problem is that AI is not a product but a technology. It comprises a wide range of methods for creating software that can enhance their own capabilities by processing and learning from data. However, while this is a core aspect of machine learning, AI also encompasses other methods, like rule-based and expert systems. As AI continues to evolve, it is becoming more complex and multifaceted. It is, therefore, not surprising that the legal definition of AI is challenging. Popular definitions, such as those from the OECD, describe what AI does and not what AI is.[7]

This problem became evident when the rule makers discovered in early 2022 that a new class of models had emerged with generative AI (GenAI). Yet, finding an appropriate regulatory approach proved difficult because GenAI serves many use cases and has become very popular. After a lengthy debate, the EU legislature decided to request transparency obligations for such models and to impose more stringent obligations, such as risk management, monitoring serious incidents, and

[4]High-Level Expert Group on Artificial Intelligence, "Ethics Guidelines for Trustworthy AI", Brussels, 8 April 2019.

[5]Commission Communication COM(2019) 168 final of 8 April 2019 on Building Trust in Human-Centric Artificial Intelligence.

[6]Two Directives, still in negotiation, aim to harmonise the legal framework for such liability claims: Commission Proposal COM(2022) 496 of 28 September 2022 for a Directive on adapting non-contractual civil liability rules to artificial intelligence (AI Liability Directive); Commission Proposal COM(2022) 495 of 28 September 2022 for a Directive on liability for defective products.

[7]Recommendation of the Council on Artificial Intelligence, OECD/Legal/0449 adopted on 22 May 2019: 'An AI system is a machine-based system that can, for a given set of human-defined objectives, make predictions, recommendations, or decisions influencing real or virtual environments.'

adversarial testing, on high-impact models, which the Regulation denotes as posing 'systemic risks'.[8] In addition, providers of such models must appoint an authorised representative to cooperate with EU and national authorities.

The distinction between these two classes seems arbitrary and may invite engineering decisions based on regulatory considerations, not performance. The Commission can adjust the thresholds and add supplementary benchmarks and indicators via a Delegated Act. In both cases, a CE mark will not be required, and the obligations will be implemented through codes of practice.

While GenAI dominated the discussion, the initial regulatory approach focused on two use cases that were considered high risk.[9] The first concerns AI embedded in already regulated products or sectors, such as vehicles or medical devices. Product- or sector-specific regulations will implement the AI Act provisions *mutatis mutandis*. In principle, the AI Act was not needed for this and could have left the necessary adjustments to the relevant domains.[10] The second category refers to AI applied in specific areas considered sensitive for people, such as law enforcement, employment, and education. The Act defines them as 'high risk', which is an unfortunate terminology. The motivation was to signal that the regulation would be focused and leave most AI applications untouched. However, the inclusion of GenAI has de facto extended regulation to the entire field as this is becoming a pervasive technology.

The AI Act extends the physical harm approach of product regulation to people's 'fundamental rights' as stipulated by the Charter of Fundamental Rights of the European Union (2012) and includes consumer protection elements. The Charter contains diverse rights; some are more relevant than others for AI-related issues. For example, non-discrimination and gender equality are closer to ethical concerns than the right to access documents or freedom of movement. The AI Act is vague about how to determine the harm it wants to prevent except for applications it strictly forbids being used in the EU, such as subliminal manipulation, emotion recognition, social scoring, and biometric identification in public spaces.[11]

The AI Act will be implemented in the following steps: At the end of 2024, there will be no forbidden use cases; in the middle of 2025, the GenAI rules will come into effect; and in 2026, everyone addressed by the Regulation must comply. The implementation of the Act relies substantially on standards that CEN/CENELEC

[8]The criterion is based on how much computing, measured in 'floating points' FLOPs, was used in the training phase. At the end of 2023, it seems that only GPT-4 and Gemini from Google would fall under these obligations.

[9]High-risk AI systems must fulfil a set of obligations regarding risk management, data governance, technical documentation, record keeping, transparency, human oversight, accuracy, robustness, and cybersecurity.

[10]The situation for medical devices is particularly complicated, as two Directives already regulate their software in detail.

[11]Several exemptions have been made for law enforcement. For example, searches for victims or persons suspected of being terrorists.

are to develop by the middle of 2025.[12] CEN/CENELEC will cooperate with ISO/IEC,[13] which has a comprehensive AI agenda by itself and might adopt standards from their work in this domain.[14] Together, they work on more than 70 projects. ISO/IEC has already published some standards, such as AI management or biases.[15]

Using standards is voluntary and not cheap, as organisations must go through a certification process. Yet, it has the advantage of compliance presumption when officially recognised by the Commission. This is not unusual, but AI is different from traditional product safety standards. AI raises value judgement issues, which need to be translated into technical parameters and process descriptions. Let's take a closer look.

Fairness and Accuracy

What do regulators mean when they talk about ethical AI? You will find references to bias, discrimination, fairness, etc., but no consistent concept. Biases have always plagued statisticians when they try to build representative models of the world. A paper published in 2019 summarises the variety of possible distortions; for example, analysts could use non-representative data, confuse cross-sectorial data with longitudinal data, or measure input in a way that pre-determines the result [5]. In machine learning, these biases can be particularly difficult to identify because of the opacity of the models.

An instructive example of the issue is COMPAS (Correctional Offender Management Profiling for Alternative Sanctions), an algorithm used in some jurisdictions in the United States. It is a risk assessment tool designed to assist judges and parole boards in making decisions about bail, sentencing, and parole based on a defendant's risk of reoffending. The system has been a subject of debate and legal challenges due to concerns about bias and fairness.[16]

---

[12] CEN/CLC/JTC 21 Artificial Intelligence. https://www.cencenelec.eu/areas-of-work/cen-cenelec-topics/artificial-intelligence/

[13] ISO (International Organisation for Standardisation) and IEC (International Electrotechnical Commission).

[14] https://www.iso.org/committee/6794475.html

[15] 'ISO/IEC 42001 is an international standard that specifies requirements for establishing, implementing, maintaining, and continually improving an Artificial Intelligence Management System (AIMS) within organizations.' https://www.iso.org/standard/81230.html

ISO/IEC TR 24027:2021 '. . .addresses bias in relation to AI systems, especially with regards to AI-aided decision-making.' https://www.iso.org/standard/77607.html

[16] For an overview, see Andrew Lee Park, "Injustice Ex Machina: Predictive Algorithms in Criminal Sentencing", *Law Meets World*, 19 February 2019. https://www.uclalawreview.org/injustice-ex-machina-predictive-algorithms-in-criminal-sentencing/

Although the model did not use racial or other information considered discriminatory, it produced more false negatives for black people and more false positives for white people. However, the same percentage of white and black people were classified as being at high risk of recidivism. This is an example of a situation where applying one definition of discrimination without conflicting with another is impossible. In an article for the *MIT Technology Review* of 4 February 2019, Karen Hao asks: ‘Does fairness mean, for example, that the same proportion of black and white individuals should get high-risk assessment scores? Or that the same level of risk should result in the same score regardless of race?’

The case of COMPAS reveals the difficulties of encapsulating fairness in models when data reflect biases of the real world. Do you correct data to make them fairer? Then, models might no longer deliver adequate predictions. A solution could be in *ex post* corrections, which, when applied in the context of the AI Act, would put more responsibility on the user of an AI system than its provider.

Back to standards. Within the organisations, technical committees develop standards based on expert views and adopt them as consensus. The participants come from industry, academics, or NGOs and bring their interests and worldviews to the table. Sure, their work must be confirmed by the European Commission. However, it should be stressed again that AI touches upon societal issues. Experience will show to what extent standards, like the above-mentioned ISO/IEC standard on biases, can provide adequate assurance in AI’s fast-evolving and complex field. This complexity is a consequence of the AI Act.

International Developments

> The world wants to regulate AI, but does not quite know how.
> *The Economist*, 24 October 2023.

Before the policy interest in regulating AI took shape, tech companies had already taken action. Google, Meta, Microsoft, and others published ethical principles (who had not?), established ethics committees, and set up ethics coalitions. These commitments were met with caution by politicians and, of course, by activists. Some criticism sounded more like an attack on capitalism and big companies than a well-thought risk assessment; for example, accusing companies of ‘data colonialism’ does not lead us anywhere [6].

Organisations of different kinds worldwide have jumped on the AI ethics train. For example, the UN, the World Economic Forum, and the Institute of Electrical and Electronics Engineers (IEEE) have all issued papers and announced further work. The Beijing Academy of Artificial Intelligence already released its Beijing AI Principles in May 2019, at the same time as the OECD published arguably the most influential contribution, which it updated in November 2023.[17]

---

[17] https://oecd.ai/en/ai-principles

On 31 October 2023, the G7 leaders committed to working on a common framework in cooperation with the OECD. Meanwhile, US President Biden released an executive order that obliges AI companies to share the risk analysis of their advanced models with competent authorities.[18] The order addresses various other aspects, from standards to cybersecurity. Of particular importance is preventing AI from facilitating the development of biological weapons. This concern was shared at the AI Summit organised by the UK government at Bletchley Park in early November 2023.

At this Summit, 28 countries, including the United States, China, and the EU, agreed on a Declaration. CEOs of top AI companies participated in the discussion. The Declaration identified cybersecurity, disinformation, and biotechnology as risks and pointed to the unpredictable capabilities of frontier AI.

It is puzzling that these policy anxieties do not match current evidence. There are, of course, examples of where AI has caused problems. For instance, face recognition models were criticised for being biased against people of colour [7]. In 2024, Google's Gemini model seemed to do just the opposite. In 2016, Microsoft got into trouble with its Chatbot Tay, which was tricked by users into using offensive language and was taken down one day after it was launched. However, many problems attributed to AI have existed before; disinformation campaigns on social media are of human origin and circulate even without botnets.

Yet, AI has an accelerating effect as it makes it easier to draft authentic-looking text, manufacture fake images and videos, and imitate voices, causing a proliferation of false content. It will be more complex and harder for users to distinguish fake from real. Detection software can help, particularly when AI content is watermarked.[19] However, this helps against individuals using standard tools but not against sophisticated malicious actors. Moreover, researchers have already demonstrated how to circumvent such watermarking techniques.[20]

The effectiveness of product regulation in addressing this issue is limited, as the abuse of AI-generated content stems from malicious intent rather than flaws in the AI models themselves. Instead, addressing this challenge will require adjustments to our judicial system. AI behaves more akin to an artificial reality than exhibiting true intelligence.

Moreover, the damage does not come primarily from fake content but from its wide distribution. This puts responsibility on influential platforms for how they design their recommender systems and how good they can identify such content. This is one of the issues addressed by the Digital Services Act, which is introduced in the following chapter. However, not all risks can be contained by regulation. Society must learn how to deal with AI in a similar way as it learned to manage new media in the past, and this—to be stressed again—includes the judicial system.

---

[18] https://ai.gov/

[19] https://contentauthenticity.org/

[20] https://www.wired.com/story/artificial-intelligence-watermarking-issues/

Thus, we must learn more about the functioning of social media and the capabilities of AI. Ultimately, we may need to consider each image, video, or text as AI-generated unless it is proven otherwise. We must even be aware that a familiar voice on the phone could be faked. The focus must shift towards the ‘origin’, who posted the content, and the ‘endorsers’, who shared and liked the post. However, how do you find out? Voluntary identification—remember the blue Twitter label—could be a way forward. You may disagree with someone’s opinion; it may even be AI-faked, but at least you know who is behind it.

Demystifying AI

> ... the researchers, who came to Hanover 50 years ago, thought about ways to make machines more cognizant, and they wanted to lay out a framework to understand human intelligence better.
>
> Dartmouth (New Hampshire) website[21] on the purpose of the 1956 conference where Professor John McCarthy introduced the term Artificial Intelligence.[22]

While technology has progressed towards the first goal, neuroscientists do not believe the second ambition has been reached. The FET flagship Human Brain attempted to use computer science to model and better understand the human brain but had not much impact on AI. Noam Chomsky, a renowned linguist, says that large language models are useful devices but ‘designed in such a way that in principle they can’t tell you anything about language learning cognitive processes’.[23] For him, AI is engineering and not science. Yann LeCun, a key person in developing deep learning techniques, mocked ‘machine learning as the science of sloppiness’.[24]

Yet, people involved in AI development express worries that resonate with the media and politicians: that it could supersede human intelligence, become sentient, and potentially become an existential threat to humanity. Geoffrey Hinton, for example, justifies his concerns that language models have shown unexpected emerging properties with increasing size. Yann LeCun argues against this and, like Chomsky, points out that the current models cannot plan and have no common sense. Unlike humans, the models lack cognitive knowledge about the physical world. They learn what is in the data but understand little of human tacit knowledge or intuition. The physics Nobel Prize laureate Roger Penrose says, ‘AI is a misno-

---

[21] https://home.dartmouth.edu/about/artificial-intelligence-ai-coined-dartmouth

[22] I already pointed to a panel discussion from 1972 about AI, in which John McCarthy also participated. The discussion at around 45′ is particularly insightful. https://media.aiai.ed.ac.uk/Video/Lighthill1973/1973-BBC-Lighthill-Controversy.mp4

[23] Interview published on YouTube by ‘Eye on AI’ #126 on 23 June 2023 entitled ‘Decoding the Human Mind & Neural Nets’.

[24] YouTube interview with Lex Fridman. https://www.youtube.com/watch?v=SGSOCuByo24

mer'.[25] Indeed, if the models were known by the name of machine learning, we would see less political excitement.

The observed harm directly attributed to AI is not proportionate to the political drama. The current concerns are a projection into the future: if these models can do this now, what will they be able to do tomorrow? There is a substantial amount of fearmongering, even coming from AI companies. 'Some people push existential risk because they think it will benefit their own company', says François Chollet, an AI researcher at Google.[26] Politicians and the media do not have the nerve to accept that technology shifts come with uncertainties. From a practical point of view, it is good that the Bletchley Summit participants concluded they would work together on '... building a shared scientific and evidence-based understanding of these risks'.

Employment and Productivity

> ... some readers may not yet have heard the name, but of which they will hear a great deal in the years to come—namely, technological unemployment.
>
> John Maynard Keynes, "Economic Possibilities for our Grandchildren" (1930), in Essays in Persuasion, New York, Harcourt Brace, 1932, pp. 358–373.

While this sounds pessimistic, Keynes drew a positive conclusion in this article: 'I would predict that the standard of life in progressive countries one hundred years hence will be between four and eight times as high as it is.' History proved him right.

Whenever technology significantly impacts the labour market, the question of employment arises; typically, this concerns the number of jobs. However, working conditions and job content have also been equally relevant. In the history of the Luddites, the workers are often portrayed as technology haters, but it was probably more of a protest against working conditions, which they expressed through attacks on the machines [8].

In their book *Race Against the Machine*, Brynjolfsson and McAfee argued that ICT would have an unprecedented effect on white-collar workers [9]. This was followed by a raft of studies and books, which screened occupations for their potential to be automated by computers and estimated high percentages.[27] However, being affected does not mean being replaced. It could well mean augmented and enriched. Labour economist David Autor argues convincingly how AI could provide middle-class workers with expertise whose jobs have been automated with opportunities. AI '... can enable workers with an appropriate foundation of expertise to

[25] Interview with Channel 4 News, 3 December 2021.

[26] "These six questions will dictate the future of generative AI", Will Douglas Heaven, *MIT Technology Review*, 19 December 2023. https://www.technologyreview.com/2023/12/19/1084505/generative-ai-artificial-intelligence-bias-jobs-copyright-misinformation/

[27] Carl Benedikt Frey and Michael A. Osborne, "The Future of Employment: How Susceptible are Jobs to Computerisation?" Oxford Martin School Working Paper, 2013. This was one of the earlier works.

level up' [10]. This is an opportunity that deserves political attention and goes beyond launching digital skills support programmes.

The expanding literature on AI and its impact on employment is set to grow significantly. As we delve deeper, drawing upon empirical evidence, a growing body of research will illuminate the subject from diverse angles. For example, Baldwin and Okubo's analysis of Japanese data reveals a positive correlation between investments in telework-enabling software and AI investments, a finding corroborated by a survey of workers. ICT engineers, business consultants, and researchers, in particular, anticipate an uptick in teleworking and an increased availability of AI tools at their disposal.[28]

Translating these insights into adjustments for both educational curricula and institutions represents a formidable yet crucial challenge. History has demonstrated that these institutions are slow to evolve, marked by significant variability across member states. The EU's influence over educational matters is circumscribed, and in some member states, educational governance even falls under regional jurisdiction. Despite the Commission's repeated proposals[29] for reforms in higher education and vocational training, uptake has been tepid, evidenced by the modest outcomes of numerous conferences, expert gatherings, and the rhetoric emanating from Council-level discussions. Against the backdrop of AI's ascent, the push for comprehensive institutional reform in education and vocational training has never been more pressing.

The scope of tasks that generative AI can automate is extensive and can be relatively precisely identified even in its early stages. These tasks include generating journalistic articles, crafting marketing slogans, producing visual content, translating and interpreting various languages, handling data entry and processing, reviewing legal documents, and facilitating customer support through chatbots. However, in most cases, these models serve as tools or technical assistants to augment the capabilities of individuals. You may trust them with specific tasks, but '... there's never one thing you can do with AI that solves that problem in full. And I think that's just a testament to the world being really big and messy, and that these systems are still evolving, they're still really in their infancy...'.[30]

---

[28] Richard Baldwin and Toshihiro Okubo, "Are Software Automation and Teleworkers Substitutes? Preliminary Evidence from Japan", *National Bureau of Economic Research*, Working Paper 31,627, August 2023, DOI 10.3386/w31627. The Covid pandemic provided a rare opportunity to obtain data from a real-life experiment.

[29] Commission Communication COM (2016) 381 of 10 June 2016 on a new skills agenda for Europe. Working together to strengthen human capital, employability and competitiveness.

Commission Communication COM(2020)274 of 1 July 2020 on a European skills agenda for sustainable competitiveness, social fairness and resilience.

[30] OpenAI COO Brad Lightcap on a talk with CNBC about the ChatGPT launch. Published on 4 December 2023 and updated on 5 December. By reading this interview, you learn a lot about innovation. The story of Europe's digital policy is rich in examples of missed innovations, which, however, is not a criticism. Policymakers are not positioned to predict innovations; even those who innovate—as the interview showed—often do not realise they are onto something big.

However, the question is whether these productivity gains specific to various occupations will cumulatively lead to a significant increase in macroeconomic productivity. This question lies at the heart of the Solow Paradox debate, which I introduced earlier and ponders why we have not seen ICT deliver productivity effects akin to past industrial revolutions [11, 12]. Can AI solve the paradox?

Despite the remarkable performance of the latest AI models, this outcome is not readily apparent. To have a substantial impact on macroeconomic productivity, AI automation must encompass a significant portion of tasks across the entire economy, particularly in sectors like manufacturing. The models must become better at planning and reasoning, decomposing complex tasks, and finding means to complete them. Additionally, societal institutions must adapt to accommodate the capabilities of generative AI and encourage innovative solutions to replace outdated practices. This leads us to the future of AI in Europe.

Burning Questions for Europe

While regulating AI is in vogue, the trajectory of the AI ecosystem and the direction of technology remain uncertain. How long will the transformer model continue as the dominant architecture? The performance of these models is closely tied to scale, requiring large datasets and extensive training efforts to generate billions of parameters. However, some AI pioneers, such as Yann LeCun and Sepp Hochreiter, believe that better alternatives are needed and are actively developing them. Yet, similar doubts were once held about TCP/IP. The next generation of AI may evolve from GenAI rather than being a complete departure. This is pertinent for Europe, as competing with US companies on large AI models will be hard without a paradigm shift.

Indeed, as of early 2024, the ecosystem is highly dynamic. Numerous companies, including a significant number of start-ups and research organisations, are training their own models. Just within a single week at the beginning of February 2024, OpenAI unveiled Sora, a text-to-video generative model, Google released Gemini 1.5, and Stability AI has open-sourced Stable Cascade, a new text-to-image model. Two European companies, Mistral (France) and Aleph Alpha (Germany), have made advancements in the GenAI market. However, many European start-ups fine-tune their models based on the top GenAI models, indicating a potential transition of the AI market into a platform business with typical network effects. They also become a target for acquisition by large players. Moreover, the United States dominates the VC investment scene in AI. From 2012 to 2023, the European share of global VC funding in GenAI was 5%, and about 90% was invested in the United States. Europe accounted for 15% of all AI areas, US start-ups garnered 63%, and China stood at 11%.[31]

[31] https://dealroom.co/guides/deep-tech-europe. Accessed on 20 February 2024.

European policymakers champion open-source software to challenge the dominance of large companies. Since these firms have been embracing open-source practices, this challenge has lost relevance. Nevertheless, open-source AI empowers smaller companies, even from traditional sectors, to enter the AI market and develop tailored solutions without compromising data access or business processes.[32] Moreover, many argue that open-source AI is crucial for fostering responsible AI development. However, concerns persist about the potential misuse of AI models that are globally available, as highlighted at the UK AI Summit mentioned earlier.

Open-source AI can manifest in various forms. Ideally, it entails making the architecture, source code, and data accessible, facilitating community-driven development. For instance, when Meta unveiled its Llama 2 model, it shared a paper detailing the architecture and methods of fine-tuning and how to reduce biases, along with a file containing the model's parameters and code for inference. However, it withheld the data and training algorithm. Another example is BLOOM, a 176-billion-parameter open-source model resulting from international collaboration. Coordinated by Hugging Face, a leading AI open-source company based in the United States, BLOOM was trained on a supercomputer in France. A final example of the vibrant open-source scene is the release of Aya, a model trained in 101 languages, by Cohere.[33] The company published a fine-tuned dataset containing annotations from speakers around the world.

Europe should embrace a global perspective. For instance, visiting the Hugging Face website reveals significant involvement from Chinese companies and their open-source models. Although names like 01.AI (founded by Kai-Fu Lee) and Qwen (from Alibaba) may not be as familiar as GPT-4 or Gemini, substantial activity is occurring in China and other regions worldwide.[34]

The Commission continues to stress Europe's strengths in vertical industries and the availability of industrial data as a competitive advantage. This is highlighted in a policy paper on AI innovation and start-ups published by the Commission in January 2024.[35] The goal is to leverage existing support programmes across various sectors, from chemicals to healthcare, in order to promote the adoption of AI. While this approach is logical, it may not necessarily alter Europe's competitive position in AI.

Another aspect of the plan involves making existing supercomputers accessible to European researchers and expanding their capacity. While this will benefit researchers and SMEs, it is unfortunate that the capacity will still fall short of what major US tech companies can deploy for their next-generation models. Additionally, the efficiency of resource allocation remains uncertain. There is a difference between

[32] The AI Act exempts open-source models under certain conditions from certain provisions.

[33] Cohere was cofounded by Aidan Gomez, one of the authors of the "Attention is all You Need" paper.

[34] https://www.blog.aiport.tech/p/the-first-truly-global-generative?utm_source=turingpost&utm_medium=email&utm_campaign=genailandscape

[35] European Commission COM(2024) 28 final of 24 January 2024 on boosting startups and innovation in trustworthy artificial intelligence.

having allocated computer time and having unrestricted access to use the computer as needed. AI development still requires an artisanal approach, with teams needing the flexibility to experiment with various architectures and test ideas by running the model multiple times. 'Llama 2-Chat is the result of several months of research and iterative applications of alignment techniques, including both instruction tuning and RLHF, requiring significant computational and annotation resources [13].'

The plan outlines the scope of actions achievable at the EU level. However, a more ambitious strategy would involve the member states. Leveraging the Digital Decade Policy Programme 2030 could serve as a platform to rally and synchronise national efforts. The absence of such coordination is puzzling, especially considering its potential significance for the public sector. Initiating joint AI procurement projects, emphasising scalability, presents one avenue. For instance, public employment services could harness AI to assess job seekers and design and implement training programmes. This is just one example. The opportunities are vast and, with political determination, can be exploited.

References

1. Kai-Fu Lee, *AI Superpowers. China, Silicon Valley and the New World Order*, Boston, New York, 2018. p.1.
2. Steven Levy, "8 Google Employees Invented Modern AI. Here's the Inside Story", *WIRED*, 28 March 2024.
3. Madhumita Murgia, "Transformers: the Google scientists who pioneered an AI revolution", *Financial Times*, 23 July 2023.
4. Regulation (EU) 2024/1689 of 13 June 2024 laying down harmonised rules on artificial intelligence and amending Regulations (EC) No 300/2008,(EU) No 167/2013, (EU) No 168/2013, (EU) 2018/858, (EU) 2018/1139 and (EU) 2019/2144 and Directives 2014/90/EU, (EU) 2016/797 and (EU) 2020/1828 (Artificial Intelligence Act).
5. Ninareh Mehrabi et al., "A Survey on Bias and Fairness in Machine Learning", 25 January 2022. https://arxiv.org/pdf/1908.09635.pdf
6. Melissa Heikkilä and Joy Buolamwini, "We're giving AI companies a free pass", *MIT Technology Review*, 29 October 2023.
7. Arianna Johnson, "Racism And AI: Here's How It's Been Criticized For Amplifying Bias", *Forbes*, 25 May 2023.
8. Miriam A. Cherry, "The Future Encyclopaedia of Luddism", *The MIT Press Reader*, 2021. https://thereader.mitpress.mit.edu/the-future-encyclopedia-of-luddism/
9. Erik Brynjolfsson and Andrew McAfee, *Race Against the Machine*, Digital Frontier Press, 2012.
10. David Autor, "AI Could Actually Help Rebuild the Middle Class", *Noema*, 12 February 2024. https://www.noemamag.com/how-ai-could-help-rebuild-the-middle-class/?mc_cid=8e7d3a34e9&mc_eid=6dec9e96fd
11. Robert J. Gordon, "Is U.S. Economic Growth over? Faltering Innovation Confronts the Six Headwinds", 2012, *NBER Working Paper 18315*. http://www.nber.org/papers/w18315
12. Nicholas Oulto, "Long-term implications of the ICT revolution: Applying the lessons of growth theory and growth accounting", *Economic Modelling*, Volume 29, Issue 5, September 2012, pp. 1722-1736.
13. Hugo Touvron et al. "Llama 2: Open Foundation and Fine-Tuned Chat Models." *arXiv:2307.09288*, 19 July 2023, p.8.

Chapter 9
Seeking Digital Sovereignty

The 2020s began sadly: the Covid pandemic cost millions of lives, stifled the global economy, and disrupted supply chains. However, it boosted a new vaccine technology based on mRNA, which could help humanity with other diseases. Connectivity kept the economy, education, and social life afloat.

Europe is committed to fighting climate change and promotes a twin transformation: green and digital.[1]

On 1 December 2019, the Ursula von der Leyen Commission took office. Digital was one of its six priorities: 'Europe fit for the Digital Age'. This begs the question of whether the digital age has just begun. It is somewhat perplexing to be preparing for something that has already been around for 40 years. Margrethe Vestager, as Vice-President, and Thierry Breton, Commissioner for industry and digital affairs, most likely did not bother about such semantics.

If You Can't Beat Them, Regulate Them

> Because of the increasing direct or indirect influence of electronics in practically all aspects of industrial life in the Western world, what was just technological dependence in a few specialised areas in the past is now threatening to become industrial and economic dependence, plain and simple. In these conditions, the identity of Europe and, eventually, its political independence will be seriously at stake.
>
> Commission Communication COM (83) 258 final of 2 June 1983 on Esprit: First European Strategic Programme for Research and Development in Information Technologies.

[1] 'We should harness this transformative power of the twin digital and climate transition to strengthen our own industrial base and innovation potential.'

Ursula von der Leyen, Speech to the European Parliament, 27 November 2019.

D. Eckert, *40 Years of European Digital Policies*, Professional Practice in Governance and Public Organizations,
https://doi.org/10.1007/978-3-031-61641-9_9

In its first strategy document, Shaping Europe's Digital Future, the Commission assembled a long list of actions a few months into the mandate, making it a document like many others.[2] However, the paper is noteworthy as it puts forward the notion of technological sovereignty. Since then, this narrative has been repeated in various flavours as the terminology has shifted through strategic sovereignty, digital sovereignty, and strategic autonomy.

The sovereignty catchphrase invites interpretations. Two complementary lines of thought stand out. The first is the classical goal that Europe must master critical technologies, such as nanochips, quantum, big data, AI, and 6G. For example, Commissioner Thierry Breton devoted his speech at the Hannover Messe Digital Days in July 2020 to digital sovereignty: 'Data, microelectronics and connectivity are the cornerstones of our digital sovereignty.' Strictly speaking, Europe's problem is less about technology and more about a shortage of global companies and big-impact innovations, such as those we witnessed at the end of the 2000s with smartphones and social media. Innovations are not programmable and do not follow a linear trajectory from science and inventions. Innovations are the result of entrepreneurship, as Schumpeter would have understood it. A complex web of societal institutions, national culture, and legal frameworks influences the probability of innovations emerging.[3]

The second meaning of sovereignty refers to legislation. The EU possesses a well-oiled legislative machine of high quality, which is competent to deal with cross-border issues. Thus, by issuing rules for its internal market, the EU, by the same token, sets rules for the global industry. The GDPR is a good example. Other countries find copying at least part of this Regulation efficient, and international companies translate European rules into their products and processes. This has become known as the Brussels Effect [1].

However, apart from the risk of burdening businesses with high compliance costs, more regulation does not make European companies more competitive. As Guntram Wolff wrote in February 2020: 'Europe may be the world's AI referee, but referees don't win.'[4]

---

[2]Commission Communication COM (2020) 67 final of 19 February 2020 on Shaping Europe's digital future.

[3]In the 1980s and 1990s, substantial literature emerged about how to foster innovation. Christopher Freeman, a British economist, is considered one of the founders of the economics of innovation. He proposed the concept of National Innovation Systems. Chris Freeman, The "National System of Innovation" in historical perspective, *Cambridge Journal of Economics*, Vol. 19, No. 1, Special Issue on Technology and Innovation (February 1995), pp. 5–24. 'The concept of national innovation systems directs the attention of policymakers to possible systemic failures which may impede the innovative performance of industry.' OECD, *National Innovation Systems*, Paris 1997, p. 41.

I met Chris in 1984 when I was a visiting fellow at the Science and Policy Research Unit (SPRU) in Brighton. We kept in touch for quite a while, and I have kept his thank you note for my comments on one of his books as a memory. He was a fabulous person and a great economist. Mary Kaldor wrote an obituary for him in The Guardian of 8 September 2010.

[4]https://www.bruegel.org/2020/02/europe-may-be-the-worlds-ai-referee-but-referees-dont-win/

Much of this chapter will be devoted to the regulatory agenda of the Digital Decade, which is impressive in volume and scope. It covers cybersecurity, semiconductors, digital services, artificial intelligence, and connectivity. But beforehand, we should talk about methods and money.

The Open Method for Coordination Revisited

In March 2021, the Commission proposed a long-term agenda to the Parliament and the Council—the 2030 Digital Compass: The European Way for the Digital Decade.[5] It's nice to see that after 30 years, the narrative of the first action plan, Europe's Way to the Information Society, is almost repeated. According to the document: 'The European way to a digitalised economy and society is about solidarity, prosperity, and sustainability.' This is in the tradition of Europe 2020's vision of a 'smart, sustainable and inclusive economy'.

The Digital Compass consists of 12 quantitative targets for 2030,[6] such as ensuring that all households are furnished with gigabit connections (following in the footsteps of the Digital Agenda). It set the scene for a formal Decision by the Parliament and Council establishing a policy programme.[7] Through this Decision, the Digital Decade programme was formulated as a legal framework and not only endorsed through Council Conclusions—a step change in digital policymaking.

The Decision confirmed the 12 targets, established a process to benchmark member states, committed them to submit national roadmaps, and set a framework for multi-country projects. The Commission will publish regular reports about the state of the Digital Decade.[8] This process mimics the European Semester and the Open Method of Coordination (OMC) of the Lisbon agenda.

The OMC is still applied in several policy domains, particularly in employment policy, which is reinforced by Article 148 TFEU, stipulating a similar process of benchmarking and guidelines. One interesting element not included in the Digital Decade process is multilateral surveillance, where member states, not the Commission, evaluate each other and make recommendations.

In the European Semester procedure, the Commission publishes an Annual Growth Survey; member states present national reform plans, and the Commission evaluates each country. It proposes recommendations, and finally, the Council

---

[5] Commission Communication, COM (2021) 118 final of 9 March 2021 on 2030 Digital Compass: the European way for the Digital Decade.

[6] These targets are clustered in four domains (called 'cardinal points'): digital skills, secure and performing digital infrastructure, digital transformation of business, and digitalisation of public services.

[7] Decision (EU) 2022/2481 of 14 December 2022 establishing the Digital Decade Policy Programme 2030.

[8] 2030 DIGITAL DECADE. European Commission report on the state of the digital decade 2024. https://digital-strategy.ec.europa.eu/en/policies/2024-state-digital-decade-package

adopts country-specific recommendations with legal implications, which is not the case with the Digital Decade process.[9]

The Digital Decade strategy is complemented by digital principles, highlighting its underlying values. A Declaration by the European institutions stipulates several values, mainly to ensure human centricity in the digital age.[10] This approach reflects the zeitgeist that people need a guardian against unchecked digital transformation.

Money for the Digital Decade

What are the means to finance the ambitions of the Digital Decade? At the EU level, three programmes provide funding: Horizon Europe, Digital Europe, and the Connecting Europe Facility.

One of the core lessons from the past is that EU funding alone is subcritical, even with private co-investment, which is required to participate in the programmes. Therefore, the Commission is increasingly setting up mechanisms to mobilise additional funding from the member states. The Joint Undertaking (JU) concept is an example of this approach. Although the involvement of member states can lift project sizes to a higher level, they often pale against the efforts of global companies or other nations. This is why the programme's rhetoric and market reality often do not match, for example, in the case of AI.

FP9: Horizon Europe

Horizon Europe is equipped with 95 billion euros, even without the United Kingdom, an increase of about 22% compared to Horizon 2020.[11] It has thankfully maintained the three-pillar approach, albeit with modifications. The pillars are Excellent Science, Global Challenges and European Industrial Competitiveness, and Innovative Europe. When simplified, you get Science, Technology, and Innovation, miming the classical but misleading linear innovation model.

[9]In 2023, Germany was the only country to which a comprehensive digital-related recommendation was issued. While the lack of digitalisation is a topic in the country, this recommendation did not make any headlines, nor did it trigger a policy discussion.

[10]European Declaration on Digital Rights and Principles for the Digital Decade, signed by the Parliament, the Council, and the Commission on 15 December 2022.

[11]Regulation (EU) 2021/695 of 28 April 2021 establishing Horizon Europe—the Framework Programme for Research and Innovation, laying down its rules for participation and dissemination, and repealing Regulations (EU) No 1290/2013 and (EU) No 1291/2013.

Council Decision (EU) 2021/764 of 10 May 2021 establishing the Specific Programme implementing Horizon Europe—the Framework Programme for Research and Innovation, and repealing Decision 2013/743/EU.

Let's focus on the second pillar, which combines application and technologies. This pillar is divided into eight clusters,[12] with digital technologies bundled with industry and space into one common cluster. Digital technologies are no longer stand-alone, which was already the case with applications in Horizon 2020. Therefore, the amount earmarked for digital technologies is not straightforward to predict. However, the Commission estimates that about a third of the budget is related to digital because of its pervasive character.[13]

The digital cluster addresses many, if not all, familiar technologies, such as photonics, micro- and nanoelectronics, and high-performance computing. AI stands out in Horizon Europe as it receives a long overdue boost.

Innovation actions are now assembled in the third pillar and are no longer an add-on to other priorities. This goes back to a report from a high-level group mandated to make recommendations for FP9—Horizon Europe. The report says:

> Breakthrough innovation, the type that creates new markets, is rare in Europe. This is due to a range of factors, including a lack of venture capital, a deep-rooted aversion to risk and an inability to exploit the scale that an economy of half a billion people represents.[14]

In line with the group's recommendation, Horizon Europe has introduced a new entity called the European Innovation Council (EIC). The EIC manages various functions, including venture capital, organising business advisory services, and awarding grants. However, the EIC may not meet expectations. While its size and openness are commendable, they may strain its management capacity. Moreover, no innovation programme can guarantee innovation regardless of its scale. It needs to be stressed again: innovation is influenced more by institutions, economic incentives, and cultures than by financial support programmes.

The Digital Europe Programme

This programme responds to the recognition that research alone is insufficient to match industrial policy expectations.[15] The EU needs to invest in building the capacity of digital infrastructure. This is the aim of Digital Europe.

Endowed with 7.6 billion euros over seven years, it has been financing actions in AI, cybersecurity, high-performance computing, and digital skills. For example, it supports the establishment of a network of Digital Innovation Hubs, which are

[12] In Horizon 2020, these were called specific objectives.

[13] https://digital-strategy.ec.europa.eu/en/activities/funding-digital

[14] Investing in the European future we want. Report of the independent High-Level Group on maximising the impact of EU Research & Innovation Programmes. Published by the European Commission in 2007, p.12.

[15] Regulation (EU) 2021/694 of 29 April 2021 establishing the Digital Europe Programme and repealing Decision (EU) 2015/2240.

centres to help SMEs in their digital transformation. With the Chips Act, budget distribution changed to finance pilot installations for advanced chip production.

The Connecting Europe Facility

The Connecting Europe Facility (CEF Digital), significantly underfinanced during the previous MFF, was relaunched with a doubled budget of 2.1 billion euros.[16] CEF 2 Digital will support 5G roll-out (mainly along cross-border transport routes), backbone networks for European cloud federations, and the Quantum Communication Infrastructure initiative (EuroQCI).

The EuroQCI is interesting. This infrastructure can distribute encryption keys by exploiting a feature of quantum mechanics (entanglement). Recall that the Internet relies on public key cryptography to distribute encryption keys. In the future, nobody knows when, and even if ever, quantum computers could break its algorithm. So, a solution is needed, and quantum technology theoretically offers one. The quantum state of the encryption keys makes it impossible to intercept them without destroying them and revealing the presence of an eavesdropper. So far, quantum encryption only works in controlled experiments, so scaling this technique to serve billions of Internet users will be highly challenging.

The initiative combines financial means from all three programmes. It builds on the Horizon 2020 Open QKD project and the Quantum Technology FET Flagship. Digital Europe will finance applications, while the CEF will invest close to 200 million euros to connect national fibre networks and the links between the terrestrial and the space segments. The space agency ESA will be responsible for the satellite launch and operations.

China has already taken the lead. Jian-Wei Pan, a former student of the Nobel Prize laureate in physics, Anton Zeilinger, started a project in 2011.[17] In a talk at the University of Vienna on 25 January 2022, Zeilinger recalled that in the early 2000, he could not find support for a project involving launching a satellite in Europe. When his student called him ten years later to propose such a project, Zeilinger asked about the budget. The answer was 'one hundred million USD, but this is only a number'. On 29 September 2017, a satellite link established a secured video conference between Vienna and Beijing by deploying encryption keys encoded in entangled photons.

To be successful, EuroQCI must overcome some inherent problems, notably scaling, costs, and authentication. While you exchange the key securely, how do

[16]Regulation (EU) 2021/1153 of 7 July 2021 establishing the Connecting Europe Facility and repealing Regulations (EU) No 1316/2013 and (EU).

[17]Martin Giles, "The man turning China into a quantum superpower", *MIT Technology Review*, 19 December 2018: 'Jian-Wei Pan, China's "father of quantum", is masterminding its drive for global leadership in technologies that could change entire industries.'

you ensure that you do it with the right party? This is why we need more options. The concept of post-quantum cryptography is currently the most promising candidate.

Post-quantum cryptography (PQC) refers to cryptographic algorithms believed to be secure against attacks using quantum computers. These algorithms typically rely on mathematical problems considered difficult even for quantum computers to solve. Examples of such mathematical problems include lattice-based, code-based, multivariate polynomial, and hash-based cryptography.

ENISA has released a comprehensive report summarising and analysing methodologies, advancements, and obstacles in the field.[18] The report highlights efforts undertaken by member state organisations like the French ANSSI and the German BSI. ENISA underscores the substantial endeavours that lie ahead, acknowledging the absence of a guaranteed path to success in achieving robust and scalable algorithms. Transitioning from legacy PKI systems to a new paradigm poses formidable challenges. Therefore, the Commission emphasises the necessity for improved coordination among member states' initiatives.

NIST (The US National Institute of Standards and Technology) has been leading standardisation efforts. Its standardisation process involves multiple rounds of evaluation and selection to ensure that the chosen algorithms are secure and practical for real-world deployment. On 5 July, it announced four candidates for standardisation.[19] Besides NIST, there are efforts by ETSI and IETF, but they do not match the progress made by their American counterpart.

After this glance at the future, let's turn to the problems caused by malicious people and organisations.

Cybersecurity

> There's a gathering cyber storm. This storm is brewing, and it's really hard to anticipate just how bad that will be.
>
> Sadie Creese is a professor of cybersecurity at the University of Oxford—interview at the World Economic Forum's Annual Meeting 2023 in Davos, Switzerland.[20]

Recall the decentralised architecture of the Internet to understand the enormous tasks of cybersecurity. So far, engineers in the IETF, ICANN, RIPE, and others have successfully defended the Internet's central functionality, such as the domain name system. Most attacks aim at the networks, computers, and devices connected to the Internet; protecting them is the user's responsibility.

Hold on, what about the IT industry? What about sloppy software? To some extent, the market will force companies to develop devices and software with as few vulnerabilities as possible. At the beginning of the Internet age, companies did not

---

[18] ENISA. Post-Quantum Cryptography. Integration study. October 2022.

[19] https://csrc.nist.gov/News/2022/pqc-candidates-to-be-standardized-and-round-4#standardization

[20] https://www.cs.ox.ac.uk/news/2134-full.html

feel too much pressure and were more concerned about usability. Although this has changed and IT companies strive to appear security-minded, vulnerabilities still pop up and are being exploited. Shouldn't they be liable?

People sometimes confuse safety with security. Engineers can test safety measures, such as electronic braking systems or airbags, and gradually improve them over time so that malfunctions become rare. That is impossible with cybersecurity, which is about fending off malicious people, organisations, or state actors constantly inventing new attack vectors. Unlike safety engineering, cybersecurity is not linear. David Aucsmith, a cybersecurity consultant, writes: 'Nonlinearity adds friction to war in the cyber domain through three mechanisms: complexity, chaos, and speed [2].' It's a cat-and-mouse game with no ending.

Regulation can oblige a company to build state-of-the-art products, not be negligent, be transparent, and close security holes. Still, it cannot hold them accountable for falling victim to unknown attacks, state-sponsored espionage, or tricky social engineering. Thus, users are not off the hook even with in-built security devices.

An entire industry has emerged to help users protect their IT systems. What started with firewalls and antivirus hardware and software now encompasses a wide range of defences, such as intrusion detection, threat management, two-factor authentication, network access control, and virtual private networks. It also comprises security services, consultancy, and training. Cyber defence falls into three categories: products (technology), processes (organisation), and people (skills). Everyone protecting IT systems needs to keep these three dimensions in mind.

Since the creation of ENISA, European cybersecurity policy has developed dramatically. The days when member states felt Europe should stay out of security affairs are gone. The number of policy papers, initiatives, and legislative actions has steadily increased. It has become a maze: EU Cert, EU-CyCLONe, NIS coordination group, national CSIRT network, Cyber Shield, Joint Cyber Unit, and Cybersecurity Competence Centre are all entities and programmes serving different but overlapping purposes. Several funds compete for 'customers': Horizon Europe, Digital Europe, and European Defence Funds. Cyber-specific regulation intersperses with safety and security regulation in specific sectors such as finance and banking. Confused? Let's dissect this a bit.

Better Cybersecurity Processes

The Network and Information Security (NIS) Directive of 2016 was the first European law that imposed cybersecurity obligations on member states and actors in critical sectors. Its motivation was like the one that created ENISA, namely member states' inaction or inability to set up sufficient national cyber defence structures. Initially, the Digital Agenda of 2010 continued the traditional approach of calling upon member states to do more and committed the Commission to intensify coordination. However, we concluded that bolder action was needed when revising the Digital Agenda. It took over three years to adopt the NIS Directive, and it was the first European regulation of its kind.

NIS II, adopted in December 2022 [4], reinforces the original Directive. It focuses on risk management for critical infrastructure such as transport, health, finance, and digital infrastructure (cloud providers, network operators, Domain Name System). The Directive also obliges member states to adopt national cybersecurity strategies, appoint a single point of contact, and define operators of essential services in critical sectors. It institutionalises cooperation between member states through the NIS coordination group.

Security Standards

The Cybersecurity Act (CSA) [5] of 2019 sets out product criteria and requirements, as well as processes and services, to obtain a security certification, which is voluntary. Lawmakers have based these criteria on Common Criteria (CC), an internationally recognised set of guidelines for evaluating the security features of digital devices. The CSA enhanced Common Criteria standards by including patch management systems, vulnerability handling and disclosure, and tighter compliance monitoring. The CSA framework will absorb the work of SOGIS, which—as the reader may recall—was once the core of European security coordination.

However, it would be hard-pressed to consider CC a success. The database of certified products shows that it consists mostly of smart cards, network devices, and VPNs.[21] Many other products have limited functionality, or only a small part of their functionality is evaluated. You will find operating systems, but upon closer look, you will see that it concerns the VPN. For more complex products, the assurance level is low (EAL1, EAL2, EAL3) when EAL4 would be required. The enhancements of the CSA help, but they do not fix the problems of high costs, delays, and the small scope of evaluation, which are inevitably linked to certification processes.

The Regulation trusts ENISA to set up the operational framework, which national certification authorities will implement. In 2023, four years after its enactment, three schemes were being developed for ICT products, cloud services, and 5G networks. Finally, in January 2024, the one for ICT products was adopted, but it will take months or even years to become fully operational. This all takes too much time. National certification bodies must keep up with the complexity and speed at which, on the one hand, digital innovations emerge and on the other, cyberattacks evolve.[22]

[21] https://www.commoncriteriaportal.org/products/index.cfm

[22] While schemes are developed by ENISA, they are formally adopted by the Commission through an Implementing Act.

Commission Implementing Regulation (EU) 2024/482 of 31 January 2024 laying down rules for the application of Regulation (EU) 2019/881 of the European Parliament and of the Council as regards the adoption of the European Common Criteria-based cybersecurity certification scheme (EUCC).

Aiming at More Secure Devices

The Cyber Resilience Act (CRA),[23] for which a political agreement was achieved on 30 November 2023,[24] aims to establish a 'security by design, in manufacturing, and during operation' principle across all products with a digital component, be it software or hardware. The EU requests a security conformity mark (the CE logo) to place such products on the market. This is a far-reaching approach because many products contain digital elements, from microwaves to toothbrushes to elevators.

Products must have appropriate protection based on risk assessment, better understood in cybersecurity as 'threat analysis'. Products may not contain known vulnerabilities, must be delivered with a 'security by default' configuration, have adequate access protection, and must protect data with strong encryption.

During the lifetime of a product, vulnerabilities unavoidably show up. Security companies and researchers routinely challenge digital products to find weak points before malicious people discover and exploit them. The CRA requires that the vendor fixes those vulnerabilities without delay, is transparent, and informs national CSIRTs (computer security incident response teams). How to involve ENISA was a sticking point in the negotiations, leading to a complex compromise. ENISA will also get the information, but member states could restrict it. The manufacturer could also request to limit the dissemination of information about the vulnerability. This is indeed sensitive. If a vendor has no patch developed yet, which must be carefully tested, revealing a zero-day vulnerability even to authorities carries risks. You cannot exclude that an authority might have fallen victim to an espionage attack. Restricting the attack surface makes sense.

The CRA proposal distinguishes three classes of products: non-critical (encompassing about 90% of products, like smart toys, TVs, and refrigerators), critical (like network interfaces, firewalls, microcontrollers, browsers, VPNs), and highly critical (like industrial firewalls, CPUs, operating systems, card readers, IoT devices). The difference lies in the ways in which the CE mark is obtained, from self-assessment and presentation of a CSA standard to third-party quality assurance.

A CE mark may provide a false sense of security. The human element remains paramount in the realm of security. It begins with individual users and employees susceptible to social engineering tactics. It extends to system administrators who may find themselves overwhelmed by the complexities of heterogeneous networks lacking clearly defined perimeters. Furthermore, it involves the threat posed by malicious insiders, often considered the most severe risk, and culminates in the ingenuity of attackers.

Therefore, prioritising the development of cybersecurity skills and raising awareness of threats among the general public and the workforce should be imperative. This could be achieved through increased funding for awareness campaigns,

[23] Commission Proposal COM(2022) 454 of 15 September 2022 for a Regulation on horizontal cybersecurity requirements for products with digital elements and amending Regulation (EU) 2019/1020.

[24] For legalistic and technical reasons, the adoption of the final text will occur later in 2024.

dissemination of best practices, and enhancement of professional curricula. However, the key lies in scalability. It is insufficient to merely launch sporadic projects or initiatives; they must become integral components of educational and training structures.

Where Is It Going?

The ICT industry has recognised the shared responsibility of enhancing protection for the digital ecosystem. However, the extent to which they effectively coordinate efforts to address vulnerabilities in the supply chain remains a subject of debate. While cybersecurity regulations can compel or incentivise companies to employ 'state-of-the-art' methods, they alone cannot devise solutions. Regulations often need to catch up with technological advancements and market trends.

A pertinent illustration of this is the emerging concept of confidential computing. Traditional computer designs fail to inherently safeguard data and programs while in use, that is, when residing in memory.[25] Suppose attackers, including a malicious insider, breach the network and computer perimeter protections and gain access to the core of the operating system. In that case, they can manipulate, access, or corrupt ongoing operations and data. Given the increasingly widespread use of computing across various environments such as on-premises, public cloud, and the edge, addressing this vulnerability has become crucial.

Confidential computing entails executing computations within a hardware-based and attested Trusted Execution Environment (TEE). But what can you trust? For instance, how can you be sure that your application operates within a trusted environment on the public cloud? Assurance is derived from an attestation process that ultimately hinges on cryptographic keys supplied by the chip vendor. This is the foundation of trust.

This evolving concept promises to enhance the protection of cryptographic keys, edge computing data, and business applications hosted on public cloud platforms. It facilitates secure data sharing and analysis for machine learning applications while preserving privacy. Notably, it holds the potential to support the implementation of the European Digital Identity Wallet, as outlined in Chap. 6. It could also alter the implementation of the GDPR's data transfer provision. When personal data are constantly encrypted, in transit, in storage, and in use, wherever they are, their location does not matter, provided you can trust the encryption keys.

Despite its significant potential, the EU's policy interest remains limited. Currently, only a handful of European companies and the Fraunhofer Institute are

[25] It is quite common to encrypt data in a database (at rest) and when sent over a network (in transit). Previous efforts to protect data in use have not been comprehensive. For instance, a Trusted Platform Module can store encryption keys in hardware (useful but insufficient), or homomorphic computing can execute a programme on encrypted data (the challenge lies in overcoming extreme performance loss).

actively engaged in the Consortium dedicated to confidential computing.[26] The relevant Horizon Europe work programme for 2023/24 encompasses a wide range of topics but lacks a specific focus on this technology.[27]

Another priority should be AI, which is set to play a pivotal role in shaping the future of cybersecurity. On the positive side, AI will aid in secure code development, network monitoring, automating incident response, and improving spam detection. AI user behaviour analysis can detect deviations from typical patterns, which can help identify insider threats. Moreover, it has the potential to predict and pre-empt cyberattacks.

The bad news, however, is that these advances can also be leveraged by malicious actors, including hackers, spies, and criminals. They can utilise AI to identify vulnerabilities, pinpoint weaknesses in network defences, and craft convincing spam messages. AI can empower them to develop novel, sophisticated attacks.[28] AI systems will be assaulted to alter their behaviour with evil intent by using various techniques, such as prompt injections, jailbreaks, or data poisoning.

Here again, we will face an arms race. AI can be an invaluable assistant, aiding security personnel in identifying, responding to, and analysing attacks. Furthermore, AI assistants can handle reporting tasks, saving administrators valuable time and generating datasets to train the AI systems involved. The future of cybersecurity resilience lies in this symbiotic relationship between human expertise and AI-driven solutions.[29]

Encryption Debate Reloaded

The encryption debate we encountered in the 1990s has not gone away. Encryption has remained a headache for law enforcement, even more so as smartphones, laptops, and messaging apps offer sophisticated out-of-the-box encryption. This protects citizens' privacy and business secrets but also criminals' communication.

The most recent push to gain access to encrypted communication and even to encrypted devices is linked to child abuse. On 9 September 2022, in London, G7

[26] The Confidential Computing Consortium (CCC), which includes hardware vendors, cloud providers, and software companies, collaborates to advance architecture and ensure interoperability. https://confidentialcomputing.io/

[27] European Commission Decision C(2023)2178 of 31 March 2023. Horizon Europe. Work Programme 2023–2024. 6. Civil Security for Society.

[28] A Forrester Study commissioned by Darktrace, The Emergence of Offensive AI. How companies are protecting themselves against malicious applications of AI, February 2020: 'Close to 80% of cybersecurity decision-makers anticipate offensive AI to increase the scale and speed of attacks.'

[29] ENISA proposed five areas for intensive research. Testbeds, penetration tools, training models for practitioners, preservation of privacy and confidentiality of information, and an observatory for AI-enabled threats. "Artificial Intelligence and Cybersecurity Research", ENISA Research and Innovation Brief, June 2023.

home affairs ministers committed to taking robust measures to fight this crime. The United States, the United Kingdom, and the EU are envisaging regulations to impose monitoring obligations on tech companies. While the proposed EU Regulation (CSAM)[30,31] does not mandate a specific detection technology, complying with its requirements would force providers of interpersonal communications to modify or terminate their end-to-end encryption services. The practical implementation of such measures is full of pitfalls.

In one potential scenario, the service provider would use a master key to encrypt session keys. If needed, authorised persons could unlock a device or read messages by using the master key. As discussed in Chap. 3, key escrow weakens security, which is particularly questionable in the current hostile geopolitical environment. Coding and operating key escrowed hardware and software are a nightmare. In this scenario, we do not have an optimal solution to reconcile public safety with privacy. However, a *de facto* provision to weaken end-to-end encryption should be avoided.[32]

The Global Semiconductor Race

> European-based integrated circuit manufacturers supply 30% of their own home market and represent 13% of world production, half of which is manufactured in the USA by subsidiaries of European companies.
>
> Commission Communication COM (83) 258 final of 2 June 1983 on Esprit: First European Strategic Programme for Research and Development in Information Technologies.

Europe has always considered semiconductors a strategic technology, and policies to bolster their industries go back to the 1980s and even earlier. Chapter 1 covered the semiconductor trade war between Japan and the United States and the failed attempts of the ESPRIT and EUREKA programmes to keep advanced memory and microprocessor chip production in Europe. Support for micro- and nanoelectronics continued with each research framework programme. In 2014, the last EUREKA project, Catrena, ended, and activities at the European level were concentrated in the ECSEL JU.

Despite these efforts, Europe's competitive position has remained mediocre. Until recently, Europe had no facility to produce cutting-edge nanometre chips. In September 2023, US-based Intel began manufacturing its most advanced chips in

[30] At the time of drafting, the legislative discussion had not been concluded.

[31] Proposal for a Regulation COM (2022) 209 final of 11 May 2022 laying down rules to prevent and combat child sexual abuse.

[32] The *de facto* qualification is important here as Article 26 in the Regulation stipulates that providers must 'ensure that the technologies employed by them cannot be used by them or their employees for purposes other than compliance with this Regulation, nor by third parties, and thus to avoid undermining the security and confidentiality of the communications of users'. The snag is that this is not possible without weakening encryption for everybody.

7 nm technology in Ireland. Moreover, European companies rely heavily on imports of materials, access to foreign technology, and production capacities abroad, particularly in Asia. However, this is true for all countries and regions, as the semiconductor industry is one of the most internationally integrated sectors in the world.[33]

Because of this deep integration, the Covid pandemic and geopolitical tensions have had a particularly disruptive effect and created anxieties about dependency and supply chain interruptions, not only in Europe but across the globe. As a result, the industrial superpowers, particularly the United States, China, Korea, and Japan, have launched national chip strategies, and so has the EU.

The Chips Act

The Chips Act[34] aspires to double the EU's global market share in semiconductors, covering the entire value chain, from 10% to at least 20% by 2030.[35] Realistically, this can only be achieved with foreign investments, such as the one in Ireland. Thus, European market share refers to European production, not EU-headquartered companies.

The EU is entering a global race to attract investment in the chips value chain, a race which is not economically healthy and distorts the functioning of an otherwise thriving global industry. Unfortunately, the political reality is such that the EU must play this game to avoid being sidelined.

The Act comes with a headline figure of a 43 billion euros investment envelope up to 2030. Do not assume the EU would mobilise that amount from its MFF budget. It is a political number that brings the EU Chips Act not only in name but also in size within reach of the US Chips Act.[36] In fact, up to the end of the current MFF in 2027, only 3.3 billion euros have been earmarked or reallocated to support the Chips Act. This is less than what the EUREKA project JESSI once mobilised. Most of it will be spent through the new Chips Joint Undertaking.[37] The 43 billion euros figure mainly

[33] A Staff Working Paper accompanying the Chips Act gives a comprehensive and good-to-read overview of the technology and the industry. Commission Staff Working Document SWD(2022) 147 final of 11 May 2022: A Chips Act for Europe.

[34] Regulation (EU) 2023/1781 of 13 September 2023 establishing a framework of measures for strengthening Europe's semiconductor ecosystem and amending Regulation (EU) 2021/694 (Chips Act).

[35] The Digital Decade target refers to 'cutting-edge', but the Communication outlining the measurement methodology does not specify this term. Commission Communication COM (2023) 7500 final of 27 September 2023 establishing Union-level projected trajectories for the digital targets.

[36] The US government will spend $50 billion over 5 years, $11 billion on advanced semiconductor R&D and $39 billion to support domestic chip production, of which $6 billion will cover direct loans and loan guarantees. https://www.nist.gov/chips

[37] This is the former Key Digital Technologies JU, relabelled and refocused. Its initial budget of €1.8 billion was increased to €4.175 billion. The JU will also support non-semiconductor research and innovation activities with 1.3 billion.

represents expected private investments and member state subsidies for significant investments by multinational chip companies.

The Chips JU will focus on areas where the EU is still leading or at least competitive, such as chips for automobiles, manufacturing, telecom networks, and chip production technologies, in which the Dutch-headquartered ASML is a world leader for lithography. Unlike in the past, the emphasis will be on pilot lines and testing facilities. In addition, the initiative will support competence centres, providing access to technical expertise and experimentation, helping companies, particularly SMEs, improve design capabilities and develop skills.

Launching an industrial strategy based on a legal act is a novelty. Besides the convenience of reorienting existing support programmes in one go, it provides a framework for building investment consortia and policy coordination. One key objective is to enhance the resilience of the EU against future supply chain disruptions. The Regulation establishes a monitoring and crisis response mechanism that should help identify possible supply bottlenecks and enable the EU to take necessary actions to address them, such as pooling procurement. An advisory body, the European Semiconductor Board, will play a role in managing supply chain issues.

The Act provides the political backing to allow member states to grant significant subsidies to build advanced semiconductor facilities. We should not forget that the Treaty obliges the Commission to assess all subsidies and only permit them when justified. The Chips Act defines criteria the Commission will use for this purpose, and here, the crucial concept is that the investment must concern a 'first of its kind' facility to allow member states to hand out exceptional amounts.[38]

The initiative differs from previous strategies as it attempts to mobilise sufficient resources beyond research and adds a resilience dimension. However, the global wave of subsidies could lead to over-capacities and revisions of investment plans. Instead, the EU could intensify its efforts to find silicon alternatives. Unfortunately, graphene, photonic, and neuromorphic chips have not yet matured enough to become the foundation of a new computing paradigm. Similarly, quantum computing still needs to overcome fundamental difficulties due to the laws of physics and will complement classical computers, not replace them. While US companies are leading, Europe has potential in terms of research and start-ups. The story of the British company ARM is an instructive example of how Europe can compete against dominant companies and establish an alternative technology platform.

The Story of ARM

Look at your smartphone. A chip designed by ARM almost certainly powers it. ARM-designed chips power over 95% of smartphones worldwide and are inside many other devices such as laptops, navigation systems, modems, car electronics,

[38] Articles 13 and 14 of the Chips Act.

and data centres. Recently, the company went public on the US Nasdaq, with a big success. ARM is a beacon of the European semiconductor industry—forget Brexit. Its history teaches some lessons.

In the 1980s, the BBC developed a computer literacy programme and, in collaboration with the Education Department, aimed to bring computers to schools. In those days, electronic shops were filled with different home computer brands. IBM introduced the PC only in 1981.[39] The BBC, excluding foreign companies, organised a competition, which the computer company Acorn won.[40]

Acorn Computer Ltd. was founded in 1979 by Hermann Hauser,[41] an Austrian physicist linked to Cambridge, and Christopher Curry, a British engineer. The BBC Micro, introduced in December 1981, sold well—1.5 million units—and provided Acorn with the financial means to expand. Their engineering team, led by Sophie Wilson and Steve Furber, soon realised that they needed a more powerful processor and eventually decided to design one themselves. They were inspired by the RISC (Reduced Instruction Set Computer) architecture, particularly by the Berkeley RISC project, which allowed for a more straightforward processor design. The first Acorn RISC Machine (ARM1) processor, manufactured by VLSI Technologies in the United States, became operational in 1985 and exceeded performance and power efficiency expectations.[42]

After running into financial difficulties, Acorn was taken over by Olivetti, one of the Big Twelve involved in the ESPRIT programme. Eventually, in 1990, the processor unit of Acorn was spun out as a joint venture of Apple, VLSI, and Acorn and named Advanced RISC Machines—the story of the Acorn and ARM split.

Apple incorporated the ARM chip in its personal digital assistant device, the Newton, which, ahead of its time, was not a success. I remember Roland Hüber, the RACE programme director, demonstrating its handwriting capabilities to me. We had no idea that its commercial failure would be a turning point for mobile communication as ARM management changed its business model. Instead of selling the processor, it would sell licences to use its technology. Because of their low power consumption, ARM-designed processors were ideally suited for mobile devices. Eventually, they found their way into the booming GSM business. The Nokia 6110, a hugely popular phone launched in 1994, was the first ARM-powered GSM device. The rest is history. Comparatively, with 2.7 billion euros in annual sales (2022) and a market capitalisation of above $50 billion, ARM is not a huge company, but its technology has been a revolution.

---

[39] Atari, Sinclair, Commodore, Amstrad, and Apple were popular brands then.

[40] The BBC produced a movie, Micro Men, telling the story of how the team at Acorn won the competition. It is available on YouTube.

[41] Hermann Hauser was one of the authors of the vision paper preparing for Horizon Europe.

[42] The processor was produced in 3 μm or 3000 nm. Today's state of the art is around 3 nm, 1000 times smaller.

The story of ARM demonstrates what increases the likelihood of innovations: a climate for striving entrepreneurs, talented technical people, and risk capital. Often, the success of innovators can be traced back to a specific customer. Intel, for example, designed the first microprocessor, the 4040, for a Japanese customer.[43] In the case of Acorn, it was the BBC, and for ARM, there were Apple and, eventually, Nokia. Who would have thought that a public computer literacy programme would lead to one of Europe's most prominent digital successes?

Taming Big Tech

After a lengthy investigation, the Commission fined Microsoft in 2004 for its abusive behaviour in the server and media player markets. Microsoft was fined again for non-compliance, and the case concluded in 2007. The origins of the complaints about licensing and interoperability go back to the early 1990s.

At the same time, a rising Google committed to a 'don't be evil' slogan, portraying themselves as the 'good guys'. Google grew further, became powerful, and ended up, well, in antitrust cases both in the United States and Europe. Bundling its Android OS with its own apps and untransparent search results looked like the Microsoft cases.

These are two examples of numerous other antitrust cases in the digital realm that the Commission conducted over the last two decades. As important as they are, each case took a lot of time, including the time for the European Court of Justice to decide on the appeals the companies routinely filed. *Ex post* competition measures come into effect when the damage is done. The Commission, therefore, decided to establish an *ex ante* competition regime for digital platforms and proposed the Digital Market Act (DMA), which was adopted in September 2022.[44]

Regulators grapple with the characteristics of the digital industry. Network effects, free services to lure customers, bundling, untransparent algorithms, and two-sided markets belong to these head-scratching issues. The dominant ecosystems become hard to penetrate. Thus, the DMA undertakes to foster contestable and fair markets.[45]

The DMA introduces the notions of 'core digital services' such as operating systems, online platforms, browsers, and search engines, and 'gatekeepers', companies that are so big and dominant they can prevent effective competition and scare off potential entrants—not unlike the telecom framework, which designates operators with significant market power in pre-defined markets. On 6 September 2023, the

[43] https://www.jstor.org/stable/20013439

[44] Regulation (EU) 2022/1925 of 14 September 2022 on contestable and fair markets in the digital sector and amending Directives (EU) 2019/1937 and (EU) 2020/1828 (Digital Markets Act).

[45] For a detailed analysis of the DMA see, for example, A. De Streel (ed.) "Implementing the DMA: Substantive and Procedural Principles", Centre on Regulation in Europe (CERRE), January 2024.

Commission designated six gatekeepers (Alphabet, Amazon, Apple, ByteDance, Meta, Microsoft) with, in total, 22 core platform services.

Gatekeepers must demonstrate that they respect rules depending on their core service: no cross-use or combining of personal data, restrictions on targeted advertisements, prohibition of self-preferencing, data portability, interoperability with third-party software, interoperability of messaging and video communication services, and no price-setting restrictions for business customers of an online platform. By 7 March 2024, the gatekeepers must have notified and implemented changes to their services.[46] How much these changes will effectively impact business practices and user experiences remains to be seen.

The DMA details complex implementation processes, the power of which lies mainly with the Commission. The gatekeeper must demonstrate compliance through regular reporting. The Regulation wisely offers the possibility for adjustment, dialogue, and interpretation. It touches upon technical details and requires understanding the algorithms, criteria, index mechanisms, and more. This is complex stuff. The Bruegel Institute in Brussels demonstrated this regarding 'self-preferencing' [3]. Therefore, the implementation will require substantial resources and will take time for the machine to run smoothly.

The DMA is a landmark piece of regulation. It will resonate worldwide and serve as a model for platform laws in other countries or at least guide antitrust cases. However, the DMA will most likely not fundamentally change the competitive position of European players. The DMA will bring more fairness to the market, but network effects will keep Big Tech in charge. In 5 years' time, the reader might compare my prediction with the evolution of the tech markets.

History has shown that dominant market positions will eventually be challenged through disruptive innovation. Microsoft's Internet Explorer was once the market leader; today, it is Google's Chrome. Google was stunned by Facebook's success. And Facebook/Meta was puzzled by TikTok. Spotify—yes, finally a European player—set up a convincing music (streaming) model to rival Apple's iTunes. Twitter/X was challenged by Telegram. Therefore, Europe's chance would be a home-grown disruptive innovation.

Content Moderation versus Free Speech

Many European politicians expressed dismay when Donald Trump was barred from Facebook and Twitter.[47] It was not that they felt any sympathy for the former President, but they believed that these platforms should not have the authority to silence him. That is an interesting bias. Why is it okay when a badly behaving Mr. Jones is banned but doubtful when it is someone with power?

[46] https://www.theverge.com/2024/3/6/24091592/eu-dma-competition-compliance-deadline-big-tech-policy-changes

[47] In 2024, X (former Twitter) and Meta (Facebook, Instagram) have reversed their decisions.

Social media allow ordinary people to reach a large audience and not only talk to each other. Their media consumption is no longer constrained by what professional journalists report or think. They can listen to other people's views and express their own. At the outset of this development, we were excited by the ability of the Internet to give people a voice. Soon, another reality emerged: shitstorms, hate speech, fake news, and defamation. Has Al Gore's vision of 'information at your fingertips' become 'disinformation at your fingertips'?

Harmful content also exists in traditional media. Opinion bubbles did not suddenly pop up with social media. What has changed is that we are aware of them. Platforms like Twitter/X allow us to watch what people and groups think, believe, and discuss in real time. What has also changed is the ease with which these opinion bubbles form, driving polarisation, which—often overlooked—is intermingled with traditional media. For Jonathan Haidt, the origin of the problem lies in the fact that radical groups on the left and right, trolls, and hostile countries '... were suddenly given the power to dominate conversations and intimidate dissenters into silence'.[48] This leads to the paradox that social media free speech suppresses free speech. All of this creates a different form of public discourse from the past, leading us to the Digital Services Act (DSA).

For more than two decades, the eCommerce Directive provided the legal framework for online businesses. Since 19 October 2023, the Digital Service Act has become its companion.[49] The DSA transferred the liability provisions of the eCommerce Directive to its legal corpus and introduced rules for search engines, social media networks, and online marketplaces, making them accountable for moderating content.[50]

The regulatory approach is straightforward with illegal content; it may not be distributed. However, what is unlawful in one country may be legal in another. A service provider must respect the law of the country of destination of its service. The country-of-origin principle does not apply here. In this context, the DSA somewhat harmonised the notice and takedown process. For example, the DSA obliges big platforms to be proactive on illegal content, a concept we previously encountered with copyright infringements.

The situation becomes more complex when the Regulation addresses harmful content. This is a vague concept; how you define it often depends on your worldview. For example, what is disinformation for some may be a legitimate opinion for

[48] Jonathan Haidt, "Yes, social media really is undermining democracy. Despite what Meta has to say", *The Atlantic*, 28 July 2022. You might not share all the views of the author, but the way he discusses them and the numerous references in this article are instructive.

[49] Regulation (EU) 2022/2065 of 19 October 2022 on a Single Market For Digital Services and amending Directive 2000/31/EC (Digital Services Act).

[50] Beyond content moderation and crisis management, the DSA contains several other provisions for online search engines and eCommerce providers. These provisions are to ensure clarity about advertising, measures against abusive notices by users against other users, and information obligations.

others, which can lead to an emotionally loaded skirmish.[51] Some opinions may be unacceptable for a majority or controversial, but should they be taken down or debated in public discourse?[52] This points to a trade-off that stems from our democratic constitutions: content moderation versus freedom of speech or expression.

Technically, content moderation means providers block or delete posts or videos uploaded on their platforms and even stop allowing certain people to use their service. Isn't this censorship *per se*? Not quite. Social media are private entities and, within the boundaries of the law, are free to define their terms and conditions. The problem starts when network effects create a dominant platform, which becomes an influential media outlet. Being present on such a platform can be essential for the profession and career of politicians, influencers, and journalists. However, even as a celebrity, you do not have the prerogative to be accepted by every platform. Freedom of speech means being protected against the State and not ending up in prison for criticising your government. While there is no right to be heard, people have a right to fairness and non-discrimination. The DSA tackles this problem with transparency provisions. The terms and conditions must be clear and applied in a non-discriminatory manner. Users must be given the means to contest decisions taken by the platform.

The gravity of harmful content for society depends on the size of the platform audience. This is why the DSA provides stronger rules for very large platforms.[53] The risk for society also depends on the context. It matters when and in which situation dubious content is published. The DSA identifies these contexts as risks to fundamental rights, democratic processes, civic discourse, electoral processes, public security, and public health. Very large platforms must set up a risk management system, report on their actions, and become subject to audits.

In addition, the DSA introduces a crisis response mechanism and a voluntary crisis protocol. The first one was subject to intense negotiations during the EU legislative process because it entails obligations that civil societies felt could tip the balance too far in the direction of censorship. Here is the gist of it.

Based on a recommendation of a board composed of member state representatives, the Commission can declare a crisis (only) for public security and public health reasons.[54] It can oblige platforms to assess the role of their services in this crisis, take appropriate measures, and report on their actions. The Regulation does not explicitly say what follows this process. Platforms are supposed to know how to react best, while the Commission will monitor and assess their actions. In practice, the

[51] On 22 January 2017, NBC host Chuck Todd asked Trump's senior adviser, Kellyanne Conway, about why the White House claimed that Trump's inauguration was visited by the largest audience ever. She said: 'You're saying it's a falsehood. And they're giving – Sean Spicer, our press secretary—gave alternative facts.' Todd responded: 'Alternative facts aren't facts, they are falsehoods.'

[52] Someone like Elon Musk defends a libertarian approach to free speech.

[53] Very large online platforms are defined as having more than 45 million users.

[54] The crisis duration is limited to three plus three months.

Commission and a provider must somehow agree on the appropriate measures. Yet, there is no guarantee that the process will work smoothly.

The DSA is an example of managing the pitfalls of content moderation in a democracy and market economy. The regulator will not tell providers which content to block or delete but imposes a due diligence process on them. The DSA process has many dimensions and will put particularly large providers within a highly complex compliance system. Time will tell whether it makes the online world safer without unduly interfering with the freedom of business and people.[55]

Thoughts

Not every initiative of the last three years, such as the Data Act and the Data Governance Act, could have been included in this chapter. The number of legal initiatives has reached an impressive level, and each legal measure has become more complex than its predecessor. This is an increasing burden for companies, particularly for smaller ones.

Taking a comprehensive view, one can discern that these pieces of legislation each have their own unique rationale. This inclination to develop policies independently based on specific considerations has persisted over the long term. It is challenging to perceive them as cohesive elements of a unified approach. The reason for this can be attributed to an imprecise narrative shaping the formulation of these strategies.

The various support programmes have struggled to create critical mass and tend to address too many issues. They are repeatedly over-optimistic about what could be achieved by financing thousands of projects. It is illusionary to expect innovation programmes to generate breakthrough innovation, especially not at a discernible scale. Improvements have been introduced, notably through Joint Undertakings, FET Flagships, and enhanced capacity-building projects. Another promising approach is exemplified by the European Research Council, which rigorously supports excellence in science based on the credentials of the scientist.

Inspiration can be derived from DARPA, the renowned US Defence Advanced Research Projects Agency, which played a pivotal role in developing the Internet by funding early research in computer networking. The DARPA approach is mission-focused and offers greater flexibility in funding mechanisms compared to European programmes. Projects under DARPA typically operate on fast-paced timelines, aiming to deliver results within a relatively short period. Most notably, DARPA empowers its programme managers with implementation authority, which is a

---

[55] 'The DSA is largely a procedural tool that creates a lot of new evidence about what is going on in the digital ecosystem.' Martin Husovec, "The Digital Service Act's Red Line: What the Commission Can and Cannot Do About Disinformation", 10 January 2024. https://papers.ssrn.com/sol3/papers.cfm?abstract_id=4689926

significant departure from our framework programmes: "DARPA goes to great lengths to identify, recruit and support excellent program managers – extraordinary individuals who are at the top of their fields and are hungry for the opportunity to push the limits of their disciplines".[56]

Making management, particularly the selection of projects, leaner and smarter through artificial intelligence could become a promising avenue and help European companies deliver solutions. Whatever the shape of FP10, the basic idea should be to focus on scale, excellence, and smarter management.

References

1. Anu Bradford, "The Brussels Effect: How the European Union Rules the World", *Oxford University Press,* USA, 2021.
2. David Aucsmith, *A Theory of War in the Cyber Domain, An Historical Perspective*, Tera Nova Books, Seattle (WA), 2023, p. 26.
3. Christophe Carugati, "How to implement the self-preferencing ban in the European Union's Digital Markets Act", Bruegel Policy Brief, 2 December 2022.
4. Directive (EU) 2022/2555 of 14 December 2022 on measures for ahigh common level of cybersecurity across the Union, amending Regulation (EU) No 910/2014 and Directive (EU) 2018/1972,and repealing Directive (EU) 2016/1148 (NIS 2 Directive).
5. Regulation (EU) 2019/881 of 17 April 2019 on ENISA (the European UnionAgency for Cybersecurity) and on information and communications technology cybersecurity certification and repealing Regulation (EU) No 526/2013 (Cybersecurity Act).

[56] https://www.darpa.mil/about-us/about-darpa

Chapter 10
Gigabit Connectivity

> Take telecoms and look at the numbers. The average number of clients of Chinese operators [is] 420 million, [that of] an American operator 110 million. And the European operators? Five million.
>
> Enrico Letta interviewed about his forthcoming report on the future of the single market in today's new strategic reality, by Martin Sandbu of the *Financial Times*, 8 February 2024.

The Commission White Paper on 'How to master Europe's digital infrastructure needs?' begins with a statement heard many times: 'A cutting-edge digital network infrastructure is the foundation for a flourishing digital economy and society.'[1] While this is true, I want to ask the ultimately heretical question—don't we have it already?

In EU countries, at the beginning of 2024, approximately 80% of the population is covered by Very High Capacity Networks (VHCN),[2] with almost two-thirds comprising fibre to the home. Coverage of 4G is widespread, and 5G reaches close to 90% of the population.[3] Europe may lag behind its global partners and competitors in some aspects of connectivity, but not in all. For instance, the EU boasts higher fibre penetration rates than the United States. Moreover, the disparities observed are not as pronounced as those in cloud computing, social media, or semiconductors. The most significant gaps will diminish over time, given the current investment trend. While the EU may fall short of its 2030 connectivity targets, predictions indicate a trajectory towards seriously impressive infrastructure.

---

[1] Commission White Paper COM (2024) 81 of 21 February 2024 on How to master Europe's digital infrastructure needs?

[2] Fibre to the premises (FTTP) and cable DOCSIS 3.1.

[3] "FTTP availability, . . . , continued to grow at an increasing rate compared to previous years, . . . , to pass nearly two thirds (64.0%) of EU homes at the end of June 2023. FTTP was the fastest growing broadband technology." OMDIA, Point Topic, Broadband Coverage in Europe 2023. Mapping progress towards the coverage objectives of the Digital Decade. A study carried out for the European Commission. Published in 2024.

D. Eckert, *40 Years of European Digital Policies*, Professional Practice in Governance and Public Organizations,
https://doi.org/10.1007/978-3-031-61641-9_10

The key point is that many scenarios involving advanced digital services and applications, such as remote healthcare, traffic management, or drone controls, are already feasible today. Certainly, having greater capacity facilitates the development of such solutions. While it is possible to envisage challenging edge cases that are difficult to implement under current circumstances, many of these remain hypothetical and require validation of their business viability. For instance, the challenge with health telematics applications, even those with compelling business cases, lies not with the network but with data protection issues, organisational inertia, and legacy systems.

The primary challenge lies not in connectivity but in enhancing the competitive position of the European telecom industry within the global digital economy. Georg Serentschy, former BEREC chair, and his co-authors write: '. . .it seems that digital policy activism may be based on too much reliance on the broad impact of regulation and too little focus on business models, innovation policy, and investment' [1]. Fundamentally, policymakers must address two key questions. First, how can Europe harness its telecommunication ecosystem to assume a more significant role in the global digital economy? Second, what direction should the telecom regulatory framework take? Is there a need to recalibrate the regulatory model, which has evolved since 2002?

The Ambitions of the European Telecom Operators

Let's delve into the first question. Throughout this book, there have been references to the dissatisfaction within the telecom industry regarding the disparity between high investment and low returns on their side, compared to the low investment and high returns observed by over-the-top players, now known as 'content and application providers' (CAPs). This discrepancy results from the Internet architecture functioning as a computer rather than a telecom network. Chapter 2 alluded to a 1994 study on the Internet as a 'hostile overlay', which foreshadowed the complex issues that currently concern the European telecom industry.

The telecom networks must handle massive video streaming, primarily from US big CAPs. According to an ETNO report, they consume about 70% of the operator's bandwidth. CAPs manage much of the traffic themselves, owning submarine cables and content delivery networks, but their investment is significantly smaller than what operators must invest. CAPs focus on data centres and cloud computing, which will increasingly influence network management.

ETNO writes:[4]

> This entails a shift from dependence on proprietary hardware to virtualised, open hardware within a cloud-native network. It also requires a rethink in relation to partnerships, with

[4]ETNO. State of Digital Communications 2024. Report prepared by Analyses Mason. January 2024, p. 59.

operators looking to multi-vendor partnerships to help them identify and respond to new customer needs.[5]

The Commission worries about this trend:[6]

As hybrid networks, edge computing, and full cloud migration change the architecture of connectivity infrastructure, the historical strength of Europe in the network equipment and service industry is at risk.[7]

This trend is inevitable. Telecom operators have indicated the need to become more efficient and agile. They appear determined to involve more partners in managing their physical assets, for example, by embracing Open RAN. Ironically, the competitive position of the two European champions, Nokia and Ericsson, might face serious challenges from American, Japanese, and Korean companies rather than, as feared, Chinese vendors. Operators will offer connectivity as a platform service and continue efforts to compete directly with CAPs. Thus, the relationship with CAPs will involve cooperation and competition, with the former being more straightforward and the latter, given experience, more challenging.

European telcos are disadvantaged compared to their international peers, particularly regarding earnings and investment capacity. This is crucial when competing with Internet content and application providers while also hampering investments in VHCN.

For a long time, telecom companies have attempted to monetise their assets, both connectivity-based and beyond. While net neutrality rules have not prohibited 'managed services', they have not facilitated them either. Data protection rules have made monetising customer data hard. The yet-to-be-adopted or shelved ePrivacy Regulation proposed in 2017 would have further complicated the use of 'metadata'. Operators' market share in the video streaming market remains small.

The focus is shifting to non-connectivity-based business services (mainly provided through the cloud), such as software-as-a-service, IoT management, or cybersecurity services. The overall share of operators in these markets is approximately 13%, largely determined by the cloud dominance of US actors (see the section in Chap. 5 on losing the competitive edge).

The Commission is eager to facilitate this transition, particularly through the mobilisation of its various programmes, such as Horizon Europe. One idea that appears to have garnered the Commission's interest is the notion of a European

[5]Virtualisation allows telecom operators to run multiple network functions on shared hardware, reducing the need for dedicated hardware for each service. Operators can dynamically allocate resources on demand, which typically happens through a cloud service, and can easily add or remove capacity as needed. This agility enables them to respond quickly to changing demand and, most interestingly, allows them to offer network-as-a-service.

[6]White Paper (2024), p. 20.

[7]Edge computing brings computation and data storage closer to the location where time-sensitive operations take place. It is suited for real-time applications that require quick processing, such as traffic management, control of robots and drones or augmented reality. It also provides geofencing options to keep sensitive data under local control.

Telco-Cloud. Already in 2021, several European cloud providers and telecom companies articulated a vision to shape the next generation of cloud infrastructure for Europe. This initiative promises much if only its outcomes could match the grandeur of its title.

This concept echoes the Internet of the Future initiative from a decade ago, which is discussed in Chap. 6. At that time, the focus was on integrating smart networks with the Internet, potentially leading to the development of new protocols. Then, as of now, the initiative was propelled by the telecom industry, though it was met with limited success. Another pertinent initiative is GAIA-X, which does not concentrate on edge clouds. According to the White Paper, a more comprehensive scheme is expected to be unveiled in 2024. It is to be hoped that the stakeholders will carefully consider the lessons from previous endeavours.

Here is a suggestion. While EU support programmes are beneficial, they often do not allocate a sufficient budget to effect significant change. Consider public procurement, as recommended in relation to AI. To genuinely propel European edge cloud computing forward, member states must unite behind a joint procurement initiative. This initiative should transcend traditional concepts of pre-commercial procurement and achieve a grander scale. We need a moment of inspiration akin to the Mitterrand/EUREKA initiative, aiming beyond the EU's conventional means. Drawing inspiration from the US Inflation Reduction Act, and as proposed by ECTA,[8] we could introduce a Buy European Act. A crucial factor will be implementation. Europe has a penchant for procedures and rules. It's time we place our trust in people. Identifying individuals with the necessary competence, integrity, and creativity to oversee such initiatives—and allowing them the freedom to operate—could be transformative.

Financial support is essential, yet refining the regulatory framework, starting with a thorough review of existing regulations, could have an even greater impact. This leads us to the second question.

Is It Time for a Regulatory Revolution?

The ongoing debate about the future of telecom regulation continues, pitting former incumbents against competitors regarding the optimal strategy to encourage investments and consumer benefits. This dichotomy has pulled telecom regulation in two divergent directions, leaving neither party satisfied. Incumbents bemoan internationally uncompetitive low revenues and investment challenges, while competitors appreciate the lower costs for European citizens and argue that competition spurs investment.

[8] ECTA MANIFESTO. "A Vision for an Innovative, Competitive, Inclusive, and Greener Europe", 5 March 2024.

Looking back to 1998, the liberalisation of infrastructure represented the final piece of the puzzle. Our guiding principle was the freedom to invest, viewing regulation of access to the legacy network as a temporary measure, eventually to be superseded by antitrust policies. However, it became evident that pre-emptive regulation based on competition law would ensure a smoother transition to a landscape marked by fewer, yet still competitive, unregulated markets. The 2002 framework, which adopted this methodology, has been successful, reducing the number of regulated markets from 18 to just 2: Internet access and the market for wholesale access and call origination on public telephone networks at a fixed location, enabling competitors to offer voice telephony services to end-users.

The political sensitivity of access regulation escalated with the advent of the Internet. Internet access has emerged as a vital social and economic need, underlining the push for ambitious political broadband connectivity targets. The 2010 NGA Recommendation (Chap. 6) and the co-investment provision in the Code reflected the EU legislators' intent to adopt more adaptable access regulations while maintaining necessary regulatory safeguards. The White Paper initiates a consultation, potentially marking a significant shift in telecom policy and heralding a post-'Code' era. The impetus for a comprehensive reform of the telecom framework is driven by evolving market dynamics, such as network-cloud convergence, the predominance of American cloud providers, and the recognition that the cost of building physical infrastructure represents a significant hurdle.

Early 2024, the Commission has already taken preliminary steps towards this future. It updated the 2010 NGA Recommendation, providing insights into its view of the future regulatory landscape, and proposed amendments to the Broadband Cost Reduction Directive, tackling the costs associated with physical infrastructure more assertively, a move that co-legislators have supported. Let us delve into the core aspects, one at a time.

Gigabit Recommendation

Like its predecessor, the Gigabit Recommendation[9] offers guidance to National Regulatory Authorities (NRAs) on accessing telecom networks of operators with significant market power. Compared to the 2010 Recommendation, its 2024 counterpart focuses entirely on promoting gigabit connectivity and VHCNs.[10]

[9] Commission Recommendation (EU) 2024/539 of 6 February 2024 on the regulatory promotion of gigabit connectivity.

[10] The Recommendation applies to VHCN as defined by the 'Code' and includes fibre to the building and customer premises and coax cable (DOCSIS 3.1, soon DOCSIS 4.0) connected to the fibre backbone. DOCSIS 3.1 (Data Over Cable Service Interface Specification) is a standard that allows for up to 10 Gbps downstream and 1 Gbps upstream Internet speeds.

The Commission advocates that *ex ante* regulation should concentrate primarily on the remaining competition bottlenecks, with a particular emphasis on accessing civil engineering infrastructure to deploy VHCNs.

The 2024 document calls for a balanced approach to price control obligations on VHCNs, considering the potential impact on investment incentives and the dynamics of competition. This stance marks a departure from the previous emphasis on ensuring competitive conditions through a broader array of regulatory instruments. NRAs are encouraged to consider geographic differences in competitive conditions, which may lead to geographically segmented remedies based on objective criteria.

Furthermore, the Recommendation promotes the rapid decommissioning of legacy technologies within a 2- to 3-year timeframe and the deployment of gigabit networks, underlining the urgency of transitioning towards more advanced, high-capacity telecommunications infrastructure.

Gigabit Infrastructure Act

At the outset of 2020, it became clear that the Broadband Cost Reduction Directive of 2014 (discussed in Chap. 6) would not achieve its intended objectives of diminishing administrative costs and expediting network deployment. On 6 February 2024, the co-legislators concurred to substitute this Directive with a Regulation as proposed by the Commission the year before.[11]

The aim is to refine and standardise national and local administrative procedures for operators seeking permission to construct networks and requiring access to existing facilities. Although this is a Regulation, its implementation into administrative and legal frameworks will, with certain exceptions, span 18 months.

The scope of regulated issues largely remains unchanged: access to existing physical infrastructure, transparency concerning physical infrastructure, coordination of civil works, transparency regarding planned civil works, the process for granting permits and rights of way, access to in-building physical infrastructure, digitalisation of single information points, and dispute resolution. The significant distinction from the previous Directive lies in the meticulous detail of the articles. Such specifics are typically left to the discretion of the authorities and the Commission's Implementing Acts. However, this Regulation aims to precisely synchronise these details.

For instance, Article 7 on permissions in the original Directive contained just four paragraphs. In the Regulation, this article elaborates on these provisions across more than 20 detailed paragraphs. The provision allowing a 4-month period for authorities to grant permission, subject to exceptions, remains unchanged. The Commission's

[11] Regulation (EU) 2024/1309 of 29 April 2024 on measures to reduce the cost of deploying gigabit electronic communications networks, amending Regulation (EU) 2015/2120 and repealing Directive 2014/61/EU (Gigabit Infrastructure Act).

proposal for 'tacit approval' following the expiration of this deadline, allowing for intervention by affected third parties, has been made optional.[12] Article 7 also specifies that small-scale civil works do not require permission, detailing what these entail, the applicable exceptions, and the potential obligation for operators to notify such works before commencement.

The Regulation's drafting strategy initially grants operators more latitude vis-à-vis infrastructure owners and authorities, then outlines exceptions and offers member states considerable flexibility. Overall, the Regulation contributes more substance than it removes. Two instances illustrate this.

First, operators may seek access to infrastructure owned by public entities, such as rooftops, light poles, billboards, toll frames, or tramway stops, aiding the densification of 5G networks and future 6G deployment.

Second, a provision mandates that new buildings or those undergoing major renovations 'shall be equipped with a fibre-ready in-building physical infrastructure, including in-building fibre wiring up to the point where the end-user connects to the public network' (Article 8.1). Several member states, including Spain and France, have proactively enforced regulations mandating the installation of fibre optic cabling in new or significantly renovated buildings to facilitate high-speed Internet readiness.

The 6 February agreement elicited mixed responses. Leading telecom organisations such as ETNO, ECTA, GIGAEUROPE, and GSMA expressed scepticism and dissatisfaction, particularly regarding the 'tacit approval' provision being downgraded and criticised the Regulation's extension of price caps on intra-EU calls and SMS.[13]

The White Paper also refers to 5G and 6G, emphasising spectrum policy. Let's examine the development of mobile communications.

The Future of Mobile Communications

Early 2024. We have arrived at the end of our 40-year story of digital policies. The story will continue, but in this book, it will end where it started, with mobile communications.

The GSM standard became Europe's most significant achievement in the digital world. We witnessed the catastrophic launch of 3G-UMTS in the early 2000.

[12] *Member States should be able to derogate from the tacit approval provision if they make available to the operator an alternative remedy to the noncompliance by the competent authority … Such alternative remedy should include either a mechanism to allow the operator to claim compensation for damage resulting from the delay in the procedure, or the possibility to refer the case to a court or to a supervisory authority, …*. Recital 42.

[13] https://www.ectaportal.com/news/ecta-press-releases/1675-ecta-etno-gigaeurope-gsma-joint-statement-european-telecom-operators-are-united-in-voicing-strong-concerns-regarding-the-current-gia-negotiations

4G-LTE became a global success and was the prerequisite for the success of smartphones and the app economy. Without the mobile ecosystem, social media would not have flourished as they did. And now, 5G is being deployed, and 6G is already on the horizon.

The 5G Vision

Vendors and operators cherished 5G as a revolution. With several Gbps download speeds, super-short reaction times, and the ability to connect millions of devices, it would pave the way for a new industrial paradigm, Industry 4.0. The 5G technology will indeed overtake 4G connections in Europe by around 2025. However, an industrial revolution is still to come, 5 years after 5G was first launched in South Korea in April 2019.

What makes 5G faster than 4G? The short answer is more spectrum coupled with clever antenna technology.[14] The 5G standard also contains other improvements over 4G, but spectrum and antennas generate the big leap. While 5G can operate on a broad spectrum range, it achieves optimal performance when it uses the 3.5 GHz band, also called the C-band, as this spectrum offers an attractive combination of reach and speed.[15]

5G operating on the 700 MHz bands will not reach the widely advertised 10 to 20 times faster. Deploying 5G on the 26 GHz mm-wave spectrum offers high-speed connections only over relatively short distances. Consequently, this spectrum primarily supports Fixed Wireless Access, providing an alternative to fibre to the home or replacing Wi-Fi in urban hotspots.

In Europe, many operators initially implemented 5G atop their existing 4G networks. This approach allowed them to leverage the coverage and infrastructure of the established 4G networks. However, non-stand-alone deployments lack certain advanced functionalities. Recently, operators have started to transition to stand-alone architectures, ensuring that all components, including the radio access network and core network, are 5G-native. This shift enables capabilities like network slicing, allowing operators to create virtual networks tailored to specific industrial use cases. However, by August 2023, only 10 out of 114 commercial networks were stand-alone.

[14] In traditional systems, you might have one or a few antennas at the base station and on your device. MIMO technology takes this to the next level by using many antennas, both at the transmitter (base station) and receiver (your device). Antennas with 64 input and 64 output elements on the base station are quite common.

[15] Higher frequency signals can carry more data due to their shorter wavelengths, but they also have limitations. Higher frequency signals have a reduced propagation range as they are more susceptible to being absorbed or scattered by obstacles, including the air. This necessitates the deployment of more antennas to ensure adequate coverage for a given area.

The 5G core alone may not suffice for extremely low-latency industrial applications. An edge computing infrastructure is needed to manage devices on industrial campuses or road infrastructures, or computing must occur close to the action, such as with moving robots—see the previous sub-chapter. Therefore, 5G is not a plug-and-play technology for industry; its performance hinges on factors like network readiness, spectrum availability, and device capabilities.

Furthermore, investing in 5G competes with alternative mobile technologies such as LTE-M, Wi-Fi, Zigbee, NB-IoT, and Lora. In specific scenarios, these existing technologies might offer sufficient capabilities, rendering an upgrade or investment in 5G less justified from a business perspective. While many analysts predict substantial economic benefits associated with 5G,[16] it is prudent to approach these studies with a degree of scepticism.[17] During our journey, we have repeatedly seen policymakers eager to embrace such grand predictions, aspiring for their countries to emerge as global leaders, and the EU is no exception.

EU 5G Action Plan

Surprisingly, the 5G Action Plan, adopted in 2016, was the first of its kind. In the past, the Commission supported mobile communications through its research programmes and attempted to align spectrum assignments of member states. The Action Plan brought these and other actions into a context, presented a narrative to create a favourable investment climate and tried to achieve closer coordination among member states.[18]

The Connecting Europe Facility, CEF 2, supports 5G corridors, which aim to establish seamless connectivity on transport roads, particularly for 5G-enabled applications, such as automatic driving.[19] The 5G-PPP in Horizon 2020 invested about 700 million euros in over 90 5G projects, first focusing on core technology and later on applications in vertical industries, such as transport, healthcare, manufacturing, and smart cities. Funding continued with Horizon Europe as part of the Smart Networks and Services (SNS) JU, emphasising large-scale projects. What remains to

---

[16] For instance, a 2020 study by Analysys Mason, commissioned by Ericsson and Quantum Technologies, predicted an incremental cost/benefit of 46 billion euros/208 billion euros for Europe over 15 years. Another study conducted by Huawei in collaboration with STL Partners projected a global gain of $740 billion in manufacturing by 2030. DLA Piper's European Tech Index report also identified significant potential in smart cities.

[17] This is not to argue about the impact of the mobile industry on the economy, which makes up, on average, around 5% of GDP, but the studies estimated the incremental effects of 5G deployments.

[18] The Commission established an excellent observatory website that has been monitoring progress in policy and market development in the EU and to some extent internationally. Data used here are from this observatory. https://5gobservatory.eu/

[19] https://5gobservatory.eu/5g-corridors/

be seen is whether these projects will scale to become viable business solutions, potentially serving a global market. This will depend on operators upgrading their networks to 5G and enterprises embracing 5G.

In this context, several EU countries have reserved spectrum for private networks to bolster the industrial uptake of 5G. Others leave the spectrum to operators, expecting them to enable local applications through network slicing. This fragmented approach makes cross-border enterprise solutions complex. Unfortunately, the current information about stand-alone architecture deployment and 5G private networks is not comprehensive but anecdotal.[20]

Member states assigned spectrum according to their own schedules and methods. By the end of 2023, just over 70% of the envisaged spectrum was assigned, which was less than the Action Plan aimed for. In particular, the mm-wave has not been popular, with less than half of the member states using it.

Nevertheless, in all member states, at least one commercial 5G network is available, and the number of subscribers has risen to around 140 million, representing a third of the EU population, by 2022. Globally, South Korea and China are leading with a subscriber penetration of about 50%. The EU is ahead of Japan and the United States by 12% and 24%, respectively. More relevant is base station density, which is double in China and even five times higher in South Korea due to the intense usage of the mm-band.

Because of its size and technology-affine population, China's role in mobile development is remarkable. The country has more than three million 5G base stations in operation. The 5G subscriber base of around 700 million in 2023 will grow to more than 1 billion by 2025. Two telecom vendors, the state-owned ZTE and private Huawei Technologies, have been instrumental in China's mobile development—and Huawei gained significant market share in Europe during the 2010s. Yet, geopolitical developments, particularly tensions between the United States and China, have resulted in a de-coupling policy. Trust on both sides is dwindling, which could affect the development of 6G.[21]

Towards 6G

Operators still have a lot of work to do with 5G deployment. Vendors and 3GPP have been further developing 5G capabilities, a process called 5G Evolution. Coupled with this, research to develop 6G has begun. The SNS JU is Europe's main instrument for advancing on both fronts.[22]

[20] https://www.gsma.com/mobileeconomy/wp-content/uploads/2022/10/051022-Mobile-Economy-Europe-2022.pdf

https://5gobservatory.eu/5g-private-networks/

[21] See also the GSMA report: The Mobile Economy, China 2023. https://www.gsma.com/mobileeconomy/china/

[22] https://smart-networks.europa.eu/6g-research-gets-a-130-million-eur-eu-funding-boost-in-europe/

Research teams worldwide have already posted some ideas for 6G.[23] The characteristics of 6G will depend on its spectrum, which will probably lie between 100 GHz and 1000 GHz (1 THz).[24] This spectrum will allow much higher data rates but at considerably shorter distances. The 6G standard will most likely also work with 5G frequencies, enabling smooth transition and hybrid solutions. The IMT-2030 specifications could be finalised by 2030.

The cell structure will be replaced by immersive radio access. Antennas will be tiny, and there will be lots of them. This will allow cell-free, ultra-massive MIMO (multiple-input and multiple-output), which is not necessarily visible as antennas but embedded everywhere. Entire building facades could be used as radio reflectors. We will end up with extreme connectivity. Devices could be powered wirelessly using an over-the-air interface, replacing batteries.

The properties of the spectrum would allow the network to function as a sensor. The radio could, for instance, measure particles to manage air quality or carry out precision localisation for controlling indoor drones or other vehicles.

Researchers agree that AI software will control the air interface (access mode) and network management. While 5G was introduced as a cloud-native network, 6G will be AI-native. AI would also support services, such as algorithms to identify objects. In extreme cases, one might generate a digital twin in any place by combining network sensing capabilities with AI object recognition.

Despite the industry's rhetoric, 5G is an evolution from 4G, whereas 6G could emerge as a new paradigm mainly because of the spectrum characteristics. As soon as the specifications of 6G become more explicit, we can expect European technosceptics to raise concerns about radiation and privacy intrusion. Sensibly responding to these worries while keeping up entrepreneurial spirits will be crucial, in addition to funding research projects. Most importantly, harmonising spectrum policy and accepting market consolidation will be essential to rebuild European leadership in mobile communications.[25]

Remarks

With this outlook on the future, the story concludes, but the book's Epilogue elaborates on what lessons the past four decades can teach policymakers.

I wrote the last four chapters as an observer with background knowledge as I retired from the Commission in 2017. After retirement, I worked for two and a half

[23] https://5g-ppp.eu/wp-content/uploads/2022/12/6G-Arch-Whitepaper_v1.0-final.pdf

[24] The World Radio Conferences (WRC) in 2023 and 2027 will further clarify which frequency ranges could be made available for 6G.

[25] Kalvin Bahia and Pau Castells, "The dynamic effects of competition on investment: the case of the European mobile communications industry", *Journal of Information Policy*, Volume 13, 2023, p. 249–309.

years in Shenzhen for Huawei's global government relations team. During this time, I experienced life in Shenzhen, which, as a smart city with over 70,000 5G base stations, was and still is ahead of European cities despite all our programmes.

China has learned much from the West, particularly the United States and Germany. Interestingly, we seem to believe that China cannot teach us much. During my time in DG Connect, we had many interchanges with the Chinese authorities. We held regular dialogues. The Commission even financed development projects in the digital realm for China. Since then, the geopolitical climate has changed.

Reference

1. Georg Serentschy, Paul Timmers, and Marja Matinmikko-Blue. "Toward Anticipatory Regulation and Beyond", p.231. In: Petri Ahokangas and Annabeth Aagaard (eds), "The Changing World of Mobile Communications 5G, 6G and the Future of Digital Services", *Palgrave Macmillan*, 2024, pp. 221-251. https://doi.org/10.1007/978-3-031-33191-6

Chapter 11
Epilogue: Aspirations and Reality

> Productivity isn't everything, but in the long run, it's almost everything. A country's ability to improve its standard of living over time depends almost entirely on its ability to raise its output per worker.
>
> Paul Krugman, The Age of Diminished Expectations: U.S. Economic Policy in the 1990s. *The Washington Post Company,* 3rd edition 1997, p. 11.

The story I told in this book is positive, yet it is not a success story. How can I explain this supposed contradiction? The EU has managed to lessen fragmentation, substantially extending the Single Market to the digital realm. Many areas are now governed by a European legislative framework, which is necessary but insufficient to make Europe a leader in the digital world.

This is when the story becomes gloomy. American and Asian companies dominate the global digital markets. Europe depends on foreign companies to deliver cutting-edge microchips, computers, software, smartphones, social media, video streaming services, cloud computing, and app stores. Europe has only a few top-notch players in the game, such as SAP (founded in the 1970s), ARM (founded in the 1990s), ASML (founded in the 1990s), and perhaps Spotify. Europe's digital strengths are linked to its industrial base, mainly automotive, to which companies like Bosch, ST Micron, or Infineon are testimony. Nokia and Ericsson are still thriving in mobile networks but are heavily challenged by Chinese, Korean, and American competitors. A recent study calculated a digital dependency index and concluded that the United States has widened its lead over all countries except China and South Korea. The authors write:

D. Eckert, *40 Years of European Digital Policies*, Professional Practice in Governance and Public Organizations,
https://doi.org/10.1007/978-3-031-61641-9_11

> The key message is that EU members' degree of digital dependence is far greater and more pervasive than often assumed. As a result, current initiatives to enhance European digital autonomy do not recognize the magnitude of the challenges ahead.[1]

Most disappointing was the absence of Europe from five of the six events heralding breakthrough innovations that would create markets comprised of a wave of new companies. These events have disrupted the course of history and were decisive for the digital economy and the world.

On 12 August 1981, IBM put its PC on the market. On 1 January 1983, ARPANET transitioned to TCP/IP. On 1 July 1991, the first GSM call was made in Finland. Netscape Navigator was released on 15 December 1994. Steve Jobs presented the iPhone on 17 September 2007. OpenAI released ChatGPT on 30 November 2022.

The question of 'why' resounds forcefully. Asking this question and seeking answers should be the starting point for future digital strategies. What explains that Europe, despite its technological potential, educated people, and impressive research performance, cannot take leadership in digital developments? Why are we not even catching up?

A candidate for an answer is entrepreneurship. Entrepreneurs like Steve Jobs, Elon Musk, Sam Altman, and Mark Zuckerberg are rare in Europe. They and many others are the product of American culture and its institutions: a mindset of competition, a willingness of venture capitalists to take risks, and talented people from all over the world. It is fiendishly hard to replicate culture, apart from the fact that people generally prefer to stick with their own culture. And European policymakers are adamant that they do not want the American model.

European countries may vary in their cultural predispositions, yet they collectively share a significant set of values and, through the EU, have established common institutions. The diverse digital agendas, from the information society to the digital decade, reflect these shared values. Initially, they focused on competitiveness and highlighted inclusion, often expressed as addressing the digital divide. Over time, the narrative has gained complexity, and the list of goals has expanded. Today's digital strategy is burdened with a multitude of societal objectives. Digital policies, for instance, are supposed to prioritise being human-centred, fundamental rights-based, inclusive, transparent, and open. They should uphold the Union's principles, rights, and values and ensure accessibility. These are commendable aspirations; however, the predicament lies in their overwhelming nature for the channels of digital policy in general and at the EU level in particular. Furthermore, a notable absence is an emphasis on increased productivity, a crucial factor in driving economic growth.

Today's living standards result from centuries of cumulative productivity increases. However, productivity growth often instils anxiety, as it is perceived as

[1] Maximilian Mayer and Yen Chi-Lu, "Digital Autonomy? Measuring the Global Digital Dependence Structure", Center for Advanced Security, Strategic and Integration Studies, Bonn 2022, pp. 19–20. The index comprises data related to ICT trade, platform ownership, and IPR.

destroying jobs and negatively impacting lives. In contrast, innovation, although a key component of productivity, carries a positive connotation. Innovation is a favourite policy objective and gives rise to numerous programmes. While innovation is the holy grail of technology policy, you rarely encounter a programme targeting 'productivity growth'.

Industrial strategies, including those involving digital industries, predominantly revolve around the notion of competitiveness. In simple terms, competitiveness denotes the capacity to thrive in global markets. Yet, this concept diverges from productivity. A country may excel in selling goods and services due to low wages while grappling with low levels of productivity. Europe aspires not merely for competitiveness but also for prosperity, necessitating a surge in productivity. While a competitive industrial landscape is advantageous, the attainment of Europe's ambitious social and environmental objectives hinges on productivity.[2]

However, the extent to which digitalisation, encompassing investments and the adoption of ICT, stimulates productivity growth is far from straightforward. The answer eludes the simplistic optimism of digital advocates and is intricately linked to the Solow Paradox, introduced in Chaps. 4 and 8. While research findings vary, overarching patterns emerge [1].

The 2000 Lisbon strategy drew inspiration from the remarkable surge in productivity observed in the United States between 1995 and 2005, a trend that significantly influenced the monetary policies of the Fed. During this period, the average annual growth rate of private business productivity soared to an impressive 2.9%.[3] It is widely acknowledged that this surge was driven by investments in and utilisation of ICT. Much of this transformative impact was indirect and encapsulated within the overall growth of total factor productivity. This is logical, considering that during those years, eCommerce and advanced communication technologies permeated across various sectors of the economy, enhancing the productivity of both capital and labour.

Subsequently, however, productivity growth experienced a notable decline, averaging a mere 0.9% over the subsequent decade. This downturn posed a perplexing puzzle, especially considering the concurrent rise of Big Tech and the consolidation of the United States as the global leader in digital innovation. However, stock market values and contributions to the economy differ. The proliferation of income inequality, the escalation of market dominance, and diminished competition all act as impediments to progress. Furthermore, a significant portion of ICT production has

[2] '... what does it mean when people talk about U.S. "competitiveness"? The answer, sadly, is that it almost always means that they don't know what they are talking about.' Paul Krugman, supra in main text, p.14.

[3] Ibid. The paper used the EUKLEMS database, which stems from a Commission research project in 2003–2008. The database has been updated several times, involving a wide academic network. https://euklems-intanprod-llee.luiss.it/

Figures from the OECD or the US Bureau of Labor Statistics differ, but the overall picture is consistent.

shifted to Asia, exemplified by Apple's decision to manufacture its chips in Taiwan and assemble the iPhone in China.

In Europe, between 1995 and 2005, labour productivity growth failed to match the impressive figures witnessed in the United States and continued to decline in subsequent years, persistently trailing behind US levels. The EU allocated comparatively less investment towards ICT and consequently failed to fully harness the dividends of its investments. This does not align with our positive views about digital strategies. While we gauged success using a variety of output indicators, we overlooked the crucial aspect of how policy measures shape the efficiency of deploying digital technologies.

We require a more profound comprehension of the reasons behind the absence of an automatic correlation between digital policies and investments and increased productivity. Scholars like Robert J. Gordon posit that the ICT revolution, though transformative, may not wield as much significance as earlier revolutions, such as those brought about by steam engines or electricity. However, conventional economic metrics fail to account for the full impact of digital technologies on the economy. Improvements in the quality, accessibility, and variety of digital services might not be fully reflected in economic statistics. More importantly, there is consensus that it will take time for both the economy and society to fully embrace digital technologies. The productivity benefits of digital technologies do not manifest automatically upon adoption. Individuals across various roles, including workers, students, managers, or engineers, must learn to leverage ICT for enhanced productivity.

A study by European Central Bank staff members delved into the intricate dynamics between digitalisation and productivity at the firm level, offering further insight into this complex relationship.[4] Their analysis revealed that, on average, digital companies do not exhibit higher levels of productivity, with the exception of a small number of firms that demonstrate superior and sustained levels of productivity. The authors conclude:

> Digitalisation seems to be a productivity gamechanger only for some firms, but it is more like a productivity sideshow for other firms who invest in digital technologies but are not able to adequately reap the productivity gains from digitalisation.[5]

It is not surprising that many IT projects fail.[6]

---

[4]Robert Anderton et al., "Digitalisation and productivity: gamechanger or sideshow?", European Central Bank Working Paper Series, No 2794, March 2023.

The study used a panel dataset of 19.3 million firm-level observations of nearly 2.4 million distinct firms.

[5]Ibid. p. 7.

[6]McKinsey found that 70% of digital transformation projects failed. Perspectives on transformation | Transformation | McKinsey & Company

Recently, productivity in the United States has experienced an upturn, while in the EU, it has stagnated or even shown negative growth [2].[7] Whether this trend will persist remains uncertain. Furthermore, the surge in US productivity may be attributed more to increased investments propelled by public initiatives like the Inflation Reduction Act rather than solely to advancements in digital technologies. Nonetheless, regardless of the driving forces behind these trends, their continuation would yield significant consequences, with positive outcomes for the United States [3] and negative implications for the EU.

Expressing concerns, the European Central Bank advocates action to address structural weaknesses. This includes measures such as finalising the Banking Union, bolstering European integration in the services sector, enhancing public investments, and promoting competition. The ECB emphasises the need to reduce '. . . the cost of firm entry and expansion as well as the cost of closing a failing business' [4].

The challenge lies in effectively integrating digital policies into a comprehensive macroeconomic reform agenda. It necessitates acknowledging that digital policies should be an integral part of a broader plan. Recall that digital policy played a minor role during the financial and Euro crises in the EU. While the Europe 2020 strategy and its reform agenda focused on financial stability and labour market reforms, little attention was directed towards stimulating digital investments.

Hence, it is also imperative that we draw lessons from Europe's early challenges during the ICT revolution. These challenges included the failure to effectively translate digital investments into innovation, comprehend the dynamics of the Internet, establish globally successful digital enterprises, and modernise public services.

Europe does not face fundamental problems of technology or infrastructure. At the dawn of the Internet, broadband was essential, and enhancing fibre connection and fostering ubiquitous 5G have remained important, but these measures no longer address the most critical bottlenecks. These bottlenecks can be found in missing complementary investments such as in skills and administrative agility. Policymakers must avoid the mistake of overemphasising specific technologies and stop rushing headlong in pursuit of the latest hype.

We need an approach that transcends the realm of digital policy as we know it. Let's exemplify this with the notion of mass flourishing introduced by Edward Phelps, Nobel Prize laureate in economics. His concept highlights the involvement of diverse individuals and groups in the innovation process [5]. According to him, societies that promote individualism, creativity, and entrepreneurship create an environment conducive to meaningful work and shared prosperity. This philosophy aligns more closely with the European way of thinking than the Silicon Valley type

---

[7] The US Bureau of Labor Statistics published a 2.6% increase in labour productivity in the nonfarm business sector for the fourth quarter compared to the same quarter of the previous year. According to Eurostat, productivity (GDP per hours worked) decreased by 0.7% for the same period. Although the datasets are not the same, they overlap sufficiently to be compared.

https://www.bls.gov/news.release/prod2.nr0.htm

https://ec.europa.eu/eurostat/en/web/products-euro-indicators/w/2-08032024-ap

of capitalism. Given Europe's diversity, there will not be a master plan agreed on by all countries. However, the EU can establish a direction and refocus its resources on what truly matters, motivating people in various roles to become digital innovators. This involves improvements in education and training, attracting international talents, and mobilising the creativity of individuals. Institutional reforms may well become more important than funding or legislation. The next European digital strategy could usefully take inspiration from Phelps' thinking.

After enacting a series of legislative measures, European policymakers might be inclined to adopt a self-congratulatory attitude. But they risk overlooking global dynamics. The world may not necessarily be impressed by the EU's regulatory achievements. First, European and national authorities must demonstrate that they can implement the rulebooks effectively and without impeding innovation. Second, they should recognise that structural weaknesses significantly contribute to the underachievement of Europe's considerable pool of talent in developing digital business: *inter alia*, high cost of capital, punitive insolvency laws, and overly heavy taxation of incipient success.

As the EU reflects on its *acquis communautaire*, there is an opportunity to learn from other regions and reflect on the potential for simplification and deregulation. There is an inherent desire of public administrations and lawmakers to regulate every perceived problem with increasing detail. Comparing the individual size of EU legal texts over the past four decades and the immense complexity that has emerged makes you wonder where this process could end. If we want more dynamism, perhaps we should give innovators more space to breathe.

Achieving scale at the European level is crucial for establishing digital leadership. Despite advancements in creating the internal market, Europe remains fragmented in many areas, placing us at a disadvantage compared to the United States, China, and potentially India. This fragmentation is tellingly highlighted in the recent Commission paper on the future of telecommunications. Achieving scale is a political decision. Member states must shift their mindset and embrace a true internal market for telecommunications, with enhanced oversight from BEREC and complete harmonisation of spectrum allocation, as a promising starting point.

However, we must explore additional avenues. Pooling public procurement, while not a novel concept, is an effective strategy to bolster the digital economy and support European companies, especially start-ups. However, it is often limited to pre-competitive procurement within research programmes. We must think on a larger scale.

Public procurement is not typically geared towards fostering innovation and competitiveness. It is bound by strict regulations and entrenched traditions, which makes integration into an innovation strategy challenging. The difficulties are amplified when aiming to centralise purchasing power at the EU level, as demonstrated by experiences with the COVID-19 vaccine and munitions procurement for Ukraine. Nevertheless, overcoming such hurdles is the essence of strategic planning.

The Digital Decade Policy Programme 2030 outlines a similar concept but predominantly refers to existing initiatives and focuses on technical fields. True scalability is achieved when addressing significant sectors such as education, healthcare, transportation, public administration, and national security. The Recovery and Resilience Facility (RRF) could provide one source of funding.

The bottom line is that Europe needs an increase in productivity. The shifting power in the world poses significant challenges. Productivity growth will help to maintain the social model, invest in defence and security, and tackle climate change. The digital strategy could be coupled with the European Semester, and the narrative synchronised with the Annual Growth Survey.[8] This would allow the extension of digital policies to the realm of economic policy at large. The Semester offers a framework to address structural reforms essential for entrepreneurship and market dynamism.

Throughout this book, I have identified lessons for consideration, aiming for a holistic view of a historical process. Of course, the value of these lessons depends on one's perspective. However, it becomes evident that Europe's path forward entails less regulation, structural reforms to stimulate entrepreneurship, and a reorientation of the research agenda. Ultimately, member states must unite to consolidate resources and achieve scale. The meta-critique of digital policymaking set out in this conclusion is intended to offer helpful insights based on 40 years of experience so that in the future, we can avoid reinventing the wheel, repeating past slogans, or advancing digital policies with too narrowly focused an agenda. Perhaps we may then finally see the rise of a generation of European tech entrepreneurs with global impact.

References

1. Robert J. Gordon, Hassan Sayed, "Transatlantic Technologies: The Role of ICT in the Evolution of U.S. and European Productivity Growth", NBER Working Paper Series, Working Paper 27425. http://www.nber.org/papers/w27425
2. Delphine Strauss et al., "Europe faces 'competitiveness crisis' as US widens productivity gap. Washington reaps benefits from green fiscal stimulus, rehiring and surge in new businesses." *Financial Times*, 9 March 2024. https://www.ft.com/content/22089f01-8468-4905-8e36-fd35d2b2293e
3. Charles Atkin et al., "Rekindling US productivity for a new era", McKinsey Global Institute Report, 16 February 2023. https://www.mckinsey.com/mgi/our-research/rekindling-us-productivity-for-a-new-era#at-a-glance
4. Isabel Schnabel, Member of the Executive Board of the ECB, "From laggard to leader? Closing the euro area's technology gap", Inauguration lecture, EMU Lab, European University Institute, 16 February 2024.
5. Edward Phelps, *My Journeys in Economic Theory*, Columbia University Press, New York, 2023, pp. 158-186.

[8] https://commission.europa.eu/publications/2024-european-semester-autumn-package_en

The manufacturer's authorised representative in the EU is Springer
Nature Customer Service Centre GmbH, Europaplatz 3, 69115 Heidelberg,
Germany. If you have any concerns regarding our products, please
contact ProductSafety@springernature.com

Printed and bound by CPI Group (UK) Ltd, Croydon, CR0 4YY
01/10/2026
02225854-0020